SEX IN CHINA

China Today series

SEX IN CHINA ——————————

Elaine Jeffreys with Haiqing Yu

polity

First published in 2015 by Polity Press

Polity Press
65 Bridge Street
Cambridge CB2 1UR, UK

Polity Press
350 Main Street
Malden, MA 02148, USA

ISBN-13: 978-0-7456-5613-7
ISBN-13: 978-0-7456-5614-4(pb)

A catalogue record for this book is available from the British Library.

Library of Congress Cataloging-in-Publication Data

Jeffreys, Elaine, 1960-
    Sex in China / Elaine Jeffreys, Haiqing Yu.
        pages cm. – (China today)
    Includes bibliographical references and index.
    ISBN 978-0-7456-5613-7 (hardcover : alk. paper) – ISBN 0-7456-5613-7 (hardcover : alk. paper) – ISBN 978-0-7456-5614-4 (pbk. : alk. paper) – ISBN 0-7456-5614-5 (pbk. : alk. paper)   1. Sexology–China.   I. Yu, Haiqing, 1970- II. Title.
    HQ60.J44 2015
    306.70951–dc23
                        2014025918

Typeset in 11.5 on 15 pt Adobe Jenson Pro
by Toppan Best-set Premedia Limited
Printed and bound in the UK by Clays Ltd, St Ives plc

For further information on Polity, visit our website: politybooks.com

Contents

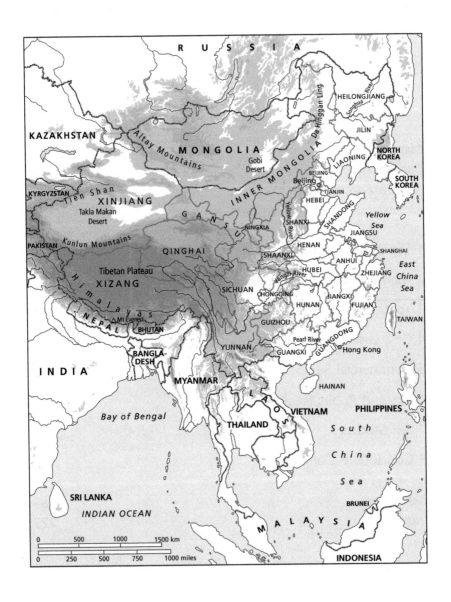

Chronology

1894–95	First Sino-Japanese War
1911	Fall of the Qing Dynasty
1912	Republic of China established under Sun Yat-sen
1927	Split between Nationalists (KMT) and Communists (CCP); civil war begins
1934–5	CCP under Mao Zedong evades KMT in Long March
December 1937	Nanjing Massacre
1937–45	Second Sino-Japanese War
1945–9	Civil war between KMT and CCP resumes
October 1949	KMT retreats to Taiwan; Mao founds People's Republic of China (PRC)
1950–3	Korean War
1953–7	First Five-Year Plan; PRC adopts Soviet-style economic planning
1954	First Constitution of the PRC and first meeting of the National People's Congress
1956–7	Hundred Flowers Movement, a brief period of open political debate
1957	Anti-Rightist Movement
1958–60	Great Leap Forward, an effort to transform China through rapid industrialization and collectivization

March 1959	Tibetan Uprising in Lhasa; Dalai Lama flees to India
1959–61	Three Hard Years, widespread famine with tens of millions of deaths
1960	Sino-Soviet split
1962	Sino-Indian War
October 1964	First PRC atomic bomb detonation
1966–76	Great Proletarian Cultural Revolution; Mao reasserts power
February 1972	President Richard Nixon visits China; 'Shanghai Communiqué' pledges to normalize US–China relations
September 1976	Death of Mao Zedong
October 1976	Ultra-Leftist Gang of Four arrested and sentenced
December 1978	Deng Xiaoping assumes power; launches Four Modernizations and economic reforms
1979–80	One-child family planning policy introduced
1979	US and China establish formal diplomatic ties; Deng Xiaoping visits Washington
1979	PRC invades Vietnam
1982	Census reports PRC population at more than one billion
December 1984	Margaret Thatcher co-signs Sino-British Joint Declaration agreeing to return Hong Kong to China in 1997
1989	Tiananmen Square protests culminate in 4 June military crackdown
1992	Deng Xiaoping's Southern Inspection Tour re-energizes economic reforms
1993–2002	Jiang Zemin is president of PRC, continues economic growth agenda

November 2001	WTO accepts China as member
August 2002	World Summit on Sustainable Development held in Johannesburg; PRC ratifies 1997 Kyoto Protocol to the United Nations Framework Convention on Climate Change
2003–12	Hu Jintao is president of PRC
2002–3	SARS outbreak concentrated in PRC and Hong Kong
2006	PRC supplants US as largest CO_2 emitter
August 2008	Summer Olympic Games in Beijing
2010	Shanghai World Exposition
2012	Xi Jinping appointed General-Secretary of the CCP (and President of PRC from 2013)

Acknowledgements

This research was supported under Australian Research Council's Future Fellowship funding scheme (FT100100238).

Elaine Jeffreys is the sole author of chapters 1, 2, 5, 6, 7 and 8.

The authors and publishers would like to thank Routledge for permission to reproduce parts of Elaine Jeffreys (2012) *Prostitution Scandals in China: Policing, Media and Society*, Abingdon, Oxon: Routledge, in chapters 5 and 6.

We would also like to thank the Aaron Diamond AIDS Research Center, ChinaAidsInitiative.org.cn, for permission to reprint figure 6.2 in chapter 6.

Elaine Jeffreys with Yu Haiqing

Abbreviations and Note on Chinese Names

Abbreviations

100% CUP:	100 Per Cent Condom Use Program
AIDS:	Acquired Immunodeficiency Syndrome
CCP:	Chinese Communist Party
HIV:	Human Immunodeficiency Virus
LGBT:	Lesbian, gay, bisexual, and transsexual
PRC:	People's Republic of China
PSA:	Public Service Advertisement
STDs:	Sexually transmitted diseases
STIs:	Sexually transmissible infections
WHO:	World Health Organization

Note on Chinese Names

Names in Chinese are usually presented as family name followed by a personal name. That practice is followed here, with two exceptions. The first is where Chinese people have a non-Chinese personal name, in which case the personal name is presented before the family name. The second is where a person with a Chinese name has indicated, usually through publication, that they wish to be known by their personal name followed by their family name.

1 | Sex in China: Introduction

Move over Mao, today's Chinese revolution is sexual.

Lynch 2003

When China opened its doors to international markets in the early 1980s, it inadvertently let in another modern phenomenon – the West's sexual culture.

Braverman 2002

The Chinese landscape – in its material and virtual, as well as geographical and social dimensions – is increasingly a sexually charged space.

Zhang, E. 2011: 109

The People's Republic of China (PRC) has been undergoing economic and social change at a rate and scale that is unprecedented in world history, ever since the country abandoned socialist-style centralized planning and adopted market-based economic reforms, with a policy of opening up to the rest of the world, in December 1978. Population mobility was severely restricted in China after 1958 to meet the requirements of centralized economic planning, a system wherein the Party-state allocated work and distributed resources, and therefore needed to know the identity and location of its workers. Along with the gradual loosening of restrictions on population mobility since the mid-1980s, an estimated 262 million people have moved from rural to urban parts of China to find work, chiefly in low-income sectors such as construction, services, transport and manufacturing (Wang, Y, 2013). Highlighting the runaway nature of China's building boom, the PRC's 'cement industry has been the largest in the world for at least the past 20 years', reportedly accounting for more than half of the globe's cement consumption in 2011 (Edwards, P. 2013). The pace of development and urbanization in China has been so fast that some commentators claim it is the equivalent of Europe's Industrial Revolution, only collapsed into the space of thirty to forty instead of 150 years ('The second industrial revolution' 2004).

These changes have been accompanied by equally dramatic changes in public discussions and expressions of sex and sexuality. Numerous scholars contend that during the revolutionary Maoist era (1949–76), and especially during the Cultural Revolution period (1966–76), 'to discuss any aspect of personal life, romantic relationships or sex was considered bourgeois and hence taboo' (Honig 2003: 143). 'There was a dearth of both public and private discussion of sex during the Cultural Revolution', says anthropologist Mayfair Yang (1999: 44). In fact, the 'slightest suggestion of sexual interest was considered so ideologically unsound that gendered tastes in hairstyle and dress were coerced into a monotonous uniformity of shape and colour…. a sexual sameness, based on the defeminization of female appearance and its approximation to male standards of dress', says historian Harriet Evans (1997: 2).

In China today, sex and sexuality have become visible and publicly discussed components of everyday life, as the quotations at the start of this chapter suggest. Unlike in the Mao era, when public expressions of sexual intimacy were rare, young and elderly couples holding hands and kissing are now common sights in Chinese streets, parks and eateries. Advertising billboards, replete with sexualized images of young men and women promoting 'must-have' consumer goods, adorn the exterior walls of upscale shopping malls, alongside government public-service advertisements. Glossy images of young 'sexy' bodies feature on the cover pages of the many men's and women's fashion, beauty, celebrity, health, and lifestyle magazines that are displayed on streetside newspaper stalls. Nightclubs with pole dancers and transsexual karaoke shows vie for custom with bars trying to attract more male drinkers by offering free drinks for women on 'ladies' nights'. Dating shows are a popular reality-television format and 'talk-back' radio shows offer advice on sex-related matters. The development of the Chinese Internet has also resulted in a proliferation of sites for engaging with sex-related matters, including: gay and lesbian support services; commercial matchmaking sites; sex blogs; soft pornographic images; and celebrity and political sex scandals.

The dramatic nature of these changes when compared to the perceived sexual austerity of the Mao era has led numerous commentators to claim that China is undergoing a sexual revolution ('China undergoing sexual revolution' 2003; Lynch 2003; Pan, S. 2009: 22; Zhang, E. 2011). For some, the use of the expression 'sexual revolution' is simply a shorthand means to capture the altered nature of China's contemporary sexual culture when compared to that of the Maoist period. For others, it indicates that the PRC is embracing western-style modernity, as demonstrated by claims that Chinese sexual practices will soon 'catch up' with those of western societies ('China undergoing sexual revolution' 2003). For yet others, it is a signifier of broader and arguably more significant political change. As one earnest young scholar explains:

> There is a revolution going on in China. It is not the Long March, The Great Leap Forward or The Cultural Revolution. There is no great Helmsman at the fore. No one person caused this revolution. The Revolution is a revolution of the senses, the mind, the body and the individual. As the party-state withdraws itself from the intervention into the personal realm, it does so concurrently with the rise of the heroes of sexual freedom, liberators of the self. (Edwards, J. 2011)

The 'sexual revolution in China' narrative has proved to be popular with English- and Chinese-speaking commentators alike because it appeals to common-sense understandings of how things were and are. It suggests that sex was repressed by the Communist Party-state during the Mao era. In contrast, the 'natural' desires of the Chinese people are now being liberated as a result of the loosening of government controls and the introduction of modern western influences.

This narrative is incorrect. The next section explains why.

RETHINKING THE HISTORY OF SEX IN THE PRC

Historical studies demonstrate that 'insofar as there is a story of repression to be told', the role of the Mao-era state in repressing sex and sexuality is far from obvious, even in the Cultural Revolution period (Honig 2003: 154). The early Chinese Communist Party (CCP) initially paid considerable attention to promoting sexual equality, especially for women. The PRC's first Marriage Law was promulgated on 1 May 1950, only seven months after the People's Republic was founded. That Law outlawed China's traditional 'feudal marriage system', including bigamy, polygamy, and arranged and mercenary marriages, and implemented a new system of free-choice, monogamous marriage based on equal rights for both sexes (Zhonghua renmin gongheguo hunyin fa 1950]). The early communist regime also set about eradicating prostitution and venereal diseases, describing them as emblematic of unequal class and gendered relations (Abrams 2001: 429–40; Jeffreys 2012b: 96–7). A broad range of materials were issued through the Party-state publicity system in the 1950s and early 1960s to educate the public about the new Marriage Law and its importance for women, and to promote sexual hygiene (Evans 1997: 2). These publications, as suggested by titles such as 'Establish a Correct Perspective on Love', and 'Talking About the Age of Marriage From a Physiological Point of View' (Evans 1997: 2), promoted a normative view of appropriate sex/uality as adult, monogamous, heterosexual and marital, rather than pre-marital, casual, extra-marital, homosexual and commercial, which may appear conservative from contemporary perspectives. But they also demonstrate that public discussions of sex and sexuality were not exactly 'taboo' in the Maoist period. It is more accurate to say that they were articulated in a different manner and in relation to different concerns from the ways in which sex-related issues are articulated today.

The role of the Mao-era state in repressing sex and sexuality during the Cultural Revolution is also unclear, despite claims that the communist repression of sex reached its zenith at this time. In an article titled 'Socialist Sex: The Cultural Revolution Revisited', Emily Honig (2003: 154) notes that there were no official declarations prohibiting non-marital romantic or sexual relationships. In fact, novels and personal memoirs released after the Cultural Revolution indicate that it provided previously inconceivable opportunities for teenagers to experience love and sex, as youthful Red Guards travelled around China together without parental supervision, and many urban youth were separated from their families and 'sent down' to the countryside to learn from poor peasants, while alleviating urban employment pressures (Honig 2003; Min 2009). Scattered statistics available from army corps suggest high levels of cohabitation and pregnancy (Honig 2003: 161). Sent-down youth were also known to have circulated handwritten copies of pornographic stories (Link 2000: 243), and imperial and Republican-era novels featuring romantic and sexual themes (Honig 2003: 157–8), which had stopped being printed or being available for sale along with the CCP's curtailment of the monetary economy and establishment of a state-controlled media.

At the same time, some members of the many different Red Guard factions bullied, harassed and condemned other people for prioritizing 'love' over 'revolution', and for being immoral (Honig 2003:153–4). Local cadres in rural areas sometimes penalized young people, and destroyed their future career-life prospects, for engaging in pre-marital sex, especially when such romances resulted in pregnancy (Honig 2003: 151–3). An official document issued in 1970 demonstrates the existence of sexual abuse and sex-related corruption, by stating that cadres who raped female sent-down youth would be penalized according to the law, and those who forced them into marriage would be subjected to criticism and struggle ('Zhonggong zhongyang wenjian zhong fa, 1970, 26 hao' 1970).

The preceding examples point to a more complicated relationship between 'sex' and 'power' than the narrative of a monolithic communist state oppressing people in a top-down fashion allows. The absence of prohibitions on non-marital sex, other than regulations designed to halt sexual abuse and sex-related corruption, show that the Party-state did not act strictly to repress sex, nor was it exactly 'silent' on the subject of sex. The perceived 'silence' on sex-related matters during the Maoist period is an effect of the primacy accorded to the imported discourse of Marxism in the state-controlled media, and the reorganization of social space to meet the requirements of centralized planning, which included the restriction of commercial spaces. Sex-related issues clearly became enmeshed in broader political and social movements, which were nevertheless interpreted differently by different people in different locations. This point is illustrated by the fact that some young people used their freedom from parental supervision to engage in sexual experimentation during the Cultural Revolution period, while others condemned them by conflating pre-marital sex with sexual immorality and 'unrevolutionary' behaviour. It is also illustrated by the fact that some local cadres used their patriarchal-style authority to penalize pre-marital sexuality, while others exploited that authority to suit their own venal purposes.

The claim that sex was actively repressed by the Mao-era state has proved to be popular, despite varying degrees of historical inaccuracy, because it appeals to what philosopher Michel Foucault (1978) calls 'the repressive hypothesis'. Foucault notes that conventional accounts of the history of sexuality in western societies posit a standard trajectory. An original period of 'natural' openness was followed by a chronicle of increasing repression that culminated in the constraints of the puritanical Victorian era, where sex was confined to marriage for the purposes of procreation. All other non-(re)productive expressions of human sexuality were stigmatized and silenced, along with the rise of capitalism and bourgeois society. Hence, the twentieth and twenty-first centuries have been characterized by multiple, but as yet unfinished, attempts to free us from those shackles, and admit the full diversity of human sexualities, as demonstrated by the women's liberation movement, and struggles for lesbian and gay rights.

Foucault (1978) challenges such narratives (the repressive hypothesis) by showing how the very 'putting of sex into discourse', from the end of the sixteenth century to the present day, has led to a proliferation of sexual identities (albeit pathologized ones), and encouraged us to speak out about sexuality as both the truth of ourselves, and an act of courage against oppression. He argues that the Christian practice of confession established a compulsion to talk about sex in relation to the inner self, which became a secularized practice after the Reformation. Public discourses on sex were further expanded by the emerging concerns of modern nation-states to ensure prosperity by managing the life, health, reproduction and longevity, etc., of populations.

By illuminating these historical links, Foucault (1978) demonstrates that power does not act strictly to repress sex; it also produces new kinds of sexual subjects and sexual subjectivities. He further suggests that we have become attached to the repressive hypothesis, despite its lack of theoretical rigour, because talking about sex in terms of liberation from repression activates the 'speaker's benefit'. That is, it gives the speaker or writer the aura of being attached to an important political cause, and even being a people's prophet or hero.

Foucault's argument concerning the positivity of power can be illustrated with reference to China's one-child-per-couple policy. The policy was introduced during 1979–80 as a means to guarantee future economic prosperity by curbing population growth (Greenhalgh 2003). Condemned by many as the most extreme example of coercive government controls over the reproductive capacities and desires of individuals in the history of the world (Scharping 2003), the one-child-per-couple policy has severed the link between sex and procreation, and dramatically altered the lives of Chinese women. Women in China are not only living longer, largely because of declines in maternal mortality flowing from the availability of contraception, better health care and reduced fertility rates, but also are spending less time on childrearing, and hence spending more time in full-time employment and other activities outside of the home (Riley 2004). The limitations placed on sex for procreation, combined with freedom from fear of pregnancy, have encouraged the expansion of public discourses on marital sex for pleasure (Pan, S. 2009: 29). The availability of contraception and abortion has also eroded former restrictions on non-marital sexuality (Pan, S. 2009: 30). Hence, government policies, whether intentionally or not, have played a significant role in promoting a new model of sex for leisure and pleasure in China.

The example of the one-child-per-couple policy also challenges the notion that China's changing sexual behaviours are an 'inadvertent' but liberating product of the PRC's opening up to the global economy and western influences. It suggests that the veritable explosion of discourses on sex that has and is taking place in reform-era China, and the emergence of new kinds of sexual behaviours and attitudes, is related to national policy developments, not just international influences. This cautions us against reiterating the tradition/modernity divide, or reifying Euramerica as the site of modern, progressive social movements, and assuming that China is more backward, traditional and oppressive, especially with regards to issues of sex and sexuality. It suggests that we should question the speaker's benefit, which, in the case of China, has the added attraction of presenting the speaker or writer as a fighter for democratic freedoms and human rights. Instead, we need to consider how different nation-states, governing strategies, economic formations, and consumer cultures, produce and uphold diverse sexual subjectivities and communities in an increasingly globalized world (Jeffreys 2009: 1).

SEX IN CHINA TODAY

Sex in China introduces readers to some of the dramatic shifts that have taken place in Chinese sexual behaviours and mores since the 1980s. The book situates China's changing sexual culture, and the nature of its governance, in the socio-political history of the PRC. In doing so, it demonstrates that government authorities and policies do not operate strictly to repress 'sex'; they also create spaces for the emergence of new sexual subjects and subjectivities. It further suggests that while the growth of a consumer society and the Internet has opened new spaces for the articulation of sex-related issues in the PRC, these spaces are not inherently empowering; they also contribute to the formation of different types of gendered and sexual social hierarchies.

Chapter 2 looks at the related issues of marriage, family and reproduction, showing how the 'modern Chinese family' has been shaped by processes of economic reform and the one-child-per-couple policy. Despite a soaring divorce rate and growing numbers of people who self-identify as gay and lesbian, marriage and parenthood are almost universal experiences for young adults in China. Marriage is a family rather than strictly personal choice for many singles, because parents and their adult children are bound by issues such as housing, social welfare and security. The high cost of housing in China's large cities means that adult children often depend on financial and other support from their families to marry in the first place. In turn, the cultural and legal expectation that children will support their parents in old age means that parents, and even grandparents, have a strong investment in the marital decisions of their children.

Following an overview of the evolution of the PRC's Marriage Law and one-child policy, chapter 2 provides four vignettes to illustrate some of the ways in which national policies and family arrangements both enable and constrain individual decision-making relating to marriage, reproduction, divorce and sexuality. The first vignette looks at some of the circumstances surrounding the marriage of a professional woman in her early thirties. The second outlines a new phenomenon known as 'cooperative marriage', that is, a marriage between a gay and a lesbian. The third looks at a short-lived spate of tax-related 'fake' divorces, whereby couples divorced to avoid paying capital gains tax on a second property. The final vignette discusses the pressures that some adult children place on divorced and widowed parents not to remarry, which has resulted in increasing numbers of elderly people cohabiting.

Chapter 3 examines the sexualization of China's youth culture, focusing on the performative sexualities of urban youth. The category of youth refers here to people born after 1979, who are predominantly only children, being born after the implementation of the one-child-per-couple policy, and who have grown up in urban environments shaped by commercialization, increased interaction with the rest of the world, changing family structures, and the spread of new media and communication technologies. Many such youth are allegedly leading China's so-called sexual revolution, as demonstrated by growing rates of pre-marital and casual sex, and the advocacy by female autobiographical novelists and sex bloggers of the right to engage in sex without emotional attachment. Other youth are using fashion and music to experiment with and express sexual personas that challenge conventional gender stereotypes, inspired in part by the cross-dressing and gender-blending practices of China's reality-television pop music idols.

Youth performative sexualities can be empowering because they challenge traditional understandings of appropriate sex and gender roles. Most notably, they challenge the assumption that expressions of female sexuality are related to heterosexual marriage and motherhood, and hence should be should be private not public. However, the performative sexualities of Chinese youth are typically limited by their articulation as individualized and commercialized acts of self-expression rather than as collective political acts.

Chapter 4 discusses the emergence and rapid expansion of gay and lesbian identities and discourses in the PRC. Although China has a documented history of tolerance of homoerotism, homosexuality was largely invisible during the Mao era, being associated with crime, sexual inversion and psychiatric disorder. Homosexuality became a topic of public discourse in the PRC during the 1980s, chiefly through medical and psychiatric texts which aimed to 'treat' or 'prevent' homosexuality. Gay identities and communities have expanded since the late 1990s in urban China, in particular, in connection with transnational lesbian and gay culture, while developing a local identity.

The PRC's actively homosexual population is now estimated at roughly 40 million people. Gay spaces catering to specific groups, for example, cruising zones, bars, restaurants, nightclubs, websites, support organizations, film festivals and pride parades, are also increasing in number and visibility. Along with these changes, new terminology is emerging as people self-identify and describe others as gay, lesbian and queer. Same-sex attracted people are also increasingly presenting their lives and experiences to others on the Internet and in film. However, despite improvements in conditions for same-sex attracted people and their hope for a better future, public discourse in China is at best ambivalent or disinterested regarding homosexuality. Many same-sex attracted people find it difficult to 'come out' because of family demands that they marry and have children, fear of discrimination at work and limited finances that constrain their capacity to live away from home.

Chapter 5 examines the development of a commercial sex industry in China, and the nature of public debates about its policing and legal regulation. Prostitution was allegedly eradicated from Mao-era China in the mid to late 1950s as an expression of the degraded position of women under feudal-capitalist patriarchy, and therefore as incompatible with the goals of building socialism and establishing more equitable socio-sexual relations. Today, the PRC has a highly visible sex market, catering to different hierarchies of buyers and sellers across all sectors of the society, with services expanding to include male–male and youth prostitution. This situation has raised questions about the usefulness of the nation's adherence to a more than three-decade-long policy of attempting to abolish the sex industry via policing campaigns.

Public criticisms of the corrupt, punitive and ineffective nature of police-led crackdowns on prostitution have resulted in important amendments to China's prostitution controls in recent years. The problems associated with the policing of prostitution have also led an increasing number of commentators –academics, bloggers, journalists, police, sex workers, and even prominent public figures with Communist Party affiliations – to openly argue that the commercial sex industry should be legalized or decriminalized to prevent corruption, promote tourism, raise tax revenue, prevent the spread of sexually transmissible infections (STIs), and give sex workers legal protections. However, there is no consensus to date about the actual shape of such policies and how they might be implemented in practice.

Chapter 6 explores China's altered responses to growing rates of sexually transmissible infections, especially the Human Immunodeficiency Virus (HIV) and Acquired Immunodeficiency Syndrome (AIDS). In 1964, the CCP made world history when it announced to the World Health Organization that active venereal disease no longer existed in mainland China, following a series of campaigns involving mass education, the virtual eradication of the prostitution industry and the large-scale provision of costly penicillin. Since the mid-1980s, the reported incident rate of STIs in China has risen sharply; and, since the 2000s, the spread of HIV has become linked to domestic sexual transmission, rather than 'foreigners', shared needles and contaminated blood transfusions.

Initially slow to respond to the policy imperatives of AIDS, the PRC government now actively promotes STIs-HIV prevention work. This shift has led to the introduction of: (1) national sentinel sites to monitor the spread of new infections and identify populations 'at risk'; (2) improved access to medical testing and treatment; (3) celebrity-endorsed public-service advertisements encouraging acceptance of people living with HIV; and (4) programs promoting safer sex and condom use, especially for populations identified as 'high risk', such as sex workers and men who have sex with men. As in other parts of the world, the success of these efforts is challenged by issues of shame, fear and secrecy, and the stigmatizing and often restrictive effects of identifying certain populations as being 'more at-risk' than others because of their sexual behaviours.

Chapter 7 examines the history and development of sex studies in the PRC. After the founding of the PRC in 1949, academic disciplines were subordinated to the organizing principles of Marxism-Leninism and the overarching goal of socialist development. In the 1950s, disciplines such as sociology were banned as 'anti-socialist', based on the assumption that since socialism had been realized in China there were no longer any socio-economic problems to study, especially from a non-Marxist perspective. Hence, sex studies were accorded a low priority until the early 1980s, when Deng Xiaoping's call for intellectuals to 'free their minds' and assist China's modernization revived interest in fields such as anthropology, sexology, sociology and psychiatry.

Throughout the 1980s and 1990s, studies of human sexuality in China were chiefly characterized by a medical and moral focus on identifying and 'correcting' unhealthy sexual bodies and minds.

A considerably smaller number of studies were concerned either to document the history of China's sexual culture and ethnic minority sexual cultures, or to use quantitative-style sociological surveys to identify the PRC's changing sexual behaviours and attitudes.

Since the 2000s, a small but growing number of researchers have focused on sexual diversity and sexual rights, conducting large-scale surveys of the sexual behaviours of Chinese citizens, advocating for legal acceptance of commercial sex, group sex and same-sex marriage, and running conferences about China's transforming sexual culture and sexualities. Chapter 7 explores these changes by reviewing the growth of publications on sexuality in reform-era China and the work of two of the PRC's most famous 'sexperts' – Li Yinhe and Pan Suiming.

Chapter 8 concludes the book by restating the key arguments of *Sex in China* and highlighting some avenues for future research.

2   Marriage and 'Family Planning'

This chapter discusses the related subjects of marriage, family and reproduction in reform-era China. Marriage and parenthood are almost universal experiences for young adults in China, despite growing numbers of divorcees and people who self-identify as gay and lesbian (McMillan 2004: 205). According to the 2010 Population Census of the PRC, only 1.9 per cent of men and women aged forty years and over had never married (Population Census Office under the State Council and the Department of Population and Employment Statistics, the National Bureau of Statistics 2012b: 1862; the percentage was obtained from household data from the long form of the 2010 Census given in Table 5-3 of Book III ('Population by age, sex, educational attainment and marital status'), and was calculated by dividing the sum of men and women listed as having never married in the age group forty to sixty-five plus by the sum of men and women in the same age group who filled in the long form (Population Census Office under the State Council 2012b: 1862–7)).

Marriage is also the social arrangement within which children are legitimately born, and the majority of pregnancies out of marriage end in abortion (McMillan 2004: 205–6). China is estimated to have one of the highest abortion rates in the world, with somewhere between 9 and 13 million abortions a year being performed mostly on unmarried women under twenty-four years of age (Oleson 2011). Abortion in China is relatively inexpensive and free from stigma, largely as a result of the introduction of the one-child-per-couple 'family planning policy' (*jihua shengyu zhengce*) in 1979–80.

The social expectation that everyone will marry and then have a child is highlighted in a satirical diagram titled 'Speeches at a Family Gathering', which outlines a concept called 'Chinese-style forced marriage' (*Zhongguoshi bihun*) ('Zhongguoshi bihun' 2012). The diagram was posted on numerous online forums and reposted over 50,000 times solely on Sina.com microblogs between January and February 2012. It suggests that young adults are often reluctant to attend New Year family gatherings because, unless they are married with a child, their older relatives will compel them to become so (see also Sun and Lu 2012).

The diagram describes the 'universal' imperative to marry and reproduce by detailing the following series of hypothetical situations faced by young Chinese adults at New Year family gatherings. Upon arriving at the family gathering, seldom-seen older relatives will ask: 'Are you married and do you have a child?' If you have a spouse, then older relatives will want to know everything about them, especially how much money they earn. If you have a child, then the child will have to perform for them, for example, by singing, dancing, telling jokes or demonstrating their ability to speak English. In contrast, if you are married but do *not* have a child, then older relatives will urge you to get 'pregnant' that very day; and, if you are *not* married then they will beseech you to get married and have a child without delay ('Zhongguoshi bihun' 2012).

If you have a boyfriend/girlfriend, you will be told to 'strike while the iron is hot' rather than risk rejection by your partner and being unable to find another partner, then ultimately becoming old and unmarried, and socially ostracized as someone who obviously has 'a problem'. The ensuing discussion about the inevitable awfulness of becoming a social outcast should you delay in marrying will make you promise to register to get married the following day. If you do *not* have a boyfriend/girlfriend then you will be told to find one immediately because being single contravenes the laws of nature, civilization and science, and is basically an 'anti-revolutionary' crime that harms the well-being of 'one's parents, grandparents, Chinese society, the Chinese Communist Party and the Chinese nation!' Your older relatives will conclude by offering to introduce you straightaway to a suitable person whom you should promptly marry, and have a child with, to stop everyone from worrying that you will grow old alone and be forced to 'beg for food on the streets' ('Zhongguoshi bihun' 2012).

The reality behind this satire of heteronormativity is demonstrated by weekly matchmaking events held in urban parks across China, each of which are attended by thousands of middle-aged parents hoping to find a suitable match for their adult child. At such events, parents holding placards that advertise details such as their child's age, height, educational background, occupation, salary, place of household registration (*hukou*), home-ownership status, and personal characteristics and interests, are approached by other interested parents (Shi, Y. 2013: 1, 6). All hope to find a spouse for their child and to become grandparents. As women in China usually retire at the age of fifty, and men at sixty years, many of these people view caring for their grandchild as an optimal family arrangement not only for reasons of personal satisfaction, but also because it contributes to the future security of the extended family by allowing their child to continue working.

The chapter examines the major forces shaping the 'modern Chinese family', focusing on the significant role played by national policies and laws. It first outlines the evolution of the PRC's Marriage Law and related regulations. It then explores some of the consequences of the introduction of China's one-child-per-couple policy in 1979–80. Finally, it provides a series of vignettes about late marriages, 'fake heterosexual marriages' between gays and lesbians, 'fake tax-related divorces' and elderly cohabiting couples. Contrary to suggestions that the Chinese conjugal family is a static state-enforced institution, the chapter illustrates how changing national policies and family arrangements both enable and constrain individual decision-making relating to marriage, divorce, reproduction and sexuality.

MARRIAGE AND DIVORCE

In the PRC, as elsewhere, legal frameworks define who can enter into and exit a marriage. These frameworks typically reflect and entrench heteronormative sexual mores – marrying partners should be single, adult members of the opposite sex. Such frameworks are sometimes condemned from contemporary perspectives for institutionalizing heterosexual marital monogamy (Kam 2014), and leaving 'no discursive space for women – or men – to choose difference, whether this means simply not marrying, having a lover outside marriage, or rejecting heterosexuality' (Evans 1997: 212). However, the promulgation of the PRC's first Marriage Law in May 1950, less than a year after the PRC was founded in October 1949, also represents the early Chinese Communist Party's claim to have revolutionized socio-sexual relationships by abolishing the feudal-patriarchal marriage and family system that had oppressed Chinese women for centuries (Information Office of the State Council of the People's Republic of China 1994a, 1994b). As these opposing viewpoints suggest, there is little that is universal, 'natural' or 'private' about marriage as an institution: 'marriage' is an evolving institution with enculturated and contested histories.

Marriage and family relations in China are governed by the Marriage Law of the PRC, first promulgated in 1950, and revised in 1980 and 2001. The 1950 Marriage Law abolished polygamy, together with arranged and mercenary marriages, and established a new marriage and family system based on the free choice of (heterosexual) partners, monogamy and equality between the sexes (Zhonghua renmin gongheguo hunyin fa 1950). Campaigns to implement the new Marriage Law were followed by a spate of divorces as women, in particular, sought to dissolve 'old-style marriages'. However, the initial support of the Communist Party for unilateral divorce was soon halted because of the unpopularity of this policy with male peasants, who constituted both the mainstay of the military and early CCP support (Huang, P. 2005: 175–6), as well as with members of the older generation who felt their control of family affairs was threatened (Croll 1978: 234; Johnson 1983: 115–37). Some historians conclude that the communist regime reneged on its promise to revolutionize marital and family relations, while others note that the CCP paid considerable attention to eradicating polygamy, slave girls, and mercenary and forced marriages, throughout the 1950s (Huang, P. 2005: 177).

Whichever the case may be, the PRC's divorce rate remained extremely low throughout the 1960s and 1970s for three reasons. First, although divorce was permitted in theory, it was discouraged in practice unless there were compelling political reasons to warrant such an action. By the end of the 1950s, it was assumed that all 'feudal' forms of marriage had been eradicated or dissolved and therefore only 'good, socialist forms' remained (Huang, P. 2005: 155). Second, the early communist regime's distaste for the 'bourgeois legal system' resulted in a general decrease in access to legal institutions. As a result, 'ordinary' disputes such as divorces were exhaustively mediated by Party organizations, with relevant procedures being geared towards reconciliation rather than dissolution of a marriage (Woo 2009: 65). Finally, divorce was complicated in practice by the introduction of centralized economic planning, a system wherein the Party-state allocated work and distributed resources, and therefore needed to know the identity and location of its workers.

Population mobility was severely restricted in the PRC between the late 1950s and mid-1980s to meet the requirements of centralized economic planning. The implementation of a household registration system (*hukou*) in 1958 tied urban Chinese and rural agricultural producers to their place of work and/or birth. Household registration denied citizens of the PRC the right to move from one city to another, and from rural to urban areas, unless they had official permission to do so. Such permission was difficult to obtain; it depended on a complicated system of employment quotas and associated education opportunities as specified in national and local economic plans (Lu Yilong 2002: 127; Whyte and Parish: 1984: 18).

People in rural areas became tied to the communities formed by agricultural collectives and the majority of urban Chinese spent their day-to-day lives in the closed community of a socialist work unit (*danwei*). A *danwei* refers to state-run places of employment, such as factories, schools and universities, which aimed to overcome the alienation of labour by merging life and work. Until urban reform began in the early 1990s, a *danwei* not only provided lifelong employment for its employees, but also the other necessities of daily life – food, clothing, housing, education, entertainment, health care, and retirement benefits (Jeffreys and Sigley 2011: 14).

The introduction of the work unit and household registration system had a significant impact on marriage and divorce patterns across the country. Restrictions on population mobility meant that the place of residence of a PRC citizen became an important determinant of opportunities for socio-economic advancement through marriage. Urban citizens strove to marry residents of work units with better working and living conditions (Lavely 1991: 291), while China's rural citizens became second-class citizens because of their limited access to state-provided welfare services when compared to urban citizens (Xu, F. 2011: 39–43). In this context, marriage to someone with a superior place of residence or urban residency became a means to achieve social and intra- and inter-provincial mobility, especially for rural women (Fan and Huang 1998: 230–4; Fan 2008: 75). Such marriages often involved the marriage of a young, rural woman to a significantly older man with failing physical and/or mental health. However, his land or urban residence offered improved living conditions and employment opportunities for the young woman and ultimately her natal family (Fan and Huang 1998: 235; Huang Youqin 2001: 261).

Restrictions on population mobility also dissuaded many couples from applying for a divorce because there was no practical way to exit an unhappy marriage. Applying for a divorce meant making one's 'private' circumstances known to other members of the local community. Moreover, until the introduction of economic reforms and the opening of China's labour and property market, most potential divorcees would have been unable to move and access other work and accommodation. As sociologist Deborah Davies puts it: 'In the socialist era, people were really nailed to a place. You were stuck with the neighbors you had, as well as the spouse you had' (Davies, cited in Tan, T. 2013: 3).

In 1980, a revised version of the 1950 Marriage Law was approved, which contained amendments designed to promote China's economic development and the one-child-per-couple policy (Zhonghua renmin gongheguo hunyin fa (xiuzheng) 1980). Between late 1979 and 1980, the PRC government determined that adopting a policy of 'one couple, one child' for the next thirty to forty years was the only solution to prevent an estimated massive growth in population that would jeopardize the goal of modernizing China and raising overall living standards (Greenhalgh 2003: 169, 184–5). That goal involved keeping the population within a projected target range of 1.2 billion people by the year 2000 to raise per capita income levels to around USD 800–1,000, and ensure the adequate provision of services and infrastructure (Greenhalgh 2003: 167, 184). The 1980 Marriage Law, effective 1 January 1981, consequently raised the legal age of marriage from eighteen to twenty years for women and from twenty to twenty-two years for men, and enjoined couples to practise family planning (Zhonghua renmin gongheguo hunyin fa (xiuzheng) 1980: Articles 5 and 12).

These amendments were accompanied by changes to the PRC's national marriage registration system – a marriage is legal in the PRC only when it is registered with an appropriate department of civil affairs. In November 1980, new Marriage Registration Procedures came into effect, replacing procedures that had been in place since 1955. These Procedures were amended in 1986, and replaced by the Marriage Registration Management Regulations in 1994. A new system of Marriage Registration Regulations was introduced in 2003 (Hunyin dengji banfa 1955; Hunyin dengji banfa (1980 nian) 1980; Hunyin dengji banfa 1986; Hunyin dengji guanli tiaoli 1994; Hunyin dengji tiaoli 2003).

All of these regulations require parties applying for marriage registration to appear in person before the relevant authorities to verify their identity and confirm that they are single and entering into a marriage of their own free will. Prior to 1994, PRC applicants had to produce two types of documentation: a certificate of household registration or a resident identity card; and a certificate issued by their work unit, indicating the applicant's name, sex, date of birth, marital status, and other identity-related details (Hunyin dengji banfa 1986). Between 1994 and 2003, PRC citizens had to produce four types of documentation: a certificate of household registration; a resident identity card; a certificate issued by the applicant's work unit or local neighbourhood committee verifying their marital status; and a pre-marital health check-up report issued by a hospital designated by the marriage registration department (Hunyin dengji guanli tiaoli 1994). Mandatory pre-marital health check-ups aimed to protect the health of future one-child generations by ensuring that potential spouses were of good mental and reproductive health, and free of hereditary, major and communicable diseases (Sleeboom-Faulkner 2011).

In 2003, the 1994 Marriage Registration Management Regulations and all supplementary regulations governing the procedures for registering a marriage in the PRC were replaced by the current Marriage Registration Regulations (Hunyin dengji tiaoli 2003). The 2003 regulations simplified the procedures for registering a domestic marriage by removing requirements that applicants produce a certificate issued by their work unit to verify their marital status. This requirement became unworkable along with the opening of the PRC's labour market and the loosening of former controls over population mobility, which also led to the gradual decline of the *danwei* system in favour of private enterprise. The 2003 regulations further simplified the procedures for registering a domestic marriage by removing requirements that applicants undergo a mandatory pre-marital health check-up. Such testing became voluntary in 2002. This action reduced state health-care costs and side-stepped domestic and international criticisms of the eugenicist nature of compulsory testing, which strongly discouraged the marriage and procreation of people with mental and physical health issues (Sleeboom-Faulkner 2011). Voluntary testing makes individuals rather than the state responsible for any concerns about their physical and reproductive health, and that of prospective marriage partners, in the context of the one-child-per-couple policy.

Domestic applicants for marriage registration in the PRC now have to produce a certificate of household registration, a national identity card, and a signed declaration stating that they are single and not a close blood relative of their intended spouse (Article 5). A marriage between two people of direct lineal descent or collateral consanguinity within three generations is viewed from a medical standpoint as increasing the possibility of congenital disorders in children. When applicants present these documents at a local marriage registration office, and sign relevant documents in front of a delegated representative of that office, they are issued a marriage certificate stating that they are legally married (see figure 2.1). Wedding celebrations typically take place several weeks or even months after the legal formalities.

The 2003 regulations also simplified the procedures for registering a divorce. The 1980 Marriage Law stipulated for the first time that the People's Courts would grant a divorce in cases where couples had experienced a 'breakdown in mutual affections' (*ganqing que yi polie*)

Figure 2.1 Couple posing with marriage certificates
Source: ©Imaginechina/Corbis; reproduced with permission

and attempts at mediation had failed (Zhonghua renmin gongheguo hunyin fa 1980: Article 25). The 1994 marriage regulations supported easier divorce in theory by stating that the marriage registration department would process divorce applications that met the criteria for divorce within one month (Hunyin dengji guanli tiaoli 1994: Article 16). However, PRC citizens could only meet the criteria by providing a supporting letter from their work unit or an equivalent authority (Article 14), which was extremely difficult to obtain in practice because of an emphasis on the mediation rather than dissolution of troubled marriages. The revised Marriage Law of 2001 clarified the conditions for obtaining a divorce. Article 3 prohibits domestic violence, bigamy and the cohabitation of a married person with any third party (Zhonghua renmin gongheguo hunyin fa 2001). Article 31 states that a couple who present appropriate documentation to the relevant civil affairs department, and confirm that they both consent to an uncontested divorce, will be granted a divorce forthwith. In the event that one party does not consent to a divorce, Article 32 stipulates that an individual may file a suit for divorce with the People's Courts and that a divorce shall be granted in cases involving the alienation of mutual affection (Zhonghua renmin gongheguo hunyin fa 2001). The 2003 Marriage Registration Regulations further facilitate divorce by removing the requirement that divorce applicants must provide relevant authorities with a letter of support from their work units (Hunyin dengji tiaoli 2003).

These changes, in conjunction with increased job mobility and access to private housing, have contributed to soaring divorce rates. As figure 2.2 illustrates, only 319,000 couples registered a divorce in

Figure 2.2 China's rising number of divorces

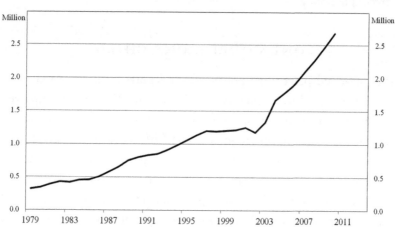

Source: Chart adapted from figures provided by Zhonghua renmin gongheguo minzhengbu [Ministry of Civil Affairs of the People's Republic of China (2011) 'Lihun banli' [Divorce registration], Zhongguo Minzheng Tongji Nianjian, Beijing Zhongguo tongji chubanshe, p. 106

mainland China in 1979. That figure rose to over 1 million couples in 1995, and more than 2.6 million couples in 2010 (Zhonghua renmin gongheguo minzhengbu 2011: 106). Media reports suggest that this upward trend is continuing as more than 3.1 million couples divorced in China in 2012 (Cui, He and Wu 2013).

Although the PRC's divorce rate remains low when compared to many other countries, the now widespread occurrence of divorce points to altered expectations of love, marriage and family life. Some scholars argue that the PRC's rising divorce rate demonstrates the growing premium that many people now place on romantic and sexual love (Pan, S. 2009: 29). Other scholars suggest that the rising divorce rate may be related to the emotional and financial pressures placed on married couples in urban centres as two working people who are responsible for the care of their one child and four aging parents, given the PRC's inadequate social security system (Wang and Zhou 2010: 266). All of these considerations are related in part to the one-child-per-couple policy.

ONE COUPLE, ONE CHILD

The one-child-per-couple policy, which reportedly has averted more than 300 million births since its introduction in 1979–80, has impacted on virtually every aspect of everyday life in China (Greenhalgh 2003: 163). It immediately contributed to the PRC's already rapidly declining fertility rate. During the 1970s, the average number of children per woman dropped from just under six to just under three (Greenhalgh and Winckler 2005: 3). Following the introduction of the one-child policy, the fertility rate dropped to the 'replacement level' of around 2.1 children per woman. By the 2000s, it had fallen below the replacement level to reach an average of 1.6 children per woman (Greenhalgh and Winckler 2005: 3). The fertility rate is now just over 1.5 children per woman, according to data from the 2010 Population Census of the

Figure 2.3 China's declining population and birth rates

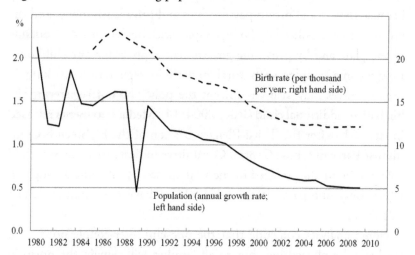

Source: Chart adapted from figures provided by 'China's population, 1969–2009' (n.d.), Chinability; at <http://www.chinability.com/>

PRC (Rothman and Wang 2013: 7). The one-child policy has therefore helped to make small families the norm, especially in urban China. Figure 2.3 offers a graphic illustration of China's declining population growth and birth rates since the introduction of the one-child family planning policy in 1979–80.

There are exceptions to the one-child rule, despite the initial draconian enforcement of the policy, which involved highly publicized cases in the western media of forced sterilizations and late abortions (Oleson 2011; Riley 2004: 12). The rule applies to members of China's dominant ethnic group – the Han. Members of the PRC's fifty-five minority ethnic groups are excluded from the policy. People in most rural areas can apply to have a second child if their first-born child is a girl. Parents with sickly or disabled children are permitted to have more than one child, and couples who are both only children are allowed to have two children (Shan 2013b: 1). Wealthy couples may circumvent the policy because they can afford to pay for fines and private schooling, and the policy is chiefly policed by fining couples with births registered outside of the 'plan', and by providing government support for one child only. Low-income couples with rural household registration working in urban centres may also circumvent the policy by not registering the birth of an additional child (Riley 2004: 14). Media statements released in late 2013 after the Third Plenary Session of the Eighteenth Communist Party of China Central Committee indicate that the one-child rule will be further relaxed in the near future, by allowing a couple in which only one party is an only child to have two children (Shan 2013b: 1).

Some analysts conclude that the one-child-per-couple policy will gradually be phased out, but small families will remain the norm in China for economic reasons, as is the case in East Asia more generally (Rothman and Wang 2013: 7). In March 2013, the PRC government announced that the National Population and Family Planning Commission (NPFPC), which was previously responsible for implementing the one-child policy, would be merged into two different organizations – the Ministry of Health and the National Development and Reform Commission, as part of a streamlining of government administration. The break-up of the NPFPC arguably signals a desire to end the one-child policy, although this conclusion is refuted in media statements about the reorganization (Deng, S. 2013; Shan 2013a: 3). Whichever the case may be, data from the PRC's 2010 census indicates that small families have become the norm in major Chinese cities, and will remain the custom even if the one-child policy is lifted. In Shanghai, for example, the fertility rate is an average of 0.7 children per woman, which suggests that many couples who are in the only-child cohort, and therefore eligible to have two children, are choosing not to have a second child, and some are choosing to have no children (Rothman and Wang 2013: 5).

The combined effects of the one-child-per-couple policy and rising expectations of living standards have meant that marriage and pregnancy are occurring at later ages in the PRC than was previously the norm. In the 1980s, women over the age of twenty-three years and men over twenty-five years were 'regarded as behind schedule in marriage both by the family of origin and by the individuals themselves' (Fowler, Gao and Carlson 2010: 346). Today, the average age of marriage is twenty-six years or later, with some people remaining single into their thirties (Fowler, Gao and Carlson 2010: 346). Moreover, around 7 per cent of women living in major cities are delaying having their first child until they are aged thirty-five years (Zhang, X. 2010).

Later marriage and single childbearing are having significant effects on the lives of Chinese women – they not only live longer than previous generations of Chinese women, but also often enjoy a higher social status and family position than those occupied by their mothers and grandmothers. Women in China are living longer largely because of declines in maternal mortality flowing from the availability of contraception, better health care and reduced fertility rates. The life expectancy at birth for both sexes was sixty-four years in 1980; it rose to just under seventy-two years by 2001, and reached nearly seventy-five years in 2010 ('Life expectancy rises in China' 2012; Riley 2004: 9). The average life expectancy of Chinese women is now around seventy-seven years, and the average life expectancy of Chinese men is around seventy-two years ('Life expectancy rises in China' 2012). Later and fewer pregnancies also mean that many Chinese women are spending less time on childrearing and are able to continue in full-time employment and undertake other activities outside of the home (Riley 2004: 24). Hence, many such women are able to negotiate more equitable marital relationships than previous generations of Chinese women.

The one-child family policy's severing of marital sex from procreation has also altered expectations of married life, opening the space for public discussions of marital romance and sex, and domestic violence and marital rape – issues which were rarely discussed publicly in China until the 1980s and 1990s (Cao et al. 2011: 546; Milwertz 2003: 631; McMillan 2004: 203; Xu, X. et al. 2005: 79). Such discussions predominantly target young adults, and especially women, as part of the commercialized romanticization and sexualization of heterosexuality that has accompanied China's economic reforms (see chapter 3), and also as newly-weds with limited experience of managing domestic conflict/violence and accessing support services. However, romance, sex and (re)marriage are increasingly presented as 'normal, natural and healthy in middle and old age' (Shea 2005: 118). For example, in large cities such as Beijing where one-child families are common, interviews with older Chinese women suggest that the majority did not view menopause as signalling the end of their physical/sexual attractiveness, because their marriage had already extended well beyond their reproductive years as dictated by national policy (Shea 2005: 129–31).

China's governing authorities have recently rebranded late marriage and the one-child family as part of a cosmopolitan lifestyle that is helping to promote sustainable *global* population growth. Banners and painted slogans displayed in residential communities across the PRC once stated that population control was necessary for national development and security. Typical slogans were: 'We have limited land and a large population, family planning is an essential national policy' (*ren duo di shao shi jiben guoqing, jihua shengyu shi jiben guoce*); 'Population security means controlling population growth and improving the quality of the population' (*kongzhi renkou zengzhang, tigao renkou suzhi, weihu renkou anquan*); and 'Ensure family happiness and national prosperity by practising planned parenthood' (*weile guojia fuqiang, jiating xingfu, qing nin jihua shengyu*) (Li Zidong 2011). Typical slogans today are: 'We share one planet; we must control population growth' (*renlei zhiyou yige diqiu, bixu kongzhi renkou zengzhang*); 'Safeguard our shared planet; please reduce population pressure' (*weihu women gongyou de xingqiu qing jianshao renkou yali*); and 'We only have one planet, please leave some space for future generations' (*renlei zhiyou yige diqiu weile zisun houdai qing liuxia yipian fazhan kongjian*) (Li Zidong 2011). In short, the one-child-per-couple policy is increasingly presented as the 'right thing' for modern citizens to do rather than a state-enforced rule.

Other banners and posters highlight efforts to address one of the documented negative effects of the one-child-per-couple policy – the 'missing girls' phenomenon. China has the world's highest-documented sex ratios at birth. In 1989, the ratio was close to normal – approximately 105 boys for every 100 girls for first births; by the end of the 2000s, there were nearly 120 boys for every 100 girls (Riley 2004: 17). According to the PRC's most recent census, the sex ratio at birth in 2010 stood at just over 118 males per 100 females, which is slightly lower than the over 119 ratio documented in 2009, but still higher than the nearly 117 ratio from the fifth national census in 2000 ('New campaign targets gender ratio imbalance' 2011). There are four standard explanations for the PRC's high sex ratios: (1) 'excess deaths of female babies through infanticide, neglect, or abandonment'; (2) 'under-reporting of female births'; (3) 'adoption of female children'; and (4) 'sex-selective abortions' (Riley 2004: 18). These problems are related to the combined effects of the one-child policy and the cultural preference, especially in rural China, for boy children to carry on the family line and support ageing parents.

The PRC government has responded by banning sex-selective abortions and launching publicity campaigns that emphasize the value of girl children. Sex-selective abortions were banned as early as 1995. New legislation came into effect in 2001 that punishes medical practitioners who use an ultrasound to determine the sex of a child and then inform the parents of the child's gender, by stripping them of their medical licence ('New campaign targets gender ratio imbalance' 2011). However, married couples who want their first child to be a boy continue to seek medical help, as demonstrated by the launching in 2011 of an eight-month-long policing campaign against medical practitioners who provided non-medical sex determinations (ultrasound scans) and gender-selective abortions ('New campaign targets gender ratio imbalance' 2011).

The prevalence of sex-selective abortion is further indicated by a community education poster seen by the lead author of this book on a street in Zhengzhou, the capital city of Henan Province in north-central China, in May 2013. The poster displays an image of a baby whose head and body is partly covered by a blanket, in a field of wild flowers. Text above the image says: 'Please don't tell anyone my gender' (*qing buyao ba wode xingbei gaosu beiren*) (see figure 2.4).

Other slogans found in public places illustrate government-led efforts to encourage the positive valuing of girl children. Such slogans

Figure 2.4 'Please don't tell anyone my gender'
Source: Photograph by Elaine Jeffreys of poster produced by the Zhengzhou Chengdong Street Office

include: 'Times have changed; boys and girls are equally good!' (*shidai butongle nannü yiyang hao*); 'A daughter is as good as a son; who says girls are worth less than boys?' (*nü'er bubi nan'er cha; shui shuo nüzi buru nan*); and 'Boy or girl? Let nature take its course!' (*shengnan sheng nü shunqi ziran*) (Li Zidong 2011).

Although males continue to be the preferred child in rural areas, the one-child-per-couple policy has encouraged a positive revaluing of girl children in major urban centres as many parents and grandparents make heavy emotional and financial investments in their only female child/grandchild. Studies suggest that urban-based parents have similar aspirations for their only child's education and career, irrespective of the child's gender (Fowler, Gao and Carson 2010: 348). Parents with an only female child also expect that the child will take care of them in the future (Fong 2004: 131). Indeed, some parents suggest that having a girl may be better than having a boy. As a mother of one young man explained, this is because grown-up girls are likely to be more filial and hardworking than their male counterparts. Moreover, the parents of a young man have to help finance the cost of housing for their child as a potential groom – ownership of an apartment, or a sizeable deposit for a mortgage, being a precondition for marriage to an educated 'quality bride/future mother' in urban China (author interview, Beijing, July 2013).

Another documented negative effect of the one-child-per-couple policy is the pressure placed on working members of the one-child-generation family unit. Many of the estimated 200 million Chinese who belong to the first one-child generation (that is, people born in and after the 1980s) face the '4–2–1' family problem, meaning that married couples may find themselves responsible for the financial support and care of four retired parents and one child (Fowler, Gao and Carlson 2010: 347; Riley 2004: 22). In cases where both parents are only children, the second one-child generation are growing up with parents and grandparents, but no aunts, uncles, or cousins (Fowler,

Gao and Carlson 2010: 348). These 'sibling-less' generations face the potential burden of supporting their parents and grandparents, given social expectations that children will care for their parents and supplement China's uneven pension system. Reiterating clauses contained in the 1950 Marriage Law and the 1954 Constitution, Articles 10–13 of the Law of the People's Republic of China on Protection of the Rights and Interests of the Elderly (1996) stipulate that sons/daughters and their spouses should provide for their parents' needs in terms of emotional, financial, housing and health-care support. The 2001 Marriage Law similarly emphasizes that children have a responsibility to support the elderly and further provides 'elderly parents with the right to sue children for support' if they fail to provide assistance (Giles and Ren 2007: 266). Confirming these responsibilities, a Chinese court supported a mother's claim of filial negligence against her daughter in July 2013, by ordering the daughter to visit her mother at least once every two months *and* also on two national holidays each year (Zhou, R. 2013).

Caring for ageing parents presents difficult and costly choices for many married couples, given that 261 million people are living somewhere other than their place of household registration, according to the 2010 Population Census of the PRC (Population Census Office under the State Council 2012a, Table 7-1: 458). Many internal migrants are young couples who have moved from rural to urban areas of China to find work. Some rural-to-urban migrants leave their child/children in their native homes with grandparents, sending money home but only physically returning for holidays and/or when they can afford it (Fowler, Gao and Carlson 2010: 344). Urban couples with one child also often live in different locations from their parents because of the decline of the urban work-unit system and escalating house prices. Hence, some analysts contend that the one-child family policy has to be relaxed to ensure adequate care for China's growing numbers of senior citizens given the declining youth population (Mu, G. 2013: 9).

At the same time, the cost for parents of supporting a child until they marry and pass the perceived threshold into adulthood is rising. As in many developed countries, the children of parents who can afford to support them through higher education are increasingly staying at home and marrying late (Chen, W. 2013: 10). Labour mobility and the partial privatization of housing mean that many young adults in China now live independently from their parents. However, an estimated 30 per cent of young adults still depend on their parents financially because of high housing costs and the difficulties associated with finding graduate employment, especially in large cities (Chen, W. 2013: 10).

Parents also finance a large proportion of the cost of their child getting married, regardless of their income levels (Lu Xin 2007). A National Marriage Consumer Survey suggests that around 56 per cent of 60,000 respondents spent more than CNY 2 million getting married (Lu Xin 2007). The most expensive marriages include the cost of home ownership or a mortgage deposit in a major city, as well as the cost of redecorating and furnishing a home. For example, in 2011, the estimated cost of a marriage in Shenzhen, Beijing and Shanghai was CNY 2.08 million, 2.03 million and 2.01 million respectively, and the estimated cost of a marriage in Wuhan was CNY 650,000 (Ma Yiqun 2013). Other marriage expenses related to the PRC's booming wedding service industry, including elaborate wedding photography and restaurant services (which were used by around 86 and 79 per cent of respondents respectively), and honeymoon travel (both domestic and international) (Lu Xin 2007). The average cost of quality wedding photographs is around CNY 5,000 plus an additional CNY 1,000 for the hire of clothing; and the cost of restaurant services can reach CNY 20,000, depending on the venue and the number of invited guests (Ma Yiqun 2013: 76). Some respondents also bought wedding outfits (traditional Chinese and/or western white-wedding-style), rather than hiring them, highlighting a growing domestic market for wedding attire – the PRC is currently the largest manufacturer of wedding outfits for the international market (Lu Xin 2007). Many parents apparently are willing to pay for elaborate weddings because Chinese parents have traditionally paid for their children to marry, and some parents want to ensure that everything is 'perfect' for their only child.

MARITAL DECISION-MAKING

National policies and family arrangements impact in diverse ways on individual decisions relating to marriage, reproduction, divorce and sexuality, as illustrated by the four vignettes below. According to sociologist Sun Peidong, choosing a marriage partner is more than a personal choice for singles in China's largest cities. It is 'a family choice', because parents and adult children are bound by issues such as 'housing, social welfare and security' (Sun, cited in Shi, Y. 2013: 6).

Story 1

In June 2013, the lead author of this book was invited to two marriage ceremonies being held for a thirty-two-year-old Beijing-based acquaintance named Chen – one in Chen's parents' home of Tianjin, and one in the family home of her thirty-two-year-old Beijing-based husband, Wang, in a village in central rural China. (names, dates and other identifying details have been changed throughout this account for reasons of confidentiality). The couple, who had been dating for over a year, had registered their marriage with a civil affairs bureau in February, and their wedding celebrations were held at a later date as is often the case in China. The dates for the two celebrations were decided through negotiation with a *fengshui* expert or fortune-teller to ensure their auspicious nature. However, the agreed-upon dates happened to fit in with the availability of venues and the respective work commitments of the couple, as well as the interests of their respective families, who were paying for the events. Chen's father paid for an elaborate banquet attended by family members and over 100 guests in Tianjin, which served in part as his retirement party. Wang's parents paid for a traditional-style village wedding. This involved the observance of numerous 'rituals', including the hiring of sedans and sedan bearers to carry the bride to the groom's family home, where traditional music was performed, and firecrackers were set off, before the entire village sat down to eat and drink at a home-cooked feast.

Chen and Wang paid for two sets of wedding photographs, which in conventional Chinese style were posed for and paid for long before the wedding celebrations. The first set depicted a modern couple in a modern setting with western wedding attire – a white wedding dress and black suit, posing beside a chic apartment. White-wedding photographs are a popular commodity in China, being viewed as both modern and romantic, and young adults wearing hired clothes and posing for wedding-style photographs are a common sight in tourist and natural scenic sites across the country. Chen and Wang's second set of photographs featured a couple dressed in traditional Chinese wedding attire – red clothing to symbolize joy, and embroidered with dragons and phoenixes to symbolize that the couple is a perfect pair. The couple were also portrayed in one of the photographs holding a red ribbon in front of the Chinese symbol for 'double happiness' (*shuang xi*), signifying that they and their families are now united.

Chen's marriage delighted her parents, who were previously concerned that their only child would be looked upon as a 'leftover woman' (*shengnü*). This is a recent and somewhat pejorative term. It was listed as one of 171 new words by the PRC's Ministry of Education in 2007, and is used to describe an educated, professional woman aged over twenty-seven years who has not yet married because she is perceived to have overly high expectations ('Shengnü' 2013). Its popular circulation has resulted in a twenty-five-episode television dating show called *Come on Shengnü!* (*shengnü jiayou*), the predictable plotlines of which involve smart, successful women doing whatever they can to get a man (Sun Hao dir. 2010). One of Chen's friends had entered a different television dating show and had encouraged her to do the same. However, Chen had confined her dating activities to occasional workplace 'match-making parties' and more or less weekly blind dates arranged by her parents, in the two years before she met Wang.

Chen jokes that she had already decided that her first date with Wang was going to be her last family-arranged blind date, and hence it was a good thing for everyone concerned that it had worked out. Chen's cousin, who lives in a provincial capital city, knows a schoolfriend of Wang's. He had told his mother about Wang, who then mentioned him to her sister (Chen's mother). The sisters agreed that the two unmarried business graduates, both aged around thirty years and working with international-orientated ventures in Beijing, might be interested in meeting each other, and set about making the necessary arrangements. Chen and Wang's original date was successful and, after a year of dating, they announced their intention to marry.

Chen and Wang's decision to marry was followed by what Chen describes as somewhat unnecessary negotiations between the two sets of parents over what each partner would bring to the marriage finan-cially. While the couple viewed their decision to marry in personal terms, their parents were also concerned about the suitability of the match. Despite Wang's rural background, he was deemed a suitable match for Chen – an urban educated woman with an overseas master's degree in business management, and the daughter of a moderately suc-cessful businessman. Wang was undertaking postgraduate study ena-bling him to apply for Beijing household registration, he was being groomed for a management position at work with a view to joining the Communist Party, and one of his uncles had offered the couple rent-free accommodation in a private property investment in Beijing. Thus, Wang, as a husband and son-in-law, would be able to provide future security in terms of household registration, housing and employment and upward career prospects.

Apart from planning for an overseas holiday-cum-honeymoon and trying to get a pay rise, Chen jokes that her main concern now is when she will be expected to have a child, and whether one will do! Truthfully or not, Chen claims to be uninterested in motherhood because she enjoys her current lifestyle. However, she believes that having a child will make her parents happy and therefore has always expected to have one, and knows that her parents will look after the child while she continues to work. However, as an only child, Chen now wonders whether her husband and both sets of parents will want her to have two children if the one-child-per-couple policy is relaxed.

Story 2

Academic and media discussions of a phenomenon known as 'cooperative marriage' (*hezuo hunyin*), that is, a marriage between a gay and a lesbian, provide a different example of the influence of social and family pressure in marital decisions (Kam 2013: 99–103; Tan, M. 2013). In recent years the subject of *tongqi* (wives of homosexuals) has attracted media attention, largely as a result of unsubstantiated claims by academics that social pressure on men to marry for the purposes of continuing the family line has resulted in 16 million Chinese women being married to homosexual men, and partly because of the activist efforts of former wives of homosexuals to provide support to other women (Shan 2012). Such activism is primarily concerned with the psychological and physical consequences for *tongqi* as women who are unwittingly involved in a marriage based on deception, arguing they are not only denied a genuine loving marriage, but also vulnerable to abuse and sexually transmissible infections (Jiang, S. 2013). In contrast, 'cooperative marriage' refers to a consensual marriage between a gay and a lesbian who perform as a heterosexual couple for family and at work, while maintaining separate gay and lesbian sex lives.

Gays and lesbians enter into cooperative marriages as a tactical response to family pressures to marry and out of fear that they will be alienated by family and friends, and discriminated against at work, if they 'come out'. Cooperative marriage is a topic of controversy in China's gay and lesbian circles. Some people view it as condoning hegemonic concepts of marriage and family; others view it as a silent form of resistance to heteronormativity. However, there are now gay websites which help individuals to find cooperative-marriage partners, and provide pre- and post-marriage advice and support (Kam 2013: 99–103; Tan, M. 2013). The existence of such websites point to the growth of gay and lesbian communities in the PRC, a development which may limit the number of such marriages in the future (see chapter 4).

Being a recent, invisible and small phenomenon, there is no detailed information available about the number of gays and lesbians that are entering into cooperative marriages and how many of these couples are having children. There is also no detailed information available about the practical and ethical problems of deceiving one's parents, in-laws, neighbours, co-workers, and other associates, for a prolonged period of time (Kam 2013: 101). Viewed positively, anecdotal stories suggest that cooperative marriages may open the space for positive intimate alliances and new family arrangements (Kam 2013: 101). In an interview with a journalist, one participant in a cooperative marriage described his wife, who he met through a gay website, as a sister and spoke of his love for their son, who his wife conceived by using a plastic syringe to insert his sperm (Tan, M. 2013). Conversely, as with the existence of 'wives of homosexuals', the phenomenon of cooperative marriage underscores the pressure felt by most young adults in China to marry and reproduce, and thus to demonstrate that they are a good son or daughter, and a conventional/'normal' citizen, irrespective of their personal interests and well-being.

Story 3

However, marriage as a legal institution is not sacrosanct in China, as illustrated by media coverage of a recent spate of divorces in Beijing and Shanghai, flowing from changes to capital gains tax (Fan, F. 2013; Feng Lanlin 2013; Xu, L. 2013). In March 2013, the State Council announced that people who owned more than one household property would pay 20 per cent income tax of the capital gains from selling such property, rather than the previous rate of 2 per cent or under. This change is part of government efforts to reduce the high cost of housing in major cities, which is linked to large numbers of investment properties (Xu, L. 2013). The announcement led to a documented spate of 'fake divorces' as some couples who owned two properties filed for divorce and agreed to split their joint property under individual names, in order to subsequently sell one property and avoid taxes, and then remarry each other (Feng Lanlin 2013). Relevant authorities apparently became concerned when they noticed a major increase in divorce applications that were uncontested and hence had been processed quickly (Feng Lanlin 2013). Disputes over property and child custody are the main reasons why divorce proceedings are delayed and end up in the courts (Woo 2009: 70). Beijing's divorce rate reportedly increased by more than 40 per cent in the first nine months of 2013 compared to the same period in 2012, a spike which many attributed to tax changes (Fan, F. 2013: 3).

The relatively widespread, albeit short-lived, nature of 'tax-related fake divorces' is illustrated by the fact that the Bureau of Civil Affairs in Minhang District in Shanghai disseminated a poster titled 'The Property Market is Risky, Be Careful When Divorcing' to warn potential applicants about the risks associated with such divorces (Feng

Lanlin 2013). As subsequent media reports explained, the property in question might be owned by one spouse and the couple may have agreed to divorce and an equal division of property, based on the assumption that they would remarry and reunite finances once the additional property was sold. However, if a former spouse who had been allocated property under amicable divorce proceedings decided not to remarry the original spouse, then the original spouse would have no legal grounds to reclaim their property (Feng Lanlin 2013; Xu, L. 2013: 3). In cases where the property-owning spouse was engaged in an extra-marital affair, a 'fake divorce' might also be a pretext to exit the original marriage quickly and without an 'equal' division of property. A lawyer explained this situation to a reporter as follows: 'if one party wants to marry someone else after the fake divorce, the other party can't stop it [and claim legal redress] by saying "it's just a fake divorce"' (Xu, L. 2013: 3).

Story 4

High property prices and medical costs have also ensured that family influences on marital and living arrangements are not restricted to top-down pressure placed on children by parents; adult children also have a say in the marital and living arrangements of divorced and widowed parents. An increasing number of 'single' retirees in their fifties and sixties are apparently cohabiting with new partners, rather than marrying them, because their children are concerned about problems relating to division of property should a parent's second marriage fail, and/or the extent of their potential financial responsibility should their parent's new partner fall ill (Zhou, W. 2013: 5). Two adult sons reportedly told their father: 'it's fine if you want to keep each other company and we don't mind if you want to live at her place or she comes to live with you. The only non-negotiable thing is getting married' (cited in Zhou, W. 2013: 5). Cohabitation is consequently becoming more common among urban seniors who desire company and/or a loving relationship with sexual relations, but require financial separation.

CONCLUSION

Marriage in contemporary China, as elsewhere, is an evolving and socially determined institution. Individual decision-making relating to marriage, divorce, reproduction and sexuality, is both enabled and constrained by changing national policies and family arrangements, as demonstrated by numerous amendments to the PRC's Marriage Law and the diverse effects of implementing the one-child policy.

A survey of young Chinese professionals' attitudes towards love and marriage points to the continued influence of national policies and family arrangements on individual decision-making. In the run-up to Chinese Valentine's Day in August 2013, an advertising agency polled around 1.6 million taxi passengers (typically young professionals) in five major cities about their attitudes towards love and marriage (Xu, J. 2013: 4). Survey responses indicate that men want to marry women with a compatible personality and good looks, and women want to marry someone with a compatible personality and money (and then good looks). Around 60 per cent of the respondents said they expected to marry and have a child before the age of twenty-nine. Only 10 per cent said they had no current plans to marry and have a child. More than 80 per cent thought an apartment or established mortgage was a precondition of marriage. Around 45 per cent claimed that they were not opposed to a 'naked marriage' (*luohun*), which is a recent expression for getting married without already owning a home, furniture and car, etc. However, less than 30 per cent agreed that they would actually enter into such a marriage (Xu, J. 2013: 4). In other words, more than 70 per cent of respondents believe that ownership of property is a precondition of marriage, and around 60 per cent believe that they will meet such criteria and marry and have a child before the age of twenty-nine.

The survey responses indicate that most young adults in China not only expect to marry and have one child or two children in accordance with national policies, but also anticipate financial support from parents to do so. This implies the ongoing influence of the extended family in the marital decision-making and other living arrangements of Chinese youth.

3   Youth and Sex(iness)

This chapter examines the sexualization of youth culture in present-day China. The United Nations defines 'youth' for statistical purposes as persons between fifteen and twenty-four years of age, including teenagers (aged thirteen to nineteen) and young adults (aged twenty to twenty-four), and excludes persons aged fourteen years and younger ('What does the UN mean by "youth"' n.d.). In contrast, the Communist Youth League of China has always defined a 'youth' as someone aged between fourteen and twenty-eight years. Both definitions underscore the broad and socially constructed nature of youth as a concept that refers to a period of transition away from the assumed innocence of childhood and towards the desired social and legal maturity of adult citizenship. The concept of 'youth' clearly varies across cultures, academic disciplines and professional organizations, and in terms of legal rights and responsibilities (Jeffreys 2012b: 39–40; Wyn and White 1997).

In China today, people refer to the younger generation colloquially as the post-1980s and the post-1990s generation, that is, people born during 1980–89 and 1990–99 respectively. People in this generational cohort are often the only child in their immediate families, being born after the implementation of the one-child-per-couple policy during 1979–80 (see chapter 2). They are sometimes described collectively in the relevant English-language literature as China's millennial youth (Hooper 1991), generation ku/cool (Moore 2005), Generation Y (Sima and Pugsley 2010) or the 'Net generation' (Liu, F. 2011). Unlike people of their parents' generation, who were dependent on the central-ized socialist state in virtually all aspects of their lives, China's post-1980s and post-1990s generation has grown up in an era marked by market-based economic reform, increased interaction with the rest of the world, changing family structures, and the spread of new media and communication technologies. They are generally viewed, and indeed sometimes view themselves, as being at the forefront of a 'me culture' and a 'sexual revolution' in China (Sima and Pugsley 2010; Zhang, E. 2011).

Chinese youth are heterogeneous. Their sexual behaviours and activities are influenced by family backgrounds, gender, and other social and cultural factors, and vary across different socio-geographical spaces. Many young people in China are bound by traditional values that present sex as a private issue, a cultural taboo, a reproductive func-tion, and an act with social and moral ramifications, and that regulate and discipline female bodies, in particular, through the cultural valori-zation of virginity and fidelity (Liu, M. 2012). In fact, a 2009 National Youth Reproductive Health Survey of more than 22,000 unmarried Chinese youth aged between fifteen and twenty-four years reveals that the average age of first sexual intercourse in the PRC is just under twenty-three years (22.5 years for men and 23.1 years for women), which is considerably higher than the USA average of seventeen years ('Facts on American teens' sexual and reproductive health' 2013; Guo et al. 2012). This finding suggests that many young adults in China view sex as largely occurring in the context of serious adult relation-ships or as a precursor to marriage.

But sexual behaviours and attitudes are changing in China and youth culture has become increasingly focused on sexual values, prac-tices and identities, and displays of sexiness. The image of the young sexed body now permeates China's public spaces both in the context of commercial advertising and as young people explore and showcase their individuality, tastes and desires through the use of the Internet, mobile phones and fashion, and in shopping malls and nightclubs, as well as on casual dates (Latham 2007; Liu, F. 2011; Moore 2005; Sima and Pugsley 2010). The young 'sexy' body is one of the dominant markers of China's consumerist modernity.

The chapter first reviews the changing sexual behaviours and mores of Chinese youth, those of urban and often highly educated youth, in particular, placing them in the context of broader cultural trans-formations. It then focuses on the performative sexuality of the post-1980s and post-1990s generation as presented in China's media. It shows how gender and sexuality can be a contested terrain and a critical site for the expression of sexual identity, by examining sexual adventurism (sex bloggers) and the androgynous personas deployed in Chinese television idol-style popular music talent competitions. Finally, the chapter reassesses the political implications of being 'young', 'sexy' and 'rebellious'. It challenges both 'the repressive hypoth-esis' in which the state is understood as censoring sexual discourse and restricting sexual freedom (see chapter 1), and the 'empowerment hypothesis' in which youthful sexual adventurism and new sexualities are understood as self-empowering. It is more useful and accurate for us to see the ways in which various social agents, including female sex bloggers, pop idols, government administrators, media representa-tives, university professors and school teachers, have participated in shaping a new sexual culture in China that is simultaneously empow-ering *and* limiting.

A YOUTH-LED 'SEXUAL REVOLUTION'

The existing literature on Chinese youth culture and sex has depicted the Chinese urban landscape as an increasingly sexually charged space (Farrer 2008; Pan, S. 2009; Zhang, E. 2011). Many Chinese youth have apparently moved away from the ethics of pre-marital sexual abstinence that were advocated in traditional and socialist China. Young people are demonstrating a growing tolerance of new forms of sex and sexuality, such as casual sex, non-conjugal sex, commercial sex and homosexuality (Pan, S. 2009). For some of them, sex is a means towards an end: a channel for self-expression and self-exploration, a window on to the revelation of human nature, a shortcut towards financial security or simply a form of play.

China's changing sexual behaviours owe much to the PRC's broader socio-cultural transformation from Mao-era socialism to reform-era 'market socialism', and associated shifts in what sociologist Pan Suiming (2009) calls 'the primary life cycle', namely, reproduction, childrearing, physical sustenance, and the social relations between men and women. These changes are linked to government initiatives. For example, the 1950 Marriage Law banned polygamy and mercenary marriage and established free-choice monogamous heterosexual marriage as the only legitimate institution for sex, with the privileged function of sex being for reproduction (see chapter 2). That link was severed in the 1980s. The implementation of the one-child-per-couple policy promoted sex not only for reproduction but also for leisure and pleasure. As a result of these policies, love and sexual pleasure have become viewed as central to a marital relationship (Pan, S. 2009: 28–31). Since the late 1990s, young people's attitudes towards love and sex in China have further changed. Sex is now sometimes viewed as independent of romantic attachment; non-traditional sexual behaviours and relationships are on the rise, and sex is increasingly presented as an individual affair and a human right.

Everett Zhang (2011) describes China's changing sexual culture as a youth-led 'sexual revolution' that has unfolded in three stages. The first stage started with the re-emergence of 'romantic love' in the late 1970s, after the end of the Maoist period (1949–76), and the promotion of sexual pleasure in the 1980s, after the implementation of the one-child-per-couple policy. As China moved away from the Mao-era emphasis on class struggle, which was associated with a period of 'sexual repression' or the 'de-sexualization' of Chinese culture (see chapters 1 and 7), many Chinese people discovered *aiqing* (romantic love) in literature. Novels such as Liu Xinwu's *The Place of Romantic Love* (1978), Zhang Jie's *Love Must Not be Forgotten* (1979), and Zhang Xian's *The Corner Left Behind by Romantic Love* (1979), were popular reading materials for young people in China in the 1980s (see Zhang, E. 2011: 134). Such literature directed young people's hearts, minds and imagination away from Maoist politics and towards public discussions and expressions of romantic love (Link 2000: 279).

The pursuit of sexual pleasure, however, did not gain prominence in public discourses until after the implementation of China's one-child-per-couple family policy during 1979–80. Government promotion of this policy played an important if unintended role in separating sex from reproduction, by justifying and introducing the use of contraceptives and abortion practices on a national scale (see chapter 2). State-run workplaces provided condoms to married couples for free and abortions (both voluntary and forced) were common. By the 1990s, an increasing number of married and single women were having abortions. Abortion became less stigmatized because of its prevalence and association with national planning. Sexual relationships and pleasure became more important in this context, generating a fundamental shift in Chinese sexual culture. Ordinary people, such as sex educators, novelists, artists, photographers, bloggers, DVD vendors, entertainers, karaoke bar managers, travellers, fashion designers, film-makers, condom sellers, rock-and-roll performers and advertisers, started doing 'the on-the-ground work that led to the sexualization of China' (Zhang, E. 2011: 139).

In the late 1970s and 1980s, youth of the day discussed topics related to romantic love in literary journals and novels, and celebrated romance through the new import of popular songs from Hong Kong and Taiwan into mainland China. The romantic songs released by Teresa Teng from Taiwan, for example, captured the hearts of people born in the 1960s and 1970s especially, and played an acknowledged role in promoting public expressions of individual desires for emotional and sexual freedom (Gold 1993; Yan, Y. 2010). The development of popular music in mainland China, and especially the rock-and-roll music of Cui Jian, further promoted the expression and cultivation of particular emotional and physical yearnings as people could dance to Cui's music or shout with him without knowing the 'language' (Chow 1990). Even government-sponsored telephone hotline services and radio call-in shows, such as *Words on the Night Breeze* in Nanjing, served as popular interactive forums to talk about sexuality, gender, marriage and family (Erwin 2000; Xin 2003), until they were surpassed by television during the late 1990s and by the Internet from 2000 onward.

The second stage of China's 'sexual revolution' began in the early 1990s, along with the expansion of commercial media, popular culture and a consumer society, which enabled more diversified presentations and discussions of sexual behaviours and attitudes (Zhang, E. 2011). Public discourses on sexual love and sexual desire among heterosexual and homosexual men and women became more pronounced. Female desires, in particular, were a new focus of attention. In the 1970s, male writers dominated the writings about romantic love. From the 1980s onward, women writers came to the fore, expressing 'female desires' through autobiographical writing. Wang Anyi (1996) is representative of those women writers who looked squarely at the sexual aspect of love. As Wang states:

> If one really wants to write about human nature, there is no way to avoid love; when writing about love one must touch upon sexual love…. If you are truly a serious writer with depth, there is no way to avoid the issue of sex. (Wang Anyi cited in Jiang Hongyan 2006: 140)

Writers such as Wang Anyi portrayed female sexual psychology and 'natural instincts', and paved the way for the so-called 'body-writing' (*shenti xiezuo*) of the 1990s.

Female body-writing, as exemplified by Wei Hui's controversial semi-autographical novel *Shanghai Baby* (1999), celebrates pre-marital sex, casual sex, inter-racial sex and bisexuality. It opens up questions about the politics of sexual storytelling and claims to sexual citizenship (Farrer 2009: 102). It also reveals the ongoing negotiation of self-identity, including sexual identity, by some Chinese youth in the midst of China's changing social structure and value system. Using sexual licence as an entry into the search for such identity, female body-writing can be taken as a metaphor for the struggle among Chinese youth to reconcile the collective value system (family and patriarchy) with their individualistic pursuits (self-expression, personal aspirations for sexual empowerment and material wealth) in a materialistic world (Weber 2002).

Body-writing re-feminizes and re-sexualizes women through explicit representations of female sexual desires and encounters. Female body-writers present women as both beautiful and sexy, and as people who express their desire through their bodies. This marks a sharp contrast to Mao-era depictions of women as 'sexless' or male-like productive labourers working in jobs traditionally occupied by men (Chen, T.M. 2003).

However, body-writing has been criticized for conforming to both male-centric consciousness and the new consumer culture that has swamped present-day China. As Zhong Xueping explains:

> The gender politics of the 1990s have shown that the turn to sexual difference or sexuality in the post-Mao era has also encountered its spectre: women could not only be turned into, in the words of Tani Barlow, 'national resources' during the Mao era's pursuit of modernity, they can also be turned into, to invoke Barlow's words, 'commercial

resources' in a consumer culture. Female body writing, in other words, when practiced in today's public domains, does not always have the power to resist being co-opted or (re)subverted by the male gaze. (Zhong, X. 2006: 654–5)

In the 1990s, Chinese youth also started to display more tolerance in public towards same-sex love and desire than was previously the case in China. Discourses on homosexuality entered the public domain along with population mobility, the growth of gay and lesbian venues, the increasing visibility of gay and lesbians, global flows of queer-themed information and the targeting of men who have sex with men as part of AIDS prevention activities (see chapters 4 and 6). In some professional circles, same-sex love and desire is even considered fashionable. A gay man who used to work for China Central Television told the second author of this book that he had a large number of gay and lesbian colleagues, and people liked to talk about their sexuality openly because it was fashionable and cosmopolitan to be gay in that circle.

In addition, both the sex trade and public presentations of Chinese 'sexual culture' became more commonplace in the 1990s (see chapters 5 and 7). Phenomena that had re-emerged in the 1980s, such as prostitution, keeping mistresses, and sex-related bribery and corruption, became more visible and widespread (Jeffreys 2008). At the same time, exhibitions on indigenous Chinese sexual culture became a feature of special-themed festivals and museums, along with the revival of practices associated with *yangsheng* (cultivation of life), and *qigong* and Daoist classics on sexual cultivation (Zhang, E. 2011: 142).

Sex talk proliferated in the public sphere in 1990s China. Such talk included that of the general public related to sexual fulfilment in or outside of marriage, that of scholarly interest in sex psychology and sociology (including homosexuality), that of public health and birth control officials; and that of reformist writers on sex and China's modernizing projects (Erwin 2000; Hershatter 1996; Wan 2001; see also chapter 7). Individuals and collectives, working sometimes with, and sometimes at odds with, government-controlled agencies and spaces, negotiated and appropriated public discourse and resources to make claims for sexual expression, recognition and rights.

This trend has continued into the new millennium – the third stage of China's 'sexual revolution' (Zhang, E. 2011). For some urban youth today, sexual desire is the dominant theme in their dating, flirting and other sexual activities. Romance is something that is viewed as desirable, but neither central nor essential to a sexual relationship. For sex radicals like celebrity blogger Mu Zimei (see the next section, 'Performative sexualities'), love is purely physical and transient. It starts with her taking off her clothes and ends with her reaching orgasm (Farrer 2007). Seeking sexual pleasure without even thinking of love, affection or emotional intimacy, let alone falling in love, is regarded as fashionable and cosmopolitan among some urban middle-class young radicals. As summarized by Everett Zhang (2011: 140), these pleasure-centred sexual practices indicate 'further detachment of sex from the relations and moral sentiments previously associated with it – reproductive, familial, romantic, and so on. It has become an independently valued means and end to the good life, no longer subordinate to other social values or experiential modes.'

Parents, educators and government authorities have attempted to control the changing sexual behaviours and attitudes of Chinese youth in various ways. Parents and teachers frequently warn adolescents of the dangers of 'premature love' (*zaolian*) and pre-marital sex (Farrer 2009: 106). Students are sometimes subjected to disciplinary measures for engaging in pre-marital sex, including expulsion (Farrer 2009: 111). While sex education was introduced in schools and colleges in the 1980s, it has yet to be taught in every school. Sex education also tends to focus on abstinence, 'good' morals and 'appropriate' gender roles, rather than on knowledge about reproduction, contraception and sexual health (Aresu 2009: 535–7; Farrer 2009: 105).

However, the privatization of housing in China has eroded many of these controls as young college students increasingly live off campus and can meet in private accommodations for sex. Even in the ostensibly 'conservative' city of Lanzhou, it is easy to find young lovers living together in rented private properties. On a visit to the precincts of university campuses in Lanzhou, the second author of this book encountered locals who claimed that students were their tenants. She also spoke to students who cited romantic feeling (*ganqing*) as the ethical justification both for living with their sexual partners, and going against the advice of their parents and school authorities. This justification is often provided by students in rural and less cosmopolitan areas. Their more 'liberal and open' counterparts in major metropolitan areas were more likely to declare that romantic love was 'so yesterday' and 'last century'. For some urban youth, sex has become disconnected from romance, personal expression or desire. Sexual activities and expressions are viewed as performances of individuality, as will be discussed in the next section with reference to the cases of celebrity bloggers Mu Zimei and Furong Jiejie, and the television pop idols of *Super Girl* and *Happy Boys*.

Today's youth define their sexual rights in various media spaces, especially on the Internet. The PRC has more Internet users than the USA (over 420 million users in 2010); nearly 91 per cent of China's netizens are under forty years of age and just over 71 per cent are under thirty years of age (China Internet Network Information Center 2010). For China's young netizens, the Internet provides aggregated sources of a rich variety of entertainment: music, games, video streaming, online literature and social networking (including instant messaging, bulletin board systems, blogging and social networking sites). It is also the space where the young get their real sex education, tell their sexual stories, become popular as sexual dissidents, experiment with novel sexual practices and search for sexual partners. During fieldwork in China between May and June 2012, high-school graduate interviewees told the second author of this book that they got sexual knowledge from pornographic videos and DVDs, Japanese manga, books and magazines, and most of all, the Internet. According to a survey conducted in 2005, around 32 per cent of over 6,000 people had a one-night stand after contacting a partner over the Internet (cited in McLaren 2007: 413).

Dating and sexual behaviours are increasingly mediated by the Internet. Online dating, cybersex, virtual marriage and in-game marriage, have become a part of Chinese youth's sexual adventures and self-discovery. They create and live out their fantasies through their avatars; they 'meet' their sexual partners online; they transcend the boundary between the virtual and physical realities, and develop offline relationships including dating and sex (McLaren 2007; Wu and Wang 2011). For some young people, sexual pleasure is now more important than love, virginity and loyalty; and they are prepared to get it in unconventional ways. In a study of 'the rhetoric of sexuality of everyday social interactions' among Shanghai-based youth, James Farrer (2002: 3) characterizes young people's sexual acts as 'play'.

For many Chinese youth today, sexual play is like a rite of passage, where private narratives and sexual stories are shared, compared and retold though digital communication technologies (the Internet and mobile phones), and through the so-called traditional media (broadcasting and print). Some of them perform and applaud androgynous personas onscreen and online as an expression of their individual identity, desire and fulfilment. They sometimes stretch the meanings of 'romantic feeling' to encompass unconventional sexual encounters, including one-night stands and homosexuality. They also sometimes employ a language of rights and individual freedom to justify their violation of school regulations and parental controls. At the same time, an examination of the performative sexualities of China's rebellious post-1980s and post-1990s generation exposes the limits of sexual citizenship, by showing how individual expressions of defiant sexuality are constrained by the conventional boundaries of gender, sex and heteronormativity.

PERFORMATIVE SEXUALITIES

This section examines Chinese youth's performative sexualities by looking at a female sex blogger called Mu Zimei, and a female Chinese pop idol called Li Yuchun. Sexualities are performative in the sense that sex and gender or sexual identity can become a marker of individuality and marketability, rather than being simply a biological trait. Sexualities are bound up with the wish for recognition by both peers and the market. Performance is not any singular act or expression, but a relatively consistent, and sometimes ritualized, symbolic production of individual and group efforts to include, and exclude, certain norms, practices and values. Performance is reiterated under constraints and even bias, and therefore can be limiting in its power to critically address the hierarchical relations between men and women, or between heteronormative and peripheral sexualities. Gender and sexual norms, particularly those related to how one behaves in public (often mediated by media and communication technologies), reflect underlying value systems and power relations, as illustrated by the controversy surrounding Mu Zimei.

Mu Zimei is a post-1980s journalist-turned-blogger who achieved fame/notoriety in 2003 by publishing details of her sexual encounters at blogcn.com, one of China's major blog service providers. Her blog attracted around 110,000 visitors per day at one stage and her diary, *Left-over Love Letters*, on Sina.com, was once accessed 20 million times in the course of a single day (Pomfret 2003). Mu Zimei has also posted podcasts of her lovemaking with various men. Some of these podcasts, which feature soundtracks of climactic groans, panting and shrieking, have received 10,000 visits a day. In late 2005, more than 50,000 people simultaneously tried to download one twenty-five-minute podcast, crashing the host server (Beech 2005). Mu Zimei has since opened several blogs at different websites, where she openly declares her manifesto of enjoying sex without love or emotional attachment (Goldkorn 2006).

Like controversial female authors such as Wei Hui (1999) and Mian Mian (2002), Mu Zimei exhibits a form of 'writing through the body'. She locates her erotic experiences in a string of one-night stands in a fashionable urban context of bars and clubs, and writes in a witty and ironic manner. Her writing demonstrates both her literary skills and her 'modern cosmopolitanism', expressed through casual sexual adventurism, and familiarity with western and Japanese films, pop music and literature.

Mu Zimei's cavalier attitude towards sex without love has attracted controversy. Opponents have accused her of being 'cheap' and 'shameless', whereas others support her activities for promoting individualism and/or a feminist standpoint on sexual freedom and rights (Farrer 2007: 14–20). As James Farrer (2007) says of the Mu Zimei phenomenon, her sexual autobiography with sexual storytelling is a tactic of power and a site of social contestation. Her self-expression through sex and writing about sex involves constantly pushing the limits of what is 'proper' and 'moral'. Her claims to freedom of sexual and literary expression have also opened the space for debate on issues relating to sexual rights, women's rights and the right to free speech (Farrer 2007: 21–6).

The Mu Zimei phenomenon illustrates how the Internet can enable Chinese youth to participate in the exhibition, exploration and marketization of sex, turning what was previously a private and somewhat taboo topic into something for public consumption. Johan Lagervist (2006: 13) points out that 'government control of, and social freedom on, China's Internet are growing simultaneously'. Censorship of sexual content on the Chinese Internet mainly targets websites featuring explicit sexual images, not texts discussing sexual topics. Netizens can freely discuss personal sexual experiences, openly search for sex partners and debate moral standards.

The Mu Zimei phenomenon also indicates that the Internet in China provides a somewhat constrained, as in gendered, platform for the performance of female sexual identity. Celebrity bloggers such as Mu Zimei and Furong Jiejie (and their copycat followers) undermine stereotypical post-reform representations of Chinese women as passive daughters, wives and mothers. Furong Jiejie became a national sensation in China in 2005 for relentlessly uploading photographs of herself in sexually assertive but unrevealing poses to highlight her 'S-shaped curves', along with 'narcissistic commentary about her extraordinary beauty and artistic abilities' (Roberts 2010: 224). As I. D. Roberts (2010: 232–6) explains, Furong Jiejie has orchestrated and sustained her fame by exploiting the spaces for self-promotion that are made available by China's uneven censorship regime, which, in banning pornography and political dissidence, also encourages 'softer' expressions of sexual nonconformity and individual rebelliousness. However, as with Mu Zimei, Furong Jiejie markets her female sexuality to a predominantly heterosexual male audience. The sexual performances of bloggers such as Mu Zimei and Furong Jiejie are performative at the individual level, with little reference to broader issues of power and gendered inequality.

A different example of Chinese youth's sexual performance is provided by the androgynous personas displayed in *Super Girl* and *Happy Boys*, China's idol-style popular-music talent competitions. In 2005, Li Yuchun, a then twenty-one-year-old tall and slim girl from Chengdu City, with short spiky hair and wearing oversized T-shirts, track shoes and baggy jeans, became an overnight sensation when she won the *Super Girl* show on Hunan Satellite TV. The show was a national sensation for its wide coverage, innovative marketing strategies and use of SMS voting. *Super Girl* was broadcast nation-wide to over 400 million viewers; it ran televised auditions in multiple cities, which were accompanied by integrated publicity tactics across all media and communication platforms; and it allowed viewers to choose their own 'idols' by sending SMS votes via mobile phones (Yue and Yu 2008).

In the context of one-Party rule, the use of SMS voting on *Super Girl* inspired debates about Chinese democracy. Some commentators praised *Super Girl* for blazing a trail of participatory cultural democracy by allowing people to choose their idols. Others accused the show of commercially manipulating people's emotional investment in reality-TV stars and offering an idealized fantasy of neoliberal democracy (Xiao 2006). The show also turned Li Yuchun into an A-list celebrity, admired for the perceived 'natural' and 'cool' way in which she performed songs written for men, and for calling herself a tomboy. Her fans were crazy about her public gender-blending and cross-dressing, and called her 'Brother Chun' (Noble 2012).

Li's tomboy image and androgynous performance on stage challenges reform-era representations of Chinese femininity as 'cute', 'soft' and 'girlish', and has become a symbol of rebellion, nonconformity and transnational fashion among the post-1980s and post-1990s generation (Yue and Yu 2008). Hui Xiao's (2006) examination of Li's androgynous body shows how Chinese youth femininity is commodified through the beauty economy (*meinü jingji*) and the branding of personalities, or the personality economy (*gexing jingji*). As a result, the young androgynous body has become a new site of global capital accumulation, celebrating both the market logic and the government-sanctioned narrative of a harmonious post-revolutionary China (Xiao 2006: 66). Li's androgynous persona has been imitated by fans who adopt a gender-neutral voice and boyish appearance like her. At the same time, the homosocial affection between Li and her fans potentially challenges patriarchal and heterosexual values. The example of Li

Yuchun thus illustrates how 'youth' can be a critical site to express non-normative gendered and sexual identities.

Androgyny and cross-dressing is also a controversial marker of an all-male music talent show called *Happy Boys* (Xinhua 2010). Launched in 2007 by Hunan Satellite TV, *Happy Boys* is a sanitized spin-off of the popular *Super Girl* show (Zeng Henglin 2007). The young men it features want to become overnight stars like their counterparts in *Super Girl*. However, following directions from the State Administration of Radio, Film and Television, *Happy Boys* contains fewer 'harsh' comments from judges and fewer depictions of 'weeping fans' than the all-female talent show (Guojia guangbo dianying dianshi zongju 2007). The show nevertheless stirred up debate on gender norms for featuring 'fake ladies' (*weiniang*), a term that has entered the Chinese lexicon from the Japanese word *nisemusume*, which refers to pseudo-girls, or 'comely boys with a female appearance' after they dress up as girls and behave like girls (Xinhua 2010). Some commentators called on young people to maintain the masculine/feminine traits associated with different genders, while others called for greater tolerance of gender performance (Xinhua 2010).

The cross-dressing tomboy idol and its male equivalent – the pseudo-girl idol on Chinese reality-television shows – are a reflection of Chinese youth mobile sexualities, which sometimes involve gender-swapping. These mobile sexualities are reflected in online gaming. As Weihua Wu and Xiying Wang's (2011) study of Chinese in-game marriage reveals, gender-swapping is a common feature of online games, with many men using female avatars to get 'married' to male avatars. Players deliberately blend femininity and masculinity through their online avatars. Such gender performances work to challenge the binary gender system and institutionalized concepts of marriage (Wu and Wang 2011: 121).

Both in-game gender-swapping and the cross-dressing idols of reality TV exemplify the 'play' element in gender and sexual performativity. Judith Butler (2009: 136 and 141) argues that gender is performative, and 'gender reality is created through sustained social performances...manufactured and sustained through corporeal signs and other discursive means'. Like the theory of gender performativity, performative sexuality 'presupposes that norms are acting on us before we have a chance to act at all, and that when we do act, we recapitulate the norms that act upon us, perhaps in new or unexpected ways, but still in relation to norms that precede us and exceed us' (Butler 2009: 11).

As discussed previously, sex bloggers like Mu Zimei market their sexual identity within the constraints of the value system and power relations that govern and regulate gender and sexual norms. Mu Zimei's seemingly liberal and loose attitudes towards love and sex do not challenge heteronormativity, even though she conceivably undermines mainstream understandings of female chastity and passivity. Mu Zimei's writings and activities also do not challenge the normative values that underline the class-based moral hierarchy of the young sexed body. At the top of this hierarchy, there are cosmopolitan and educated urbanites, who are viewed as embodying the new 'open' and 'free' China, and, at the bottom, are sex workers and rural-to-urban migrant workers, who are viewed as embodying a deteriorating social order and as being responsible for the spread of disease and criminality (see chapters 5 and 6).

In the case of *Super Girl* Li Yuchun, her androgynous persona and female masculinity is also highly performative, but neither Li nor her fans pose any serious challenge to the dominant social structures that regulate youth sexuality. Ling Yang and Hongwei Bao (2012) argue that the mainstream fans of *Super Girl* are mostly ardent defenders of gender and sexual stereotypes, while *Super Girl* Girls' Love (GL) fans are more accepting of gender and sexual differences. Girls' Love refers to an online fan fiction community devoted to the imagined romantic pairing of the female contestants of the 2006 season of *Super Girl*, which mainstream fans of Li Yuchun countered by creating a BG-only (Boy and Girl) or heterosexual romance postbar, devoted to celebrating Li's perceived sexual attractiveness to men rather than women. Yang and Bao (2012) point out that GL fans engage in affective communication virtually with not only their favourite idols, but also GL writers and friends, as a performative act of female bonding. However, both the 'mainstream' and the GL fan communities reveal the fragility and limits of same-sex intimacy. Homosocial feelings among young women are tolerated by the mainstream Chinese society, but anything beyond is still taboo. In light of this:

> fans do not 'resist' dominant social structures so much as they produce 'mattering maps' in order to make sense of the world they live in and to construct their own embodied and affective world... Through affective communication and practicing mutual care, GL fans have learned to negotiate with the gender and sexual norms of 'mainstream' Chinese society... The friendship, intimacy and homosociality that the fan communication offers construct these women's gender and sexual subjectivities that in many ways refuse the normalization of gender, sexuality and social relations. (Yang and Bao 2012: 860)

Public gender-blending and cross-dressing in idol-style shows demonstrates that while some youth performance of sex and sexuality is mobile and exploratory, the articulation of such performances in public spaces is constrained by a lack of enquiry into broader issues of power and injustice: that is, the hierarchical relations between men and women, masculinity and femininity, and mainstream and non-normative sexualities. Likewise, the female body, whether it is the androgynous body of Li Yuchun or the sexed-up body of Mu Zimei, commodifies the femininity of Chinese youth and embraces the market logic prevalent in China today. In the words of Harriet Evans (2008: 364), the young sexed body 'becomes a marker of the personal gains to be acquired through individual investment in the opportunities of the private market, and not a category of meanings that interrogates established norms of gendered and, therefore, social relationships. Sex and performative sexuality remain dominantly defined as naturalized and harmonized acts, rather than as 'a field of inequality, discrimination, and abuse produced by the inequalities of the market' (Evans 2008: 379–80).

SEXUAL (DIS)EMPOWERMENT

Some observers claim that China today is like 'one big red-light zone' where the sex industry (albeit illegal) flourishes, along with rampant consumer culture and new forms of sexual relationships organized around different types of pre-marital and extra-marital sex (Zhang, E. 2011: 124). Rapid economic and social change has led to: official corruption involving sex-related bribery and sexual advances towards subordinates; the monetization of sex, as demonstrated by escorts and paid mistresses; and casual sex in the form of one-night stands and multiple sexual partnerships. Digital erotica such as pornographic websites and DVDs have proliferated, as have sex shops and exposure to medical, commercial and media practices, organized around the treatment of male impotence (Zhang, E. 2011). In large metropolises such as Beijing and Shanghai, and in second-tier cities such as Chengdu, Nanjing and Hangzhou, 'nightlife spaces' flourish for dating, sexual play, sexual adventurism and commercial sex (see chapter 5). In massage parlours, discos, karaoke rooms, nightclubs, bars, dancing clubs, restaurants, pool halls, saunas, barber shops and beauty salons, young sexualized bodies often become the marker of the twilight zone between the acceptable and the taboo, and the legal and the illegal, as they busy themselves dancing, flirting, dressing provocatively, drinking and taking drugs, and engaging in one-night stands, casual sex and commercial sex.

Such nightlife 'play', as well as sexual 'play' mediated by the media, is both productive and constraining. It can be productive in terms of disrupting 'social boundaries and hierarchies', as well as enabling new social relations and cultural expression (Farrer 2008: 2). At the same time, such 'play' remains confined by the established norms of gendered and sexual relationships. China's urban youth-led 'sexual revolution' has consequently proved to be both empowering and disempowering, particularly for women.

The performative sexualities onscreen and online that have been discussed in this chapter are symbols of China's consumerist modernity, being born out of the upheavals, excitement and uncertainties of the shift from Maoism to market socialism. The flux of the times has created a 'desiring China' and 'desiring subjects' (Rofel 2007). These desiring individuals, and groups of desiring individuals, represent a new kind of cosmopolitan Chinese person whose self-representation and self-narratives are often associated with individualism, consumerism, transnational cultural flows and novel articulations of sexual identity. They are confined by government-controlled spaces and traditional values that guide people's behaviours. At the same time, they sometimes appropriate and challenge mainstream discourses to make claims for new sexual rights and freedoms.

China's opening up has empowered the post-1980s and post-1990s generation with the material means and discursive space to pursue their dreams, and has also disempowered them as such dreams are often individualistic, commercialized and mercenary (Palmer 2013). A telling example is Ma Nuo, a post-1980s contestant on a dating show called *If You Are the One* at Jiangsu TV. When asked by a contender if she would ride with him on his bike, she replied: 'I'd rather cry in a BMW than laugh on a bicycle'. If love and bed seem inseparable as the post-1980s and post-1990s generation explore their sexual identity, love and money form a holy unity in the search for suitable suitors and spouses (Bergman 2010; see also chapter 2).

The figure of the sexualized woman has returned and dominates the popular imagination in post-Mao China (Andrews and Shen 2002). Visitors to Beijing's Houhai bar area will see well-dressed young women dining with well-dressed young men, and young female pole-dancers performing for mainly male clientele. The market has played a key role in refashioning Chinese female sexuality by relying on a 'strategic use of the essentialism of the gender binary' for female employment (Yang, M. 1999: 47). The re-feminization and re-objectification of women has seen more and more young people, including those of college age, engaging in commercial sexual activities. Some commentators claim that '10 per cent of women' between the ages of eighteen and twenty-eight 'periodically work as sex workers' and that some college women sign up as part-time mistresses to the nouveau riche, and engage in sexual activities with government officials or foreigners as a financial transaction (Noble 2012: 62; 64). These examples illustrate some of the many ways young women sanction and try to take advantage of the gendered inequalities that characterize China today.

Sex and the young sexualized body are presented in mainstream discourses as a collection of acts, responsibilities and choices that are dissociated from broader issues of gender, sexuality, class, ethnicity and injustice (Evans 2008). For example, when cosmopolitan Han Chinese men seek exoticized and ethnicized sex from the prototypically young female minorities working in China's 'rural tourist idylls', they confirm gendered socio-economic inequalities and the internal orientalist logic of inferior, promiscuous (ethnic) women serving virile, dominant (Han) men (Hyde 2001; Schein 1997). Similarly, sex functions as a metaphor of social inequality between the female migrant domestic worker (the maid) and her urban male employer. In dominant discourses, the rural female migrant who marries her urban-based employer is typically condemned as someone who uses sex to gain social mobility (Sun, W. 2010).

Although the mass media continue to function as a public space in which to discuss sex-related topics, the Internet has become the dominant space for experimenting with new forms of sexual culture among youth. It is a gendered platform that is liberating as well as limiting. As both subjects and objects, women use their sexual appeal as a means towards personal empowerment and achievement through sexual adventurism, liaison and marriage, including transnational marriages (Liu, L. and Liu, H. 2008; Wang, P. 2015). Chinese women are known to have created new virtual networks and transformed them into 'real' social networks in order to achieve their personal goals, whether they are about sexual pleasure, life decisions or development of self-identity (Pei and Ho 2008).

The Internet is also a gendered and embodied space loaded with gender stereotyping that reinforces patriarchal structures. Women are still subject to heterosexual and masculine authority. Chinese female sex bloggers and cross-dressing idols have not been able to disrupt gender and sexual representations of women, unlike their North American counterparts who are sometimes able to unsettle conventional narratives about the eroticized and exoticized Asian woman through subversive images and textual practices in cyberspace (Hudson 2007). The rapid rise in Internet use has also been accompanied by an increase in online pornographic content, sex tourism, mail-order bride businesses and the trafficking of Chinese women (Leung, M. W. H. 2008). As these examples suggest, many young women and girls have become the victims of China's sexual 'opening up'.

CONCLUSION

Being young and sexy is burdened with the angst and uncertainties of China's post-millennial consumerist modernity. The commercialization of sexual discourse has opened up 'Chinese sexual civil society to an irreverent and polymorphous democracy of opinions', as official government voices are either disregarded or appropriated in people's rush towards the commercialization of almost everything, including sex and sexuality (Farrer 2008: 58). The ensuing polymorphous expressions and representations of the young sexed body are mediated and reiterated under the constraints of the market, tradition and established 'norms'. Young sexual adventurism and new sexualities therefore need to be understood as performances that are neither the result of 'the repressive hypothesis', with the state as the culprit, nor 'the empowerment hypothesis', with rebellious youth as the heroes (see chapter 1). China's performative sexualities are better understood as expressions of a search for new sexual subjectivities and more inclusive forms of citizenship, on the part of diverse social agents in an increasingly commercialized public sphere.

The post-1980s and post-1990s generations do not form a monolithic group, and their attitudes towards sex and sexuality vary greatly, from engaging in casual sex without love at one end of the spectrum to upholding pre-marital chastity at the other. Many young people in China now hold up the romantic standard as the path of moderation, because it allows them to be 'neither too "open" nor too "traditional"' (Farrer 2009: 121), and neither too rebellious nor limiting in terms of challenging the hierarchical relations between women and men, and heteronormative and non-normative sexualities. The tension between heteronormative and non-normative sexualities is discussed in the next chapter on gay, lesbian and queer.

4 | Gay, Lesbian and Queer ——————

This chapter examines the expansion of gay, lesbian and queer identities and discourses in reform-era China. Gay identity became a topic of public discourse in the PRC during the 1980s. Gay identities and communities have expanded in urban China, in particular, since the late 1990s, along with the increasing influence of transnational lesbian, gay, bisexual and transsexual (LGBT) culture and commercialization. The PRC's growing actively homosexual population is now estimated at roughly 40 million people (Werff 2008: 172). There are hundreds of gay cruising zones and often unadvertised gay bars, restaurants and discos across the country. There are also many gay websites and LGBT organizations, which help to organize gay rights' campaigns, AIDS prevention efforts, film festivals and pride parades. Even the mainstream media have begun to feature stories on homosexuality, despite China's media censorship.

Since the publication in 1992 of the first book on gays in the PRC, *Their World: A Study of Homosexuality in China* by sociologists Li Yinhe and Wang Xiaobo, literature about and by gay people in China has been marked by recurrent themes. These themes include: the difficulty of coming out to parents and relatives; the difficulty of living a fulfilling homosexual life while remaining in the family home; the problems associated with parental expectations that children will enter a heterosexual marriage and have a child; the economic difficulties associated with making a living in a society which accepts acts of social and institutional discrimination against gays; experiencing excitement and disappointment at the opportunities, potentials and limitations that the Internet has brought in tow; and feeling lonely and isolated (Engebretsen 2013; Ho, L. W. W. 2008; Kam 2013; Kong 2010a; Li Yinhe 1998c; Miège 2009; Rofel 1999; Zhang Beichun 1994).

In China today, publicly expressed views on homosexuality range from rejection to acceptance, although many people are growing more tolerant, especially young educated, urban people. A 2007 telephone questionnaire survey of 400 people conducted by sociologist Li Yinhe (2011) found that: (1) 60 per cent of those surveyed would make friends with homosexuals; (2) 85 per cent consider homosexuals and heterosexuals to be equals; (3) 90 per cent think homosexuals should enjoy equal opportunities in employment; (4) 55 per cent believe homosexuality-related topics should be broadcast or screened in public; and (5) 40 per cent support employing homosexuals as teachers. The survey demonstrates that tolerance does not equal full acceptance, as indicated by the low responses in support of options 4 and 5. Indeed, when asked about their attitude towards gay family members, 75 per cent of those surveyed chose the response: 'I will tolerate them but hope that they will change' (Li Yinhe 2011).

Public discourse is similarly fraught with contradictions as it advocates acceptance of and improved sexual rights for gays and lesbians on one hand, while continuing to stigmatize them as social misfits and sexual perverts who should be 'healed' or corrected, on the other. As Lisa Rofel (2007) points out, homoerotic desires are not condemned outright or fully accepted by either the government or the wider population in China. It is still difficult for Chinese men and women who engage in same-sex acts to become publicly active and visible (Li, Y. 2009). The majority of them live a closeted or double life, and are forced into heterosexual marriages for procreation (see chapter 2). 'Public morality' still regulates passion and produces self-regulating subjects.

The chapter examines the emergence of gay, lesbian and queer identities and discourses in contemporary China as follows. First, it offers a brief history of homosexuality in China. Second, it looks at the different terminology used to identify Chinese gay, lesbian and queer people and highlights the stratified nature of China's homosexual communities. Third, it reviews the expansion of public representations and self-presentations of homosexuality in China's media (film, digital video and computer/the Internet). Finally, it investigates two strategies deployed by gay, lesbian and queer people in China to resist heteronormative institutions and family structures, namely, the strategies of 'going out' and 'coming home', as opposed to 'coming out'.

SAME-SEX ATTRACTION IN CHINESE HISTORY

Historical studies of homosexuality in China suggest that homosexual practices were largely tolerated (or overlooked) by government authorities in imperial China, in part, due to the absence of a monotheistic religion; moreover, early literary depictions of such relationships tended to be light-hearted (Hinsch 1990; Volp 1994). Hence, Chou Wah-Shan (2001: 30) argues that the most distinctive features of the history of homosexuality in imperial China were neither homophobia nor homoeroticism as in many western societies, but rather classism, sexism and ageism (see also Hinsch 1990: 9–12). These factors permeated and constructed both homosexual relationships and mainstream culture.

By the start of the twentieth century, there was a rich vocabulary of poetic and allegorical terms to describe same-sex affection, which conveyed little or no moral condemnation. Terms for same-sex affection between men included 'the passion of the cut sleeve' (*duanxiupi*), which comes from an episode involving Dong Xian, a Han Dynasty imperial official, and the Emperor Ai. The Emperor awoke from an afternoon sleep with Dong to discover that the sleeve of his garment was caught under Dong's head. Wishing to rise but not wishing to waken Dong, the Emperor cut off the sleeve of his garment (Hinsch 1990: 53).

Other terms include: 'Lord Long Yang' (*Longyangjun*), which is the name of the handsome male favourite of an ancient king; 'the love of sharing a peach' (*fentaozhihao*), referring to a male favourite sharing an especially delicious peach with his lord; 'male favourite' (*nanchong*); and 'rabbit' (*tuzi*), deriving from the Rabbit God, a Chinese deity who protects homosexuals. Terms for same-sex affection between women include: 'golden orchid sisters' (*jinlan zimei*), a term borrowed from that for sworn friends; and 'polishing mirrors' (*mojing*) and 'grinding bean-curd' (*mo doufu*), both referring to acts of genital contact in female mutual masturbation.

In many parts of China, homosexual relationships between women were not explicitly denigrated or prohibited, as long as the women conformed to the patriarchal order by entering a legitimate marriage with a man, produced children (especially male heirs) and did not engage in intimacy with other men. Therefore, as Tze-lan Sang (2003: 92) argues, 'compulsory marriage, compulsory sexual service, compulsory reproduction, and compulsory chastity are more apt than compulsory heterosexuality as descriptions of women's fate'. Even during the period of the 1919 May Fourth or New Cultural Movement, which involved efforts to emancipate Chinese women by promoting education and condemning practices such as foot-binding, the 'new woman' was never free from patriarchal power structures in the family and the public domain (Wang, Q. 2004: 20).

Cultural tolerance of homosexuality began to be replaced by intolerance in the Qing Dynasty (1636–1912) 'as a result of a more stringent application of Neo-Confucian rhetoric regarding the family' and imported Manchu concepts of sexuality (Hinsch 1990: 162). Tolerance of same-sex eroticism also began to fade along with the embrace of 'modern' western ideas and science by Chinese intellectuals in the early twentieth century, which included psychiatric constructions of homosexuality in terms of sexual inversion and mental illness (Hinsch 1990: Epilogue). Non-normative or reproductive forms of sex were pathologized as intellectual and political elites accepted ideas concerning gender and sexual binaries, or the polarization of male/masculinity versus female/femininity (Dikötter 1995).

The stigmatization of homosexuality intensified during the Republican period (1912–49). While some literary elites celebrated homosexuality as a gesture against conventional social and sexual morality, cultural conservatives condemned it as symbolizing the weakness and sickness of the nation, as epitomized by China's diminishing international status and inability to repel foreign armies (Kang 2009).

This connection between nation and sexuality persisted after 1949, when the PRC or 'New China' was founded under the leadership of the Chinese Communist Party and Chairman Mao Zedong (Hershatter 1997; Kang 2009). Homosexuality was seen as a form of degeneracy originating in capitalist societies. The adoption by Chinese communist reformers of western scientism, including western discourses regarding sexuality and sexual categories, and the remaking of the Chinese literary language, involving the popularization of vernacular literature and the simplification of Chinese characters, not only enabled history to be rewritten, expunging any record of homosexuality in the Chinese tradition, but also facilitated the governing of the Chinese population through western-style divisions of people into 'normal' or 'abnormal' and good or evil (Hinsch 1990: Epilogue).

Although homosexuality per se was not explicitly prohibited by any laws in the PRC, homoerotic sex was condemned as immoral or degenerate until well into the 1990s. Homoerotic behaviour (particularly between men) was often punished as 'hooliganism' (*liumangzui*), an umbrella term referring to a wide range of social misbehaviours (Geyer 2002: 263; Li, Y. 2009: 83). Until recently, homosexuality was associated with the activities of foreigners, especially westerners, and therefore with 'decadence' and 'anti-family' behaviours, or with the activities of 'perverts' and 'psychopaths', and hence with danger, violence and crime. Gays attempting to find sexual partners at 'gay beats' were easy targets for police and security authorities, frequently finding themselves victims of policing campaigns against crime, and being blackmailed by criminal gangs because exposure of their sexuality meant harming their family, risking loss of employment and destroying their social status (Li, Y. 2009: 86–94; Wan 2001).

Homosexuality started to re-emerge in the public sphere in the 1980s along with the gradual opening up of Chinese society and the international 'discovery' of AIDS (Zhang and Kaufman 2005). Greater exposure to information and people from overseas, including overseas Chinese, and the inclusion of homosexuality in the public health regime, encouraged an expansion of personal storytelling in public culture and provided opportunities for people to explore unconventional sexual identities (Zhang and Kaufman 2005). The shift 'from taboo to open discussion' was also marked by the publication of scholarly works in the field of psychology and medical science (Wan 2001). These formal publications tended to treat homosexuality as a form of illness and focused on its 'treatment', but some regarded homosexuality as a natural part of humanity (Wan 2001). However, while these discussions acknowledged the existence of homosexuality and brought it into the public arena, they were largely limited to academic, scientific and interest-based groups.

Writings about lesbians and gays increased throughout the 1990s, as the development of the Chinese Internet made it easier for people in China to connect with members of Asian and western movements for gay rights and gay communities. These developments correlated with changes in popular understandings of homosexuality and in the legal treatment of homosexuality. For example, the PRC's revised Criminal Law of 1997 removed references to the crimes of 'sodomy' (*jijianzui*) and 'hooliganism', which had previously been used by the Chinese police to apprehend homosexuals (Li, Y. 2009: 83). The category of 'homosexuality' was also deleted from the third edition of the *Chinese Classification of Mental Disorders* in 2001 (Wu, J. 2003: 125, 133).

Some universities and academics also helped to promote social awareness and acceptance of homosexuality in China. In December 2001, the first Chinese gay and lesbian film festival, organized by gay activist, film-maker and academic Cui Zi'en and his friends, was held at the Peking University library and, concurrently, at a 'secret' location in a bar outside the university. Domestic queer-themed movies and pirated copies of international queer films were screened at both venues. Only five movies were shown at the official venue of the festival before it was shut down by the university and public-security authorities (Cui, Z. 2010: 420–22). Cui and his friends did not give up, and organized a second festival in April 2005, again at Peking University. This time it not only featured more local and international films but also had support from the international community and from non-governmental organizations that support LGBT rights. Following interruptions from university authorities, the festival was successfully carried through after it moved to '798', an old factory compound converted into an art café and workshop/gallery space (Cui, Z. 2010). These two film festivals paved the way for subsequent homosexuality-themed festivals and pride parades in urban China. Shanghai, for example, has run gay pride events every year since 2009, featuring art exhibitions and film screenings rather than a street march.

Gay and lesbian film festivals also championed the discussion of homosexuality on Chinese university campuses. Fudan University in Shanghai offered China's first postgraduate course on homosexuality in 2003, and the first undergraduate course on gay and lesbian studies in 2005 (Sun, Farrer and Choi 2006: note 3). In October 2006, the first students' association dedicated to sexual minorities was established at the Sun Yat-sen University in Guangzhou (Zhang Jing 2006).

These urban- and university-centred activities have opened new spaces for exploring same-sex sexual subjectivity and identity in mainland China. Same-sex sexual subjectivities and identities are diversified, just as the LGBT community is stratified. This argument is developed in the following section.

TERMINOLOGY AND SUBCULTURAL STRATIFICATION

An increasing number of people in the PRC have been able to identify their same-sex sexual subjectivity in recent years by using labels, terms and discourses that both connect them to the international LGBT community, and separate them into subgroups and cultures based on differences of class, gender and age. Historical terms for same-sex love continue to be used in literary and formal writings. However, a broad range of new terms has entered the Chinese vernacular as a means to identity gay, lesbian and queer people.

The most common terms used to identify Chinese lesbians and gays are *tonxinglian* (same-sex love), *tongzhi* (comrade) and 'gay'; these terms may also refer to different sectors of China's gay and lesbian population when used as a means of self-identification. The term *tongxinglian* is mostly used by older married men who have sex with men, and who look for sexual partners in old-style venues such as public gardens, toilets and bathhouses, and dance halls, massage parlours, hairdressers and saunas (Bao 2012: 112–13; Sun, Farrer and Choi 2006: 4). Clandestine sexual encounters and services are available at many such venues. However, affluent and young urban gays and lesbians are more likely to frequent gay bars, nightclubs and cafés. As Hongwei Bao's (2012) study of queer spaces in Shanghai suggests, at the prestige end of China's new gay spaces lie the commercial establishments (trendy gay bars and cafés) and cultural events that are funded and staffed by people from western societies or from Hong Kong and Taiwan. These spaces constitute a special sexual zone that local police normally avoid. The middle tier comprises urban Chinese gay cultural or sports clubs.

At the bottom are the now outdated social dance halls and public parks. Apart from frequenting different types of venues, younger gays and lesbians also prefer to use the terms *tongzhi* or 'gay' to refer to themselves. This is because the term *tongxinglian* has acquired negative connotations, being used in psychiatric texts as a medical term to describe same-sex sexual behaviour in terms of mental disorder.

The term *tongzhi*, which originally meant 'comrade', is a contemporary reappropriation of China's revolutionary legacy. It was originally used by members of the Chinese Communist and Nationalist Parties to refer to colleagues united in their fight for a common cause against a common enemy (Chou 2000: 2). It was the standard term used to address virtually everybody in China after the founding of the PRC in 1949 and up until the 1990s. In the late 1980s and early 1990s, along with increased labour mobility and the development of commercial spaces, the politicized appellation 'comrade' gradually fell into disuse. Other and more gender-specific terms such as 'Mr' (*xiansheng*) and 'Miss' (*xiaojie*) started to be used as a means to refer to young people, and especially those working in the service industry. More recently, the Chinese-language terms for 'Mr' and 'Miss' have become sexually charged, being used to refer to men and women who provide commercial sexual services illicitly in recreational venues (see chapter 5).

Although the term *tongzhi* is now considered an old-fashioned way of addressing another person, it has acquired a newfound popularity among gay, lesbian and bisexual communities. The term was first used in 1989 by Hong Kong activists as a new Chinese-language word for homosexuality/gayness and later borrowed by people in other Chinese societies, including those in mainland China. According to Chou Wah-Shan (2001: 28), the term *tongzhi* represents an indigenous endeavour to integrate and harmonize the sexual with the social and cultural; it is not only gender-neutral but also free from the homo–hetero binarism. Calling oneself 'comrade'/*tongzhi* symbolizes 'both the sexual identity of difference and a political identity of same-ness' (Chou 2000: 4).

Many Chinese gays and lesbians prefer to use the term 'tongzhi/comrade' to describe themselves and other same-sex attracted persons because the English-language term 'gay' sounds foreign, and the term tongxinglian has negative connotations. However, the term is not free from ideological burden as it circulates in the Chinese tongzhi community. In Shanghai, for example, the term tongzhi has become associated with a socially responsible sexual citizen who not only attaches more importance to qing/emotional attachment than sex, but also makes significant contributions to society by being a person of high quality (gao suzhi), that is, a person who studies and works hard (Bao 2012: 110–11). These understandings sometimes function to limit the inclusiveness of the term tongzhi.

Calling oneself gay in English, as in 'wo shi gay' ('I am gay'), has become a marker of both sexual and social status among young and educated urbanites in China. The use of the term 'gay' as a form of self-identification gestures towards identification with global 'gayness'. The self-identified gay Chinese man is cosmopolitan and cultured. He often engages with transnational gay networks and mingles with expatriate communities in metropolitan centres such as Beijing and Shanghai; he can be spotted in trendy gay bars and at gay-themed festivals, parades and other transnational events. The use of the foreign word can generate 'the "sexual capital" which places one in certain social strata with certain material and imagined privileges' (Bao 2012: 106). In other words, being 'gay' implies 'a new cosmopolitan humanity' and 'cultural citizenship within Chineseness' (Rofel 2007: 197, 198).

These associations present somewhat differently in the Chinese-language term for 'queer'. Ku'er, the Chinese transliteration of 'queer', was recently introduced to China from western societies. It is less commonly used as a means of self-identification than tongxinglian, tongzhi and 'gay'. The latter three terms may be used individually or interchangeably by a person as a means of identifying themselves and others depending on where they are and who they are with, and how they understand these terms.

As in western societies, the Chinese language term *ku'er* is used to refer to a broad range of non-heteronormative sexualities and subjectivities that disrupt the conventional binaries of male/female and normative/non-normative. However, the Chinese term *ku'er*, which literally translates back into English as 'cool', is usually adopted as a marker of social distinction by artists, film-makers and academics whose works are often too abstruse for ordinary consumption, including by members of LGBT communities (Bao 2011: 121). *Ku'er* thus remains a highbrow term representing a non-normative status or 'cool' position, and does not have the oppositional and confrontational implications of western-style queer politics (Sinnot 2010: 20).

While *tongzhi*, 'gay', *tongxinglian* and *ku'er* are some of the formal terms used by gay and lesbian communities in Greater China, including Hong Kong and Taiwan, there are numerous local and translocal terms to identify gay, lesbian and queer people in mainland China. Many same-sex attracted people now use expressions such as 'people in the circle' (*quan nei/li ren*), 'people like that' (*na zhong ren*), 'people like me' (*xiang wo zheyang de ren*), or *boli*, which literally translates into English as 'glass' but is a transliteration of BL (boy love). The term *boli* was first used to refer to same-sex attracted men, but it is now used to refer to same-sex attracted men and women.

There are also gender-specific terms to describe lesbians and gays. Same-sex attracted women are often referred to as *lala* or *lesi* (both transliterations of 'les/lesbian') or 'lily' (*baihe*, borrowed from Japanese anime and games). A wide range of colloquial terms for same-sex attracted men are used in different parts of China. These include: 'cock up gay' (*gao ji*), originally used in the Cantonese-speaking areas such as Hong Kong and Guangzhou but popularized by computer games; 'wandering men' (*piaopiao*) in Chengdu City; 'pie/pancake' (*bingzi*) or 'button' (*kouzi*) in Wuhan City; 'rubber band' (*pijin*) in Shanghai; and 'second chair' (*eryizi*) or 'rabbit' (*tuzi*) in Beijing.

A Chinese translation of the expression 'brokeback' (*duan bei*) emerged as a new phrase to describe male–male sexual attraction in the PRC in the mid-2000s following the release of *Brokeback Mountain* (dir. Ang Lee 2005), an award-winning film about male–male love in the 'American West'. The film was not screened publicly in mainland China. However, the translated use of the term 'brokeback' to describe gay men in the PRC points to global flows of queer-themed information.

Global flows of queer-themed information, media representations and civil rights movements have become an indispensable component of Chinese gay, lesbian and queer subjectivities. These flows have prompted and lent resources for Chinese sexual minorities to rethink their sexual identity and practices, and the nature of (sexual) citizenship. But this by no means suggests that Chinese lesbians and gays have adopted the gay identities and strategies developed by their western counterparts. Rather, as suggested by the appropriation and indigenization of western terminology for gays, lesbians and queers, and the development of new Chinese-language terms, the politics of homosexuality in China has translocal and transcultural dimensions that resists any 'interpretations in terms of either global impact or self-explanatory indigenous evolution' (Rofel 2007: 94).

The imagined cosmopolitanism of being gay/*tongzhi* is a social imaginary that is shaped by cultural specificity and locality, as well as one's sense of belonging and attitude towards a difference that is 'classed, raced, gendered and sexed' (Bao 2012: 102). This point is illustrated by the links between being 'gay' in China and the discourse of *suzhi* (quality humans). The rhetoric of *suzhi*, which originally came from government policies designed to regulate and administer the population, has been internalized by people to construct their own identities, and is pervasive in discussions among the gay community and society at large (Anagnost 2004; Kipnis 2006; Rofel 1999). Like other members of the Chinese population, same-sex attracted people not only recognize, but also internalize, *suzhi* as a self-regulative principle and are therefore unwittingly implicated in legitimizing hegemonic power along the axis of China's urban and rural divide (Ho, L. W. W. 2008: 498–505). The recognizable characteristics of a gay with good *suzhi* include an individual's high educational level, reasonable financial status, good social networks and shrewd cultural survival skills. His opposite is the rural-to-urban migrant money boy.

The English-language term 'money boy' is used in China to refer to men who provide commercial sexual services usually to other men, although they may self-identify as heterosexual. It is estimated that there are between four and ten thousand young male rural-to-urban migrants who offer same-sex sexual services in Beijing alone (Jeffreys 2007: 163). Money boys are stigmatized in China as rural-to-urban migrants (people who are presumed to have low levels of *suzhi*), male prostitutes, homosexuals, and as such form a perceived high-risk group for HIV and other sexually transmissible infections (Kong 2010b; Wong, F. et al. 2008; see also chapter 5). They are targeted by government authorities for engaging in the illegal practice of prostitution and condemned by large sectors of society as both 'prostitutes' and 'homosexuals'. At the same time, money boys are condemned by many members of the gay community who regard them as thieves and blackmailers, or people who spoil the quality and purity of urban homosexual culture, exploit gay men and hinder the fight against homophobia by harming the reputation of gay men (Kong 2010a; Rofel 1999: 466, 2007: 105, 2010). As Elaine Jeffreys (2007: 167) points out, many academics, policing scholars, and self-identified members of the Chinese homosexual community, 'view money boys as criminal lowlifes … whose activities need to be curbed via the implementation of stricter government controls' for the sake of public health and public security.

The 'respectable' *tongzhi* communities' rejection of money boys as a part of homosexual life in China raises questions such as 'who precisely demands the services of money boys' and 'what is considered to be the appropriate range of same-sex sexual behaviours' (Jeffreys 2007: 167). The answer to these questions undermines the *suzhi* discourse that divides the homsexual community into 'respectable' and 'unrespectable' persons and behaviours. Tong Ge's research on male sex workers in China reveals that some 'respectable' members of the *tongzhi* community may also secretly engage in 'inappropriate' forms of same-sex sexual activities. According to Tong Ge (2007a), men who buy the services of money boys are mostly middle-class men aged forty to fifty-five years, and around 40 per cent of these men are closet gays who are married with children. Foreign visitors to China from diverse walks of life, including businessmen, employees of transnational corporations, tourists, athletes, academics and students, contract the services of money boys through the Internet, gay networks and friends (Tong Ge 2007a). The classed, hierarchical logic implied in the *suzhi* discourse and politics of naming and self-identification in queer China thus elides the power relations and economy of sex and sociality that are associated with China's changing sexual behaviours and mores. As Lisa Rofel (2010: 453) puts it: 'perhaps the respectable gay identity has been misrecognized and is actually more intricately embedded in a commodified world of labor and desire than that of the money boy'.

SAME-SEX ATTRACTED SUBJECTS IN CONTEMPORARY MEDIA

Lack of access to traditional media prevented positive representations of homosexuality and homosexuals from being shown in the public arena in China until recently. With the rise of HIV and AIDS prevention and care policies in China since 2001, the lives of Chinese gay and lesbian people became more visible in the public domain through stories and discussions in magazines and newspapers and on the television and Internet (see chapter 6). However, this visibility primarily involved 'experts' talking about 'homosexuals', and functioned to stigmatize homosexuality through its association with a life-threatening disease. It did not generally involve positive self-presentation, that is, gays and lesbians talking about themselves and with other gays and lesbians.

Since the late 1990s, the Internet has proven to be 'a pioneering force in building indigenous *tongzhi* discourses in China' (Chou 2000: 134), providing a participatory and reflexive public sphere for gay, lesbian and queer people to access and share information, form relationships, and cultivate queer identities and communities (Bao 2011: 124; Ho, L. W. W. 2007; Sun, Farrer and Choi 2006; Zhang and Kaufman 2005). There has been an explosion of personal storytelling on a proliferation of websites, BBS, blog and microblog sites, video-sharing services, and other online resources, that cater to sexual minorities. Reading posts in chat rooms, BBS, personal blogs or *tongzhi* literature, one is overwhelmed by the outpouring of emotions in heartbreaking narratives about same-sex attraction and ensuing family dramas (Cristini 2005). Gay groups such as Queer Comrades and Smile4Gay now campaign for the removal of homophobic commentaries and advertisements from popular search engines and websites (Chase 2012: 165–6).

However, the supposedly free and global cyberspace is subject to constraints. Some gay, lesbian and queer people do not have the financial means to afford a computer and access to the Internet at home. They are therefore obliged to use Internet cafés, where they may fear to visit certain sites in case they are observed by others (Miège 2009: 46). Gay and lesbian-oriented websites also tend to be short-lived due to Internet regulations and controls, lack of financial resources and technical expertise, the impact of online pornography, and even hacking from other Chinese gay and lesbian websites, which can arise from personal conflicts among website operators or competition over representation (Ho, L. W. W. 2007: 57; Tong Ge 2004: 201). Some moderators of Chinese gay and lesbian websites practise self-censorship to avoid the risk of being shut down by government authorities, while many other gay-oriented websites have become commercialized and sexualized to attract traffic and advertising (Ho, L. W. W. 2007).

Although the Internet is central to gay and lesbian groups in their efforts to share information and cultivate relationships, identities and communities, online activism initiated by gay and lesbian groups has limited influence on the general heterosexual public. Lesbians and gays may talk freely about almost anything in online environments, but not many heterosexuals are interested in listening (Chase 2012: 167). Only rarely does any of their discourse migrate into the traditional media sphere and that is quite often in a sensational and voyeuristic manner, as with news on gay marriages. Access to traditional media or lack thereof has proven to be a crucial factor in determining the effectiveness of online gay activism.

Gay magazines, books and movies are more strictly censored than gay websites. Homosexuality has been explored in literature (Sang 2003), but Chinese television and film industries have typically taken a socially conservative approach (Chan 2008: 144). The topic of same-sex attraction is notably absent from Chinese-produced television dramas (Zhu, Keane and Bai 2008: 10). Moreover, while homosexuality has been featured in some television talk shows such as Hunan Satellite Television's Staying Cool (hao hua hao shuo), these discussions tend to be filtered and mediated by 'experts', whether academics, public intellectuals, public health researchers or homosexual people 'disguised' as experts (Chase 2012: 158; Cui 2002: 13; Wang, Q. 2004: 182). Video productions from the Chinese diaspora, foreign or underground films, and independent documentaries that feature gay and lesbian themes, are available online, and on DVD, and are shown at small gatherings and film festivals. However, they have not reached a mass audience due to restrictions on public broadcast and screening (Zhao, J. 2010: 81). Nevertheless, there is a lively underground film culture of video stores and screening venues in China, which introduces Chinese audiences to global and domestic homosexual subcultures.

Starting in the early 1990s, some heterosexual film-makers and intellectuals began bringing the subject of alternative sexualities into the public arena. According to Chris Berry (2001: 214), there are three types of films and videos that feature Chinese gay and queer characters. The first type is feature films with gay themes shot by straight men, which are aimed at mainstream markets and the general public, such as the *Wedding Banquet* (dir. Ang Lee 1993) and *Farewell My Concubine* (dir. Chen Kaige 1993). The second type consists of independent films and videos shot by gay Asian film-makers from the Chinese diaspora, which are aimed at gay audiences, such as *White Frog* (dir. Quentin Lee 2012). The third type is festival or art-house films, such as *Vive L'Amour* (*Aiqing wansui*) and *The River* (*Heliu*) (dir. Tsai Ming-Liang 1994 and 1997) and *Happy Together* (*Chunguang zhaxie*) (dir. Wong Karwai 1997).

Many Chinese gay-themed films are the result of production alliances between Hong Kong, Taiwan, mainland China and the United States. They engage with gay sexuality in the format of the Chinese melodrama tradition (Chan 2008), for example, the trials of gay love in *Lan Yu* (dir. Stanley Kwan 2001) and queer feelings in *Farewell My Concubine* (Hsu 2012). However, most queer films are banned from being screened publicly or being released as DVDs in China, as they are considered 'dissident films' by censors (Cui, Z. 2010: 419). Under such constraints, the Chinese irreverence towards copyright has turned out to be a blessing for Chinese gays, lesbians and queers, because they can get bootleg copies of underground films cheaply, especially those Chinese movies made for international film festivals (Cui, Z. 2010: 422).

The screening of homosexuality, whether that occurs publicly in cinemas or privately with bootleg DVDs, is enabling and empowering for Chinese LGBT communities. Cinema 'is capable of bringing about societal changes' via 'new visual representations of celluloid comrades hitherto unseen on Chinese screens' (Lim 2006: 19–20). Chris Berry and Laikwan Pang (2010) note the centrality of cinema to LGBT cultures in the Chinese-speaking world, mainly through film festivals and cyberspace. Digitalization means *tongzhi* netizens all over the world can visit dedicated websites that offer video streaming and downloading, while only a very small number of people can attend the few *tongzhi* film festivals. *Tongzhi* films can be shared online as part of community-building by a Chinese-language LGBT community in different locations (Berry and Pang 2010: 100). The limited circulation of gay and lesbian films internationally also enables Chinese sexual minorities as film-makers to participate in and expand the boundaries of global gay culture (Berry 1996).

The international fascination with Chinese cinema highlighted by and flowing from the international awards given to 'Fifth Generation' directors, such as Chen Kaige, Zhang Yimou and Tian Zhuangzhuang, encouraged the development of a variety of alternative and independent film-making in China from the late 1980s onward. Cui Zi'en, China's first self-identified gay film-maker, has written and/or directed over twenty films and documentaries on homosexual themes since 1999. Like other same-sex activists, Cui is situated in the growing field and market of Chinese independent screen products both domestically and internationally. His films are acclaimed for performing sexual dissent to illuminate China's hidden gay subculture and to help build an alternative cultural sphere, rather than engaging voyeuristic audiences (Berry 1996; Voci 2010; Zhou, Y. 2014).

Another aspect of alternative film-making relates to the Chinese New Documentary Movement, which rejected 'socialist realism' in favour of focusing on the unscripted lives of ordinary, and especially marginal, people (Lü 2010). This aspect is seen in independent documentary films such as: *East Palace, West Palace (Donggong, xigong)*, directed by Zhang Yuan (1996); *Man Man Woman Woman (nannan nünü)*, directed by Liu Binjian (1999); *Feeding Boys, Ayaya (Aiyaya, qu puru)* and *Night Scene (Yejing)*, directed by Cui Zi'en (2003, 2005); and *Tongzhi*, directed by Tao Han (2004). These films highlight a sense of immediacy and unscripted spontaneity through their focus on gay lives in private settings.

Most media representations of homosexuality in China focus on gay men rather than lesbians. Some attribute the absence of mediatized lesbian subjects to the historical lack of a specific term for 'lesbian' in the Chinese language, which made it a murky category for identification until recently (Ho, A. K. H. 2009). Others think the invisibility of lesbians in China's media is linked to the 'traditional trivialization of female sexuality' and the tendency to define women in relation to family relationships only (Zhao, J. 2010: 79).

Depictions of lesbians in the mass media in China, as elsewhere, typically turn on heteronormative definitions of gender and sex and negative stereotypes. Women in China continue to be defined in mainstream discourses by their relationships with men and their social roles as wives, mothers and daughters. Same-sex desires among women are silenced, denounced or punished; some families seek legal means to separate female couples (Rofel 2007); others seek to 'fix' the errant female by getting her raped by a male (Radio Free Asia 2013). Journalistic writings often represent lesbians in negative terms such as jealous, lascivious, violent, crazy and incomprehensible; and lesbianism is also often described in those writings as a reaction to abuse or neglect by men, or as a contingent form of sexual contact in the absence of men (Ruan and Bullough 1992).

In this context, feminist depictions of female and lesbian relationships in literature and films are especially significant. Female homoeroticism and consciousness was featured in the feminist writings of Zhang

Jie, Liu Suola and Wang Anyi in the 1980s and Chen Ran and Lin Bai in the 1990s (Liu, L. H. 1991; Evans 1997; Sang 2003). A focus on female homosexuality started to emerge from the New Documentary Movement, when female film-makers such as Li Yu, Ying Weiwei and Shi Tou focused their lenses on lesbians as gendered sexual subjects (Berry, Lü and Rofel 2010). *Fish and Elephant* (*Jinnian xiatian*), directed by Li Yu (2001), is the first lesbian feature film made in China. It is about the lives of a lesbian couple, Lin and Qun, living in Beijing – their romance, their friendship with two female ex-lovers, their relationships with their mothers and their relationships with men. Like other gay and lesbian-themed films, the film is an underground production and cannot be shown in public in China, although it has been screened at different film festivals around the world (Zhao, J. 2010: 56). Another lesbian-themed production was made in the same year as the *Fish and Elephant*, titled *The Box* (*Hezi*), directed by Ying Weiwei (2001). It is known as China's first documentary with lesbian subjects. *The Box* features the talking heads of a lesbian couple, A and B, discussing their life experiences before they met and fell in love. That discussion is interspersed with images of their intimacy and daily life together.

While both *Fish and Elephant* and *The Box* were made by straight-identified film-makers, 'lesbians with video cameras' such as Shi Tou have taken a more activist and participatory approach to representing the politics of lesbianism. *Dyke March* (*Nü tongxinglian youxing ri*), directed by Shi Tou in 2004, features a lesbian parade in San Francisco on 28 June 2002. Shi Tou's symbolic 'coming out' (when she jumps in front of the camera to join her western 'sisters' in the parade), the rainbow pattern that is featured frequently throughout the film, and the focus on the bare breasts and torsos of women in the march, evoke a sense of solidarity and queer performativity (Chao 2010). Such per-formativity can be a political strategy for Chinese and global queers to challenge the heteronormative, patriarchal, hierarchical and political regimes that constrain transcultural imagination and practice about homosexuality (Chao 2010: 93). Gay- and lesbian-themed film and video productions are part of the 'scattered, ongoing, and dynamic do-it-yourself projects [that] vitally contribute to the understanding and nurturing of queer lives' (Leung, H. 2008: 120).

The focus on the individual and the private in gay- and lesbian-themed screen productions brings to light the concealed, unendorsed, illegitimate and illicit status of queer loves and lives. However, it also reduces homosexuality to a benign practice located in the private lives and spaces of individuals, rather than portraying it as a collective and open desire. The characters in gay and lesbian screen representations are often aloof and self-contained, and have little interaction with the outside world. Gay and lesbian people sometimes share emotions, seek support and perform their *tongzhi* identity in a safe place that the *tongzhi* community provides. But the community is unstructured, fragmented and fragile, which makes building long-term relationships within the *tongzhi* circle difficult (Miège 2009: 47–9). Furthermore, it remains 'relatively confined, always under threat and ... kept completely sealed off from the rest of the society' (Miège 2009: 53). These problems indicate how formidably heteronormative institutions and family systems continue to regulate popular discourses and imaginations about gender and sexuality in China.

'GOING OUT' AND 'COMING HOME'

Literature on being gay in China, whether research papers or personal accounts, show that the major pain and dilemma felt by most same-sex attracted people in China centres on the issue of whether or not to tell their parents that they are gay or lesbian, and how to avoid heterosexual marriage. For gay men in China, the pressure to carry on the patrilineal family line is especially heavy, both from parents (to be a filial son) and society (to be a respectable man). Many same-sex attracted men have pointed out that it is 'not state oppression, religious fundamentalism, or job discrimination, but the ones they love most – their parents', that cause them the most pain (Chou 2001: 34). The traditional concepts of 'face' (*mianzi*) and 'status' (*diwei*) that are rooted in China's culture and economy continue to invoke both the family and the nation as forces to regulate social behaviours. Hence, many 'gay men shy away from telling their parents that they are gay because they fear that they will take away their family's *mianzi*, and with it their own humanity' (Rofel 2007: 102).

Both lesbians and gays are under constant pressure to get married from parents, relatives, friends, work colleagues and even supervisors (see also chapter 2). In fact, many homosexuals view entering a heterosexual marriage as 'the right thing to do', despite their sexual orientation (Miège 2009: 49–52). Gay men are especially pressured to compromise their sexual desire to meet the expectations of their families, that is, to marry and procreate. This situation has reportedly trapped an estimated 16 million Chinese women in sexless and loveless marriages to gay men ('Homosexuality in China' 2010; Lau 2010). Such women are known as 'homowives' or 'wives of homosexuals' (*tongqi*). Sociologist Li Yinhe has engaged in a broad range of publicity-generating activities to raise public awareness of the issue, including advocating since 2001 for the PRC's legislature to legalize same-sex marriage (Chase 2012: 153–4; see chapter 7).

Some lesbians and gays can avoid social and family pressures for various periods of time by 'going out' (*chuzou*), literally moving away from their place of birth and family home. Labour mobility, combined with the recent, partial privatization of China's housing market, has enabled some people to settle down in their own space and place with their same-sex partners. Metropolitan cities are places where same-sex attracted people from different parts of China can go to find a 'gay' identity and community, as is often the case in western societies.

However, 'going out' is not the same as 'coming out'. 'Coming out' is an imported discourse central to gay identity politics in western societies. Rather than sticking to the binary opposition of visibility or invisibility, or 'in the closet' or 'coming out', Chinese sexual minorities often practise a classical Chinese aesthetics of *'hanxu'* (implicitness, reticence or indirectness) when negotiating their sexual identity with their family and broader society. Many Chinese lesbians and gays choose both an 'in' and 'out' policy, being 'in' or 'out' depending on the social settings they are in and the persons they are with. As Hongwei Bao (2012: 109) explains, for Chinese lesbians and gays, '[w]hen to conceal and when to disclose one's identity, together with to whom, becomes a matter of politics'.

The aesthetics of *hanxu* also explains the 'coming home' strategy that an increasing number of Chinese *tongzhi* have chosen to adopt. 'Coming home' *(huijia)* refers in Chinese gay and lesbian circles to the act of going back to the family home with a same-sex partner but without 'coming out' or declaring one's homosexuality to one's parents. The aim of 'coming home' in this sense is to obtain parental acquiescence, rather than explicit approval, for a same-sex relationship through non-confrontational negotiation. Such acquiescence is established through mutual engagement in mundane practices, for example, eating and shopping together. Hence, Chou Wah-Shan (2001) argues that 'coming home' represents a strategy to integrate the sexual with the socio-cultural, into the family and cultural context. The act of 'coming home' can be:

> explicated as a negotiative process of bringing one's sexuality into the family-kin network, not by singling out same-sex eroticism as a site for conceptual discussion but by constructing a same-sex relationship in terms of family-kin categories. (Chou 2001: 36)

Those who can 'come home' with their same-sex partners are the lucky ones. Many lesbians and gays are not able to 'come home' with their same-sex partners. Family, social and economic pressures oblige them to enter 'heterosexual' marriages and establish their own home. 'Coming home' in this sense is not a harmonious experience, but rather one that is characterized by lies, pain and frustration.

China's lesbians and gays enter into four types of 'heterosexual' marriage. These are different from the gay and lesbian weddings organized by activists, for example, He Xiaopei's lesbian weddings and *ménage à trois* wedding to one gay and one lesbian (He 2010). Activist-organized queer marriages usually take place within queer communities as a performance or spectacle and *without* the involvement of family members, especially parents. They challenge social discrimination against queer relationships by providing a symbolic celebration of the commitment of a same-sex couple to each other, or challenge the institution of heterosexual marriage by providing an example of alternative forms of marriage.

The first type of 'heterosexual' marriage that is entered into by same-sex attracted people in China involves getting married to heterosexual people and keeping their same-sex sexual desires hidden forever. The second involves getting married to a heterosexual but having a secret homosexual sex life. The third involves getting married to a heterosexual but having an openly homosexual sex life. The fourth type refers to what is known as a cooperative or pro-forma/contract marriage (*hezuo/ huzhu hunyin* or *xinghun*), that is, a marriage between a lesbian and a gay man who present themselves to family and work circles as a heterosexual couple (see also chapter 2). The first three types of marriage involve considerable emotional trauma, being associated with the repression of individual desires and the ongoing deception or disregard of one's partner (Kam 2010: 96–9). While complicated, the fourth cooperative performance of heterosexual marriage is arguably 'an emerging queer private sphere that may offer alternative models and discourses to the heteronormative model of intimacy' (Kam 2010: 102).

Cooperative marriage is a strategy used primarily by young gays and lesbians to resolve the social pressure to marry by faking marriage *with* the recognition and presence of parents and relatives. There are gay bars such as The Box in Shanghai and websites such as chinagayles.com that are dedicated to matching lesbians and gays. Such marriages enable *lala* daughters and *tongzhi* sons to demonstrate their love to their parents, to have children and potentially bypass social and workplace discrimination (Kam 2010). However, such marriages are also complicated by the requirement to perform heterosexual love in an ongoing fashion in front of families and colleagues, legal complications regarding finances and children should the 'marriage' fail, and the gendered effects on the personal independence of lesbians (Engebretsen 2013: 105; Kam 2010). Personal accounts of cooperative marriages in online forums highlight both the benefits and limitations of such fake marriages. Cooperative marriage is described as a temporary solution to family and social pressure to get married, but also as a 'nightmare' by a lesbian who experienced difficulties dealing with her partner as a 'wife' and dealing with his 'husband' (Les Sky 2011), and as 'torture' by a gay man who described his 'wife' as unreasonable and was pressured to have a child by both his parents and his 'wife's' parents (Shutong de Gongzi 2011).

'Coming home' into a heterosexual marriage, whether real or faked, does not relieve the pressures of compulsory marriage and compulsory reproduction that many Chinese homosexuals face. It signals a tacit acceptance of heteronormative hegemony and points to the fragility of gay, lesbian and queer identities in the face of family expectations and dominant social mores. 'Coming home' is not the equivalent of coming to terms with one's sexuality.

CONCLUSION

Loretta Wing Wah Ho (2010: 5) argues that Chinese gay identity is both 'open and decentred' and 'national and conforming to state control'. Elaine Jeffreys (2007) somewhat differently argues that accusations of official homophobia in China are overstated. Her examination of the media coverage of a case involving male–male prostitution demonstrates that 'the relationship between sex and government in contemporary China is not characterized by straightforward repression, official homophobia, and a corollary refusal to embrace the rights and accompanying legal strategies that are associated with progressive, liberal sexual politics' (Jeffreys 2007: 73). As the work of these and other scholars suggests, 'the repressive hypothesis', in which the state is understood as censoring sexual discourse and restricting sexual freedom, can be an impediment to understanding the broader socio-cultural context that restricts the expression and representation of homosexuality. Traditional constraints on social behaviours and pressure on gender conformity from family, friends and social circles can be far more powerful than political oppression (Zhang and Kaufman 2005: 127).

While rejecting the repressive hypothesis, one should avoid using an essentialist cultural logic to understand homosexuality in China. As Zhao Jin (2010: 3) points out, 'Chinese queerness must be understood in the complex and dynamic political and cultural context where complementary and/or contesting powers, such as the influence of western modern/postmodern thoughts, China's feudal and predominantly Confucian cultural traditions and its communist puritan cultural ideology, coexist and interplay.'

The government's prioritization of economic development over political liberalization and the inadequate nature of social welfare provisions have impacted on gay, lesbian and queer politics in China in distinct ways. China's opening up has provided more space for lesbians and gays to break away from heteronormative regimes. However, government policies still censor media representations of lesbians and gays in the public sphere (especially in films), and they block independent audio-visual productions from public screening. There is also a classed bias towards individual sexual rights based on the discourse of *suzhi*, with urban and 'cosmopolitan' homosexuals enjoying more freedom and rights than their less-valued rural counterparts. Many gays and lesbians in China are unable to demand such 'rights' because of their continued dependence on family for subsistence (including housing), and emotional and moral support, and corollary obligations to meet their parents' expectations, including the expectation that they will marry and have children.

At the same time, there is increasing tolerance of homosexuality in the PRC and China's sexual minorities have a positive attitude towards their future. This positivity is attributed to three China-specific factors. The first consideration is the one-child-per-couple policy, which has been implemented since the late 1970s to curb population growth (see chapter 2). Many lesbians and gays jokingly remark that they should be praised for contributing to the nation's population control and development policies (personal communication 2011). More seriously, they note that their status as an only child has altered the dynamics of parent–child relationships. Many parents are willing to negotiate with and accept the non-traditional sexual and lifestyle choices of their only child. Hence, more urban-based lesbians and gays are able to 'come home' to their parents than rural-based lesbians and gays.

A second factor is the newfound and rapidly increasing mobility of young Chinese people, which creates the space to construct (stratified) gay identities and communities. This includes private and public, mediated and unmediated, spaces where people can live their homosexual and homosocial lives. There are ample opportunities and spaces for LGBT people to meet one another in cities such as Beijing, Chengdu, Guangzhou and Shanghai. However, those opportunities and spaces are neither equally distributed nor equally accessible. Commercial queer spaces are marked by hierarchies of class and the discourse of *suzhi*, and government authorities still interfere in gay lives and spaces.

A third factor is the historical and continued absence of a hostile religion. Unlike their counterparts in many parts of the world, such as South Korea (Chase 2012), Chinese gays and lesbians do not face any organized religious opposition. Instead, they are often frustrated by the primacy accorded in China to the institution of heterosexual marriage, and by the PRC's media censorship and restrictions on political speech. But digital media and communication is not a panacea to the problems that Chinese sexual minorities face. Stiff competition for traffic and attention in the digital media environment can easily diversify rather than amplify serious messages in the Chinese gay, lesbian and queer movement.

Chinese queer subjects have to constantly negotiate the disjuncture and conflicts between the pursuit of individual sexual rights and engagement with local and individual specificities. Some have chosen to join the global queer community and adopted its strategies and rhetoric in openly advocating for equal sexual rights. Others continue to be the silent majority, adopting a 'don't ask, don't tell' mentality and a strategy of 'appearing to comply with but secretly violating' (*yangfeng yingwei*) heteronormativity. Chinese queer subjects face stratified lifestyles and societal environments, depending on their place of residence, employment and class. They are therefore obliged to adopt different strategies when dealing with their sexuality and expressing that sexuality in relation to their families and social circles.

5   Commercial Sex ————————

This chapter challenges claims that prostitution in China is a taboo topic and the focus of unchanging policing controls by examining the growth of the PRC's sex industry and public debates about its regulation. A 2006 article in the *International Herald Tribune* claims that the sex industry is probably the fastest-growing industry in China, it being virtually impossible 'to walk for 10 minutes in any big Chinese city without coming across the sex trade in one of its many guises' (French 2006). The article adds that 'ordinarily' (meaning in countries other than the PRC) this situation would be 'grist for all manner of conversation', from social inequalities to the public health implications and to the need for legal reform (French 2006). It concludes, however, that '[p]erhaps the most striking feature of China's booming prostitution industry...is how little ink is expended on it, how seldom its extent is even acknowledged' (French 2006). This conclusion invokes popular understandings of the PRC as a censorial police state, but it offers a far from accurate account of the situation in China today.

Prostitution is a controversial phenomenon and a new object of governance in reform-era China because of its celebrated absence during the Mao era (1949–76). In keeping with Marxist theory (Engels 1972), the early Chinese Communist Party (CCP) viewed prostitution as an expression of the degraded position of women under feudal-capitalist patriarchy and therefore as incompatible with the goals of building socialism and establishing more equitable socio-sexual relations. Following its assumption of national political power in 1949, the

CCP embarked upon a series of campaigns that allegedly eradicated prostitution from mainland China by the late 1950s (Jeffreys 2012b: 96–7). The extraordinary nature of this feat meant that it was and is vaunted as one of the major accomplishments of the communist regime. A PRC government white paper describes the abolition of prostitution as effecting an 'earth-shaking historic change in the social status and condition of women' (Information Office of the State Council of the People's Republic of China 1994a).

Prostitution rates remained extremely low during the Mao era due to the requirements of centralized economic planning that entailed the nationalization of industry, and the curtailing of the monetary economy and population mobility. By 1957, an estimated 90 per cent of China's urban population belonged to a work unit (*danwei*), a state-owned enterprise or institution that was meant to overcome the alienation of labour by merging life and work, and which provided all manner of welfare and services for its employees – housing, education, health care, policing, consumption goods and entertainment (Jeffreys 2012b: 2–3). The Mao-era system of allocation, in conjunction with a system of household registration (*hukou*), created a geographically fixed population that was permanently open to surveillance. Most urban Chinese spent their entire lives in the closed community of a work unit, while rural agricultural producers became tied to their place of birth, because the state allocated work and major resources, and therefore needed to know the identity and location of its workers (Jeffreys 2012b: 2 –3).

The comprehensive nature of this system contributed to the absence of visible prostitution in Mao-era China by restricting the physical and moral spaces in which such activities could occur. Everyday life in urban China was organized around work and collectivist political movements until the mid-1970s. Moreover, there were few venues in which individuals could engage in anonymous or private behaviours until the PRC began to develop a hospitality and service industry in the late 1980s (Jeffreys 2012b: 2 –3).

Prostitution resurfaced in the PRC coincident with the nation's post-1978 adoption of market-based economic reforms and policy of opening up to the rest of the world. Figures relating to the number of sexual service providers in China vary according to different sources and estimates. A 2009 report by the US Department of State claims that between 1.7 and 6 million women earn their primary income from prostitution, with a further 8 to 10 million women occasionally accepting money as well as gifts or rent in exchange for sexual services (US Department of State 2009). Estimates by medical researchers focusing on prostitution as a potential bridge for the transmission of sexually transmissible infections, including HIV, suggest that there are between 4 and 10 million female sex sellers in China (Li, L. et al. 2009).

Expanding on these figures, journalists and academics often cite a Chinese economist, Yang Fan, to claim that there are 20 million sex sellers, whose consumption practices account for between 6 and 13 per cent of the PRC's gross domestic product (GDP) (French 2006; Zheng: 2009a: 66). These estimates are problematic, given the inherent difficulties involved in quantifying the share of GDP constituted by consumption of participants in a black-market sector of the economy, on the one hand, and the problem of isolating factors determining the marginal propensity to consume of so variegated a population as female sex sellers, on the other. These estimates do, however, contribute to general understandings that the sex industry is an important component of life in China.

The prevalence of prostitution in China has raised questions about the usefulness of the nation's adherence to a more than three-decade-long policy of attempting to abolish it via police-led crackdowns. Journalists, academics, bloggers, and even prominent public figures with CCP affiliations, now openly argue that the sex industry should be legalized or decriminalized in order to promote tourism and tax revenue, prevent the spread of STIs-HIV and give sex workers legal protections (Huang and Liu 2010; Ji Ruijie 2009; Zhou Ruijin 2006).

The chapter first discusses the spread of prostitution businesses and practices in the reform period. It then outlines the nature of China's prostitution controls. Finally, the chapter examines calls to legalize or decriminalize commercial sex in the PRC. It demonstrates that questions regarding the most appropriate government response to the sex industry are a feature of public debate in present-day China.

SELLERS AND BUYERS

The rapid spread of prostitution businesses and practices in reform-era China raises an obvious set of anthropological and sociological questions. Who provides commercial sexual services? What are their motivations for doing so? In what kinds of spaces do they provide such services? Who demands their services and why?

In China, as in other parts of the world, providers of commercial sexual services are usually women aged under forty years and especially between seventeen and twenty-four years (Choi 2011: 104; Sun, Deng and Qin 2009; Zheng 2010a: 35). The age of statutory consent, or the age at which people can legally have sex in China, is fourteen; youth can leave school and obtain legal employment at sixteen years of age; and a young person is considered to be an adult, or to have reached the age of legal majority, when they reach the age of eighteen years (Xi 2006: 79; Article 28, Law of the People's Republic of China on the Protection of Minors 1991; Article 17, Criminal Law of the PRC 1997). Hence, the majority of women who provide commercial sexual services are young adults, and they engage in the sex trade as a short-term means of obtaining a livelihood.

The typical 'sex seller' in China has been stereotyped in government, academic and media reports as a young and poorly educated rural-to-urban migrant worker (e.g., Yu, Y. J. 2013: 350). Numerous commentators describe China's entry into the global economy as a second industrial revolution, involving the largest rural–urban migration in human history ('The second industrial revolution' 2004). Throughout the 1990s and into the new millennium, an estimated 262 million people have migrated from poor rural areas to work in developing urban centres (Wang, Y, 2013). Male migrants usually find work as low-paid and unskilled manual labourers in areas relating to the construction of infrastructure. Female migrants often find themselves in equally 'dead-end jobs' as factory hands and domestic maids, and as cleaning and waiting staff in the service industry (Choi 2011: 105; Liu, M. 2011: 71–3; Zheng 2010a: 34). Hence, although some women are forced into prostitution by severe economic hardship or physical coercion, many women enter prostitution voluntarily as a response to underemployment and limited opportunities for upward mobility. Despite problems such as social stigmatization, client violence and police harassment, selling sexual services may provide more disposable income than other precarious forms of earning a livelihood, and for fewer and more flexible hours of work (Choi 2011: 103; Jeffreys 2012a: 1–2). In the words of three Chinese sex workers: 'It is easy to make money doing this'; '[t]his is the only job that I can do, where I can make several thousand a month'; and 'I work when I want; I do not work when I do not want to' (cited in Liu, M. 2011: 99, 126).

A now common Chinese-language term for female sex workers, *Xiaojie* ('Miss'), highlights the association of commercial sex with young migrant women working as 'companions' or 'hostesses' in entertainment establishments. The title 'Miss' emerged in the late 1980s to early 1990s as the political appellation previously used to address every Chinese person, namely, *tongzhi* (comrade), fell out of fashion, especially as a way of addressing unfamiliar (not-local) people working in new urban commercial spaces (Fan Xiaoling et al. 2004: 41–7). As 'hostesses', *xiaojies* entertained the predominantly male clientele of entertainment establishments, usually government officials and entrepreneurs, by chatting, singing, dancing and flirting, in exchange for tips and a percentage of the money generated by alcohol and food consumption (Jeffreys 2012a: 1–3). Some also provided sexual services, either in the venue or at other accommodations. In the mid-1990s, journalists began using the term *xiaojie* to describe women apprehended for selling sexual services during police-led crackdowns against illegal activities in entertainment establishments (Fan Xiaoling et al. 2004: 41–7). The term *xiaojie* has since become synonymous with the English-language expression 'working girl'. Its negative connotation as a synonym for 'prostitute' or 'whore' (*jinü*) is indicated by the fact that young women who work in the hospitality and service industry are often offended if they are hailed by the term *xiaojie*, preferring to be hailed by the neutral term *fuwuyuan* ('waiter' or 'service provider').

Female sexual service providers come from multiple sectors of Chinese society, despite the rural stereotype, as suggested by the diverse sites and prices for commercial sex. Prostitution businesses and practices can be found not only in the cosmopolitan cities of Beijing and Shanghai, but also in remote and economically underdeveloped regions such as Guizhou and Tibet ('Prostitution thriving' 2005; 'Xishui piaosu' 2009). Venues for commercial sex include high- and low-grade hotels, karaoke/dance venues, bars, health and fitness clubs, saunas, cinemas, teahouses, foot- and hair-washing salons, barbershops, truck stops and temporary work camps, as well as public spaces such as beaches, parks and underneath overpass bridges (Jeffreys 2012a: 97–8; Lin et al. 2010: 5–13).

The prices commanded for engaging in commercial sex vary according to location and the nature of supply and demand. Prices range from as little as the cost of a simple meal (CNY 10) to several hundred and even several thousand yuan, depending on whether the transaction is negotiated by an individual street walker or through intermediaries in low- or high-grade venues (Jeffreys 2012a: 98; Liu, M. 2011: 109–20; Zheng 2010a: 35, 44). In Shenzhen during the late 2000s, the price for sexual services was CNY 130 at a hair salon and CNY 200–800 in a karaoke/dance venue, and street walkers charged only CNY 20–50 (Liu, M. 2011): 116–19). Prices also vary based on the relative attractiveness of the provider and the socio-economic status of those who demand their services. In China, as in other parts of the world, prostitution is an ageist, classist, racist and sexist industry that offers short-term financial gain for those who use their bodies as sexual capital. Those who meet certain aesthetic requirements (physically attractive, exotic, educated, cultured and urbane) earn more than their less 'attractive' counterparts, with an individual's earning capacity generally diminishing rapidly as their age increases (Fang Xiaoyi et al. 2007; Sun, Deng and Qin 2009). In the words of one sex worker, 'Girls have a limited number of years during which to make a lot of money' (cited in Liu, M. 2011: 155).

Buyers of sexual services (usually men aged between twenty and sixty-five years) pay different rates depending on where they engage in commercial sex, for what reasons and with whom. Blue-collar workers are associated in stereotypical fashion with the purchase of quick, cheap sex from poor migrant workers in the streets or in low-grade venues, such as foot-washing salons, massage parlours and barber shops. Although many prostitute clients are urban workers, they are usually characterized as poorly educated migrant workers who engage in 'risky' sexual behaviours to satisfy natural biological urges, or to compensate for emotional stresses, because they are working away from their homes and perhaps their wives on a long-term basis, and are often socially isolated as second-class citizens (Lin et al. 2010: 8). Conversely, wealthy entrepreneurs, government officials and professionals are associated with the consumption of sexual services from women of recognizable quality in high-grade venues, often as part of new leisure practices connected with corporate masculinity and the establishment of business deals (Jeffreys 2008: 240–1; Uretsky 2008: 801–14; Zheng 2006: 2, 182).

Although prostitution businesses and practices are characterized by multiple venues and types, ethnographic research conducted in north- and south-eastern China suggests that female sex sellers are often subjected to violence. Fights apparently are common between drunken clients and hostesses in entertainment establishments, and hostesses are regularly verbally abused and pinched, and slapped and beaten, for failing to meet manager and client expectations (Zheng 2010a: 46–51). In a survey of 200 women, three-quarters of whom were migrant workers, nearly 50 per cent said they had experienced sexual violence: they reported being threatened and forced into engaging in oral and anal sex, and being unable to end a sexual transaction when they requested (Choi 2011: 107). In addition to physical violence, women who provide sexual services are stigmatized socially as immoral, inferior and unclean. In the words of one female sex seller, 'all people look down on us' (cited in Yu, Y. J. 2013: 354).

Originally restricted chiefly to adult heterosexual prostitution, the market for sexual services in China has expanded to include male–male prostitution, male–female prostitution, youth prostitution and child prostitution (Jeffreys 2012b). The majority of men who sell male–male sexual services are single men aged between eighteen and twenty-four years (Cui 2005; Fu Jianfeng 2004; Kong 2010b: 177; Jeffreys 2007: 163). As with their female counterparts, they often have moved from poor communities in the rural hinterland to urban and more developed parts of the PRC to look for work and sometimes to study at college or university.

Commonly referred to as money boys, many of the young men who provide commercial sexual services to other men reportedly self-identify as heterosexual, but are willing to provide male–male sexual services in exchange for relatively high sums of financial recompense. In the words of one male sex worker:

> I was a salesman in an electronic shop. But these days were very boring…and at the end, you got only 1,000 yuan a month. For me, I just did one or two clients [as a money boy], then I could earn the same amount as a whole month's salary [as a salesman]! (Kong 2010b: 174)

Other money boys define themselves as bisexual or gay and claim to enjoy experimenting with their sexuality while earning money (Chapman et al. 2009: 693; Kong 2010b: 182). At the same time, they express concern over their triply stigmatized identity as homosexuals, rural-to-urban migrants and sex sellers, and worry about the future because their ability to earn an income from commercial sex is age-related and hence short term (Kong 2010b: 180–90). Quick transactions negotiated and conducted on the street command CNY 10–30, sexual services arranged at or provided in a recreational enterprise command CNY 50–500, and an overnight stay may command CNY 1,000 (Chapman et al. 2009: 695; Fu Jianfeng 2004). Customers of money boys are middle-aged men from all walks of life, including entrepreneurs, government officials, police officers, university professors and foreign nationals (Cui 2005; Ho 2008: 506; see chapter 4).

Men who offer commercial sexual services to women – known in colloquial Chinese as *yazi* (ducks), after their female counterparts, *ji* (chickens) – allegedly are growing in numbers too. The term 'ducks' is a play on the colloquial Chinese term for prostitute, *jinü*, with the abbreviated word *ji* (prostitute) being a homophone for the word *ji* (chicken). Media reports based on anecdotal evidence suggest that middle-aged women on holidays from Hong Kong and Taiwan sometimes pay for male companionship and potential sex partners in karaoke/dance venues, as do young mainland Chinese women who desire uncomplicated and/or extra-marital sex (Miller 2006). Ethnographic research further suggests that female sex sellers in the Pearl River Delta region sometimes purchase sex from male migrants, both to have 'fun' and to affirm their higher-class status as someone who can afford to purchase sexual services from a man who sells sex and therefore has a lower social status than them (Ding, Y. 2008: 95–6; Fan, M. 2007).

Youth prostitution is another new phenomenon in reform-era China. Media reports indicate that an increasing number of female university students are selling sexual services in a voluntary capacity to pay for education fees, meet men with money and influence, and augment their social identity by using disposable income to purchase designer clothing and brand-name cosmetics (Chen Jieren 2003; 'Farenshenxing' 2009). Likewise, high-school students aged between thirteen and eighteen years have sold sexual services through informal friendship networks to affluent entrepreneurs and government officials aged between thirty and fifty years in high-grade hotels for fees ranging between CNY 2,000 and 20,000, with so-called 'virgins' commanding especially high prices (Jin, Lei and Wu 2002; 'Zhongxuesheng maiyin' 2002). Such reports highlight a perceived growing trade in sex with minors (Jeffreys 2012b: 39–59).

Figure 5.1 provides three examples of advertising cards for commercial sex in China. Such cards are a common sight in the PRC, despite the illegality of the sex trade, and are regularly pasted on street pavements, put under the doors of hotel rooms (4 star and below) and

Figure 5.1 Street advertising for commercial sex
Source: Photograph by Elaine Jeffreys

handed out to people on the street by children. In 2013, the lead author of this book saw cards advertising commercial sex pasted on the city streets of Beijing, Chengdu, Chongqing, Shanghai, Guangzhou and Yinchuan. Such advertising highlights not only the prevalence and businesslike nature of prostitution in China, but also its implicit association with young women as providers of sexual services to 'invisible' male clients. As the images and Chinese characters on the cards suggest, young women are available in 'massage', 'health' and 'student' clubs.

In short, the growth of the sex industry in reform-era China has been rapid and dramatic. Prostitution businesses and practices now exist throughout the length and breadth of the PRC. Moreover, sellers and buyers of sex come from all sectors of society, with a documented growth in recent years of phenomena such as male–male prostitution and youth prostitution. The continued expansion of China's prostitution industry inevitably has raised questions about the nature of its legal regulation and policing.

LAW AND POLICING

At the start of the reform era China adopted, and still retains, an abolitionist approach to the prostitution industry, which means in theory that Chinese law criminalizes people who organize and profit from prostitution as a business, rather than adults participating in consensual commercial sex. The PRC's first Criminal Law of 1979 contained only two Articles on prostitution, perhaps reflecting the understanding that it was a rare phenomenon. Article 140 stated that whoever forced women into prostitution should be sentenced to between three and ten years' imprisonment (Criminal Law of the PRC 1979). Article 169 stated that whoever lured or sheltered women in prostitution for profit should be sentenced to a maximum of five years' imprisonment, with additional provisions for more serious offences. The 1979 Criminal Law therefore banned all third-party attempts to profit from the prostitution of others, but it made no explicit reference to the activities of sex sellers and their clients.

Police authorities handled the visible resurgence of prostitution in the mid-1980s primarily under a system of administrative sanctions and not the criminal code. During the Mao era, the formal legal system fell into disrepute as a tool of class-based oppression and was replaced in part by a system of administrative and Party disciplinary sanctions (Starr 2001: 204–19). This system was used to police the activities of those deemed to have committed social offences or political errors, but whose criminal liability was not considered sufficient to bring them before the courts. The legal control of 'women who sold sex' (*maiyin funü*) and 'men who bought the services of illicit prostitutes' (*piaosu anchang*) was therefore effected on the basis of provincial rulings and localized policing initiatives until the introduction of the Regulations of the People's Republic of China on Administrative Penalties for Public Security (1986) on 1 January 1987 (hereafter the 1986 Regulations).

Article 30 of the 1986 Regulations stated that it is forbidden to sell and buy sex, to introduce others into prostitution and to provide accommodation for the purposes of prostitution. Policing authorities could detain suspected offenders for investigation for a period of up to fifteen days, then give them a warning and order them to make a statement of repentance, and concurrently fine them up to CNY 5,000. In more serious cases, policing authorities could detain offenders for rehabilitative education or reform through labour for periods of between six months and two years. This meant that the vast majority of prostitution-related offences – the processes of investigating, determining guilt and 'suitably' penalizing the activities of sellers and buyers of sex – were (and are) dealt with by the Chinese police, with only serious cases, such as those relating to organized and forced prostitution, being managed through the courts and criminal justice system.

In 1991, the PRC's highest legislative body, the National People's Congress (NPC), issued a prostitution-specific law – the 'Decision on

Strictly Forbidding the Selling and Buying of Sex' – which was eventually incorporated into the revised criminal law of 1997 (Quanguo renda changweihui 1991). Article 358 of the Criminal Law of the PRC (1997) stipulates sentences of between five and ten years' imprisonment for organizing or forcing other people into prostitution, with penalties of between ten years' imprisonment and life imprisonment, and even the death penalty, in serious cases. Serious crimes include forcing girls under the age of fourteen years into prostitution, forcing a number of persons or repeatedly forcing another person into prostitution, raping and then forcing others into prostitution, and causing severe injuries, death or other serious consequences, to persons forced into prostitution. Article 359 stipulates penalties of up to five years' gaol for introducing and sheltering other persons into prostitution, and a minimum of five years' imprisonment in cases involving underage girls. Article 361 states that managers or employees who take advantage of their workplace to organize or force others into prostitution shall be convicted and punished in accordance with Articles 358 and 359. Article 362 states that personnel who leak information about prospective police investigations into prostitution activities at their place of work shall be convicted for obstructing the course of justice. Once again, the revised criminal code does not criminalize the behaviours of first-party participants in consensual commercial sex, with the exception of clauses relating to sex with minors and the premeditated spread of STIs (Article 360).

These laws were issued to assist police efforts to control the spread of commercial sex throughout the PRC's burgeoning hospitality and service industry. Prostitution businesses and practices have been targeted by police-led crackdown campaigns since the late 1980s, usually as part of broader campaigns against crime and illegality, but also as part of specialized anti-vice campaigns known as *saohuang* – literally sweeping away the yellow, or the pornographic and obscene. However, both this mode of policing prostitution and Chinese campaign-style policing against crime in general has attracted criticism from international and domestic commentators.

Throughout the 1990s, western-based human rights activists criticized police-led campaigns against crime for being punitive and relying on the flexibility of the administrative system rather than the procedural rules that govern the operation of the criminal justice system. Prior to the introduction of the 1997 Criminal Law, the launching of a major campaign was often accompanied by the introduction of harsher legislation designed to facilitate easier arrests, detentions and sentencing, including the extensive use of capital punishment. At the same time, huge numbers of people were detained for arbitrary periods in centres that frequently had appalling conditions, based on the former system of administrative sanctions (Human Rights in China 1999).

In the mid-1990s, Chinese policing scholars similarly expressed concern that crackdowns on prostitution were harming the PRC's international reputation because regulations governing the types and periods of detention for participants in commercial sex were imprecise and encouraged arbitrary sentencing practices. Moreover, centres for the administrative rehabilitation of sellers and buyers of sex were overcrowded and lacked appropriate funding and personnel (Wang Dazhong 1995: 57).

By the early 2000s, domestic critics of the policing of prostitution more commonly noted that police-led crackdowns were ineffective because rates and types of prostitution had continued to rise. Entertainment establishments that facilitated sexual services closed during the campaign cycle only to reopen once it was over, while the women who worked in such venues simply went home to visit their families, moved to more secure venues or reinvented themselves as legitimate workers going under the title of waitresses and so forth (Pan, S. 2002; Zhang, H. 2009: 146). Local police also often expressed a lack of enthusiasm for such crackdowns due to their recurring nature and lack of long-term success (Bakken 2003: 135; Tanner 2005: 179).

Critics further noted that police-led crackdowns on the sex industry encouraged government corruption because the 1986 Regulations gave policing officials the authority to fine and detain people participating in consensual adult prostitution. Article 36 of the 1986 Regulations stipulated that all of the monies received from administrative punishment fines should be delivered to the state treasury; and a 1997 ruling prohibited the use of quotas and the substitution of fines for administrative detention (Biddulph 2004: 31; 2007: 239). However, local policing authorities were able to retain a significant proportion of the income derived from the issuing of fines in practice, which encouraged a strategy of fining minor prostitution offenders rather than detaining them for police-funded rehabilitation.

Criticisms of the corrupt and punitive nature of police-led crackdowns on prostitution are most forcibly expressed by human rights activists and organizations located outside of China. In the words of a posting by one anonymous netizen on a Taiwanese website: 'Each brick in every newly erected Public Security Bureau building is made up of the receipts from fines and other dirty doings' ('Lun maiyin' 2004). A 2001 report by Amnesty International more dramatically claimed that:

> Many women have been tortured, including being raped and sexually abused by police who accuse them of prostitution. Police have the power to issue an instant fine on suspected prostitutes and send them and their alleged clients for up to two years' detention for 'custody and education'. Police choose to detain and torture women in order to extract lists of alleged clients to blackmail. Many alleged prostitutes and clients have died under torture. ('China: extensive use' 2001)

The introduction of the 2005 Public Security Administrative Punishments Law, which replaced the 1986 Regulations, addresses some of these criticisms by significantly reducing the penalties for first-party engagement in adult and consensual commercial sex (Quanguo renda changwu weiyuanhui 2005). It reduces the possible term of administrative detainment for prostitution-related offences from a maximum of two years to between ten and fifteen days in serious cases, and up to a maximum of five days in less serious cases, with the possible addition of a fine (Articles 66 and 67). It gives suspected offenders the rights of appeal (Article 102) and recommends that people apprehended for first-time offences should not be detained for administrative punishment (Article 21). It further reduces the average fine meted to those apprehended for prostitution offences from CNY 5,000 to 500 (USD 800 to 80) (Articles 66 and 67) and limits on-the-spot fines, which must be issued with receipts, to a maximum of CNY 200 (USD 32) (Article 100). While statements released by the Chinese police in late 2010 indicated that crackdowns on prostitution in entertainment venues would continue, police officers are now enjoined to conduct such campaigns in a lawful manner and to treat apprehended sex sellers respectfully (An, B. 2010). Interviews with police officers also suggest that fines are no longer routinely imposed on first-party participants in the prostitution transaction: 'because the police cannot keep the fine and have to submit it to the treasury department; they have no incentive to impose the fine penalty' (Liu, M. 2011: 180).

However, an increasing number of commentators now openly contend that prostitution should be legalized or decriminalized in China. Legalization refers to the removal of criminal sanctions on the third-party organization of the sex industry, and usually to a system of administrating prostitution by licensing brothels, taxing sex workers and potentially subjecting sex workers to mandatory health checks for STIs-HIV. In contrast, decriminalization refers to the repeal of laws against consensual adult sexual activity in commercial contexts, in order to protect sex sellers from being exploited and harmed by clients, managers and police. Hence, supporters of decriminalization contend that providers of commercial sexual services should be free to determine the conditions of their work, rather than have those conditions dictated by a system of abolitionary laws, licensing regulations and other controls.

HEALTH AND RIGHTS

Public debate on the potential benefits of adopting alternative approaches to the governance of commercial sex in China has increased dramatically since the mid-2000s, in part because of media publicity surrounding the roll-out of a 100 Per Cent Condom Use Programme (hereafter the 100% CUP) (see also chapter 6). The 100% CUP refers to a collaborative programme first trialled in Thailand by representatives of the World Health Organization (WHO), local government authorities, and local sex entertainment establishments, that aims to reduce the sexual transmission of STIs-HIV by ensuring that condoms are used 100 per cent of the time, in 100 per cent of risky sexual relations, and in 100 per cent of the sex entertainment establishments in a specified geographic area (Rojanapithayakorn 2006: 42). Five pilot projects of the 100% CUP were implemented in China between 2001 and 2003, resulting in the promulgation of legislation to support the development of a nationwide programme (Jeffreys and Su 2011: 315–33). The 2006 Regulation on HIV/AIDS Prevention and Treatment (*Aizibing fangzhi tiaoli*) recognizes condom use as an effective measure to control sexually transmitted HIV infection and encourages China's mass media to publicize information about HIV prevention (Guowuyuan bangongting 2006a). The PRC's action plan for controlling, preventing and treating HIV/AIDS for 2011 to 2015 further suggests expanding health interventions that promote safer sex for sex workers, and men who have sex with men, to reach an estimated 90 per cent of those populations by 2015 (Guowuyuan bangongting 2012).

Media publicity surrounding the perceived threat posed to human well-being and national prosperity by the unchecked spread of HIV has prompted even Party stalwarts to question the PRC's adherence to a policy of abolishing prostitution. In January 2006, Zhou Ruijin (2006), a CCP member and former editor of the *Liberation Daily* and the *People's Daily*, published an article on Eastday.com, which was reposted on the *People's Daily Online*, titled 'Delegates at the National People's Congress and the Chinese People's Political Consultative Congress Should Discuss [Legalizing] the Underground Sex Industry'. In the article, Zhou stated that the NPC should repeal the policy of abolishing prostitution via police-led campaigns. Instead, the underground sex industry should be opened to a system of government management to prevent the spread of STIs-HIV and protect the interests of sex workers (*xinggongzuozhe*). Zhou further insisted that legalizing prostitution would assist the President Hu Jintao and Premier Wen Jiabao administration's policy goal of developing a civilized and harmonious society (Zhou Jigang 2006).

In March 2006, Chi Susheng, a lawyer and representative at the NPC from Heilongjiang Province composed a motion to present at the 2006 meeting of the NPC called 'On Legalizing Sex Workers As Soon As Possible' (*guanyu jinzao chutai dui xingcongyezhe xingwei guifan lifa*) (Li Yunhong 2009). Chi allegedly was motivated to compose this motion by her legal experience of handling a case involving an HIV-infected man who confessed to engaging in unprotected sex with up to 100 sex workers as an act of revenge, believing that he had contracted HIV from a female sex worker. Concerned about the consequences for public health, Chi called on the NPC to continue to criminalize forced prostitution and child prostitution, but to legalize licensed brothels in order to provide sex workers with legal protections from violent clients and managers, and to prevent the spread of STIs-HIV by making sex workers subject to mandatory health checks. Chi's petition was signed by thirty-three delegates. However, it was vetoed from general discussion on technical grounds (Li Yunhong 2009; Zhou Jigang 2006).

In October 2006, health officials at the government-run Centre for Disease Control and Prevention in Harbin City sparked widespread debate about the nation's prostitution controls when they ran a training class for fifty 'working girls' on how to use condoms and prevent the spread of STIs-HIV ('Haerbin shi' 2006; Li, F. 2006; Yang Tao 2006). These actions generated immediate media controversy with journalists capitalizing on the sex and novelty value of the story and suggesting that the provision of such training not only brought the efficacy of local policing into question, but also undermined the PRC's policy of abolishing the prostitution industry (Qiu and Wang 2006). As journalists argued, the fact that health officials had been able to invite fifty sex workers to a training class after conducting a survey of local entertainment establishments implied that previous police efforts to crack down on prostitution were half-hearted and ineffective (Mu and Xue 2006). In addition, health officials had compromised the work of policing by cooperating with sex workers and managers of entertainment establishments, and asking local police to 'go soft' on sex workers and managers that supported the 100% CUP, including halting police-led crackdowns temporarily (Chen Jiu 2006; Qiu and Wang 2006). These actions prompted numerous journalists to ask: 'Is prostitution now legal in China?' (Ding Li 2006; 'Jiangsu ji kong' 2006; 'Jiuyue wuri qi' 2006; Wu Mindong 2006).

In an interview posted on the PRC government's website (www.gov.cn) to coincide with International AIDS Day on 1 December 2006, senior health officials responded by asserting that the dual policies of attacking prostitution and popularizing health training for sex workers are complementary, not contradictory. They noted that altered circumstances meant that it was not possible to eradicate prostitution from China in the near future. Moreover, the World Health Organization identifies prostitution as a potential major source of sex-related HIV/AIDs transmission. Thus, the primary responsibility of the PRC government is to mobilize and teach all Chinese citizens how to protect their health, especially since international experience has (scientifically) demonstrated the efficacy of condom-use programmes in reaching key populations at higher risk, such as sex workers ('Tuiguang anquantao fang aizibing' 2006). Other commentators affirmed this conclusion, adding that health officials are not authorized to determine whether a person receiving sexual-health education is engaged in an illicit activity or not, and the Chinese police already assist with the primary goal of disease prevention by cracking down on the prostitution industry and sending detained offenders for medical check-ups (Dong Xue 2006; Wu Mindong 2006).

The PRC's commitment to a dualistic policy of expanding the 100% CUP *and* abolishing the commercial sex industry is highlighted in the nation's five-year action plans for controlling, preventing and treating HIV and AIDS. The action plan for 2006 to 2010 stipulated that providing public information and monitoring key populations at higher risk is of vital importance for averting an AIDS epidemic. It also stated that developing a comprehensive legal framework and management strategy for combating AIDS required relevant government departments to crack down on illegal activities such as drug trafficking and prostitution (Guowuyuan bangongting 2006b). Guidelines issued by the State Council to coincide with World AIDS Day on 1 December 2010 suggested that the action plan for 2011 to 2015 would extend health protections to reach over 90 per cent of sex workers and men who have sex with men, as recommended by the World Health Organization. They further noted that the effective extension of such protections would require the introduction of anti-discriminatory measures to end the social and legal marginalization of sex workers, homosexuals and people living with HIV. However, the same guidelines recommended expanding police-led crackdowns against drugs and prostitution (Guowuyuan bangongting 2010).

This bifurcated approach has opened the parameters of public debate in China on the most appropriate response to the existence of prostitution. Li Yinhe (2008), a sociologist and one of the PRC's most famous 'sexperts' (see chapter 7), reiterates feminist criticisms of prostitution controls in the USA, Germany and the Netherlands, to argue that both prohibition and legalization are problematic (see Jeffreys 2012a: 83–95). According to Li Yinhe (2008), prohibition is unworkable, encourages police corruption and violates human rights, but legalization is an equally problematic response for two reasons. First, legalizing prostitution for the purposes of disease control is likely to result in the imposition of expanded policing, bureaucratic and business controls over providers of commercial sexual services to ensure that they meet relevant health checks and licensing requirements. In turn, the imposition of such controls will encourage corruption and render sex sellers open to continued economic and sexual exploitation. Second, legalization in the form of the establishment of red-light districts is likely to result in community objections and thus enhanced policing and business controls. Local residents will object to the establishment of red-light districts in their general vicinity, ensuring that red-light districts are located in distant and potentially unsafe areas requiring constant police supervision. In turn, sellers and buyers of sex will object to police supervision and the inconvenience of a distant if legal location by moving to areas that they deem more suitable, thereby generating renewed community objections and the new problem of illegal prostitution.

Li Yinhe (2008) concludes that legalization is not a 'cure-all' for the problems associated with the PRC's current abolitionist response to prostitution (see also chapter 7). Instead, she recommends a laissez-faire decriminalization policy (*feizuihua*) based on the removal of legal restrictions on sexual activities between consenting adults, including those that involve commercial exchange. Li Yinhe (2008) argues that decriminalization will reduce the cost of policing and allow consenting adults who wish to engage in commercial sex to advertise and meet in discreet locations, such as massage parlours and sex shops.

In Internet blogs, Pan Suiming (2008, 2007a), another sociologist and famous Chinese sexpert (see chapter 7), somewhat differently implies that legalization may facilitate the work of AIDS prevention, but given the unlikelihood of such a radical policy shift, he advocates the rationalization (*helihua*) of China's prostitution controls in the form of permitting individual operators. As Pan (2008) argues, police-led crackdowns on prostitution are ineffective, encourage corruption and entrench the exploitation of sex sellers (who he characterizes as impoverished rural-to-urban migrants), by forcing them to rely on assistance from third parties to evade apprehension. He further suggests that police-led crackdowns and the associated practice of fining minor prostitution offenders facilitate the spread of STIs-HIV, by forcing sex sellers to move around the country and encouraging them to have unprotected sex in order to recoup lost earnings or because their 'managers' and manager-facilitated clients demand it. Pan (2007a) concludes that allowing sex sellers to run a one-person business operation from a private dwelling, as occurs in the UK and Hong Kong, constitutes a preferable response because it will remove government and third-party constraints on the ability of individuals to earn a living as sex workers.

A 2009 blog reprinted in the electronic newsletter *Xiaojie*, which its university-based publishers translate as 'Sex Workers', responds to Li Yinhe by repeating Zhou Ruijin's and Chi Susheng's calls to legalize prostitution in order to prevent AIDS and create a harmonious China. According to the blogger, Ji Ruijie (2009), the 2009 meeting of the NPC was an optimal time to legalize prostitution because of the global financial crisis. Ji argues that the existence of prostitution clearly benefits large sectors of Chinese society because the sex industry can be found throughout China, despite a thirty-year-old policy of opposing it. While agreeing with Li Yinhe that legalization may not be a 'cure-all' for the problems associated with prostitution, Ji concludes that it has seven distinct advantages when compared to China's existing prostitution controls. These perceived benefits are based on the standard arguments of civil libertarians vis-à-vis the sex industry, with some added Chinese inflections, and may be summarized as follows. Legalization will: (1) promote human rights, that is, the right to work and sex; (2) increase tax revenue; (3) reduce the number of sexual offences, such as rape; (4) help the work of STIs-HIV prevention; (5) promote the interests of sex workers, who are predominantly disadvantaged rural-to-urban migrants; (6) promote social equality by enabling ordinary men, not just wealthy businessmen and government officials, to obtain easy access to sexual services; and (7) promote a civilized and harmonious society because sex workers will be able to provide therapy and advice to couples with an unhappy sex life.

Although arguments in favour of alternative approaches are usually raised on behalf of and not by sex workers, Ye Haiyan (a self-proclaimed sex worker, sex blogger and women's rights' activist) staged what was arguably the PRC's first public event in support of prostitutes' rights in July 2010. Ye Haiyan (2011) and five other people walked down a busy shopping street in Wuhan City carrying red umbrellas, an international symbol of struggles for prostitutes' rights, and held up banners calling for the legalization of sex work (*xinggongzuo hefahua*). Ye posted details and images of this event on her blog, which show that only a small number of people were involved in the protest and that it did not attract significant attention from passers-by. Nevertheless, in a subsequent interview with a foreign correspondent, Ye claimed that she was an activist for prostitutes' rights and had organized the protest to raise public awareness of how the policing of prostitution in China harmed sex workers' rights to health and legal protections (Branigan 2010: 15).

Another public event in support of prostitutes' rights reportedly took place in February 2014 (Chang 2014). Four university students wearing masks allegedly protested outside the China Central Television Station in Beijing about media coverage of police-led crackdowns on prostitution in southern China, which had included images of naked women. The 'protestors' held up banners saying 'sex work is work and sex workers also have dignity' (Chang 2014).

CONCLUSION

There clearly is some support in China for the argument that commercial sexual activities should be legalized or decriminalized to assist the task of STIs-HIV prevention, give sex worker's legal and social protections, and enable policing authorities to focus on the problems of child prostitution and forced prostitution. However, it is equally clear that there is confusion regarding what the terms 'legalization' and 'decriminalization' actually mean. Moreover, insofar as the adoption of such policies will require some form of governing or administering the sex industry, there is no consensus as to what such policies would look like, and how they might be put in place and by whom. Adding to these problems, ethnographic research conducted among men and women who provide commercial sexual services suggests that collective organization for improvements in the working conditions of Chinese sex workers is complicated by factors other than social and legal marginalization (Kong 2010a; Zheng 2010a: 55–64, 2009b: 125–7). It is complicated by the intense competition that exists between sex workers to obtain and keep regular clients while they still can and by the fact that they move to different venues and different parts of the country on a regular basis, in order to maximize profits and minimize the effects of internal competition.

6 | Sex and Public Health ————————

This chapter counters claims that condoms are a taboo topic in China (Zheng, T. 2010b) by examining the PRC's evolving responses to growing rates of sexually transmissible infections, especially HIV. In late 2011, a Chinese netizen posted an image on a microblogging site of a poster-style Public Service Advertisement (PSA) promoting condom use and safer homosexual sex, claiming that s/he was surprised to have seen the poster on a government-endorsed community noticeboard in Beijing (Xu 2011). Such noticeboards can be found in most urban residential compounds in China and are used to post PSAs and local community information. The poster contained a close-up head-to-shoulder shot of two young and shirtless Chinese men, each holding out a packaged condom to the other (see figure 6.1). Two questions accompany the image, both reading 'dai le ma?' These questions are formed in terms of a 'play' in modern standard Chinese on the homonym *dai* meaning 'bring' in the first question: 'did you bring a condom?' and 'wear' in the second question: 'are you wearing a condom?'

The netizen expressed surprise to see a poster promoting safer homosexual sex on a public noticeboard, stating: 'I never thought government offices would print such posters, as homosexuality seems taboo in China.' S/he thought it was 'good' to see sexual health awareness messages targeting men who have sex with men, but wondered how 'elderly' Chinese would respond to viewing the poster (Xu 2011). In other words, the netizen implied that some local residents might

Figure 6.1 Are you wearing a condom?
Source: 'Yufang aizi, jianchi yongtao' [Prevent AIDS, always use condoms] (2010), National Centre for AIDS/STD Control and Prevention, China CDC, 21 December, at: <http://www.chinaids.org.cn/>

find the subject matter distasteful and was surprised that government authorities had taken the bold and positive initiative of making safer-sex messages for men who have sex with men publicly available.

As this example suggests, the PRC government is now promoting public health campaigns to combat the spread of sexually transmissible infections, including HIV. Previously described as venereal diseases or sexually transmitted diseases (STDs), sexually transmissible infections are commonly transmitted between partners through forms of sexual activity, such as vaginal, oral or anal sex. The expression 'sexually *transmissible* infections' is used in this chapter rather than 'sexually *transmitted* infections' to indicate that sexual contact does not necessarily result in the contraction of an STI.

Although the government promotion of public health has an established history in the PRC (Fang, X. 2012: 8–10), sexual health is a more recent object of concern. Following its assumption of national political power in 1949, the Chinese Communist Party declared that syphilis and gonorrhea were preventable social diseases stemming from the exploitation of man by man: their root causes being poverty, prostitution, ignorance and the subordinate status of women (Abrams 2001: 429–40). Through a combination of campaigns involving mass education, the virtual eradication of the prostitution industry and the large-scale provision of costly penicillin, the CCP announced to the World Health Organization in 1964 that active venereal disease no longer existed in mainland China, that is, it no longer constituted a public health problem (Abrams 2001: 429–40; Chen, Z-Q. et al. 2007: 132–8).

Since the mid-1980s, the reported incident rate of STIs in China has risen sharply. More than 700,000 cases were registered in 2005 compared to less than 6,000 cases in 1985 (Chen, Z-Q. et al. 2007; Rosenthal 1999; Zhang, Mao and Xia 2004). Among the most common STIs in China, non-gonococcal urethritis/cervicitis has the highest reported incidence, followed by gonorrhoea, genital warts, syphilis and genital herpes (Xing ai zhongxin 2006; Yue, Jiang and Gong 2013). Health officials suggest that under-reporting makes these figures highly conservative because STI patients frequently seek treatment from commercial clinics to avoid having their details registered with government authorities (Detels et al. 2003: 803; Yu, Y. J. 2013: 359; Zhang, Mao and Xia 2004: 41).

Government concerns about sexual health in present-day China relate to the resurgence of STIs *and* the new threat posed by HIV. This focus is based on the understanding that individuals with a current or past history of STIs are more likely to contract or transmit HIV than those without (Abrams 2001: 429–40; Chen, X. et al. 2005: 853–4; Detels et al. 2003: 803).

The chapter first provides a short history of the changing demography of HIV/AIDS in the PRC, explaining how government concerns about the spread of HIV have become focused on the sexual behaviours of people described as members of key populations at higher risk. It then examines the PRC's take-up of the United Nations' vision of 'zero new HIV infections, zero discrimination and zero AIDS-related deaths' (Joint United Nations Programme on HIV/AIDS 2010). This has involved the expansion of both monitoring and treatment systems, and government-sponsored efforts to reduce the social stigma and institutional discrimination experienced by people living with HIV. Finally, the chapter looks at two different programmes involving HIV education and condom promotion, one directed at young people through the media and the education system, and another directed at (migrant) sellers and buyers of commercial sex through low-literacy intervention programs.

CHINA'S CHANGING HIV DEMOGRAPHY AND KEY POPULATIONS

Scholars usually divide the spread of AIDS in the PRC into four stages, which highlight China's changing HIV demography and evolving perspectives on the governance of HIV and AIDS (Smith 2005: 66–8; Zhang, Mao and Xia 2004: 39–40).

Stage One (1985–8) began with the identification of China's first AIDS case in Beijing in 1985; it involved a foreign tourist. Most of the cases that were subsequently reported in this early period involved overseas Chinese and 'foreign' residents in the PRC, and were located in coastal cities that had been opened to export-orientated economic development and foreign investment (Smith 2005: 66). AIDS was therefore initially viewed as an imported disease and government policies focused on preventing its entry into China. Strategies based on exclusion included prohibiting or monitoring the importation of blood products into the PRC, and requiring long-term visitors from overseas to undertake physical health examinations prior to entry, which theoretically precluded the issue of visas to people who were HIV-positive (Smith 2005: 66).

Stage Two (1989–93) relates to the identification of HIV-infected persons among intravenous drug users in peripheral western and south-western regions of China such as the Xinjiang Uyghur Autonomous Region, and Yunnan Province and the Guangxi Autonomous Region (Smith 2005: 66). These cases were linked with drug-using cultural practices among ethnic minorities. While indicating that HIV was not a 'foreign' disease, the association of these cases with ethnic minority populations living in border regions meant that HIV continued to be framed as an 'outsider's disease', or a disease that was not associated with urban Han Chinese.

Stage Three, starting in late 1994, is associated with commercial plasma donors and the recipients of blood transfusions in poor central provinces (Anagnost 2006: 509–29; Gu and Renwick 2008: 89–91). Henan was one of many provinces during the early 1990s where commercial companies and provincial health authorities offered rural agricultural workers money for blood. The collected blood was then pooled together and the plasma was extracted, and the remaining red blood cells from an unscreened pool were reinjected into blood sellers to speed recovery time, resulting in an estimated 500,000 HIV infections in Henan Province alone (Gittings 2001). By 1998, HIV infection had been reported in all of China's thirty-one provinces, autonomous regions, and municipalities, with over 70 per cent of all reported cases being in the countryside (Zhang, Mao and Xia 2004: 39).

Since 2001, the spread of AIDS in China has reached a Stage Four pattern in that the rate of domestically generated HIV infections has increased and many new cases are linked to sexual transmission (Smith

2005). Figures published by the PRC's Ministry of Health in 2012 suggest that 780,000 people are now living with HIV in China, and nearly half of them were infected through sexual transmission (Ministry of Health of the PRC 2012: 6). Cases relating to sexual transmission rose from around 33 per cent in 2006 to more than 76 per cent in 2011 (Ministry of Health of the PRC 2012: 5–6). Hence, the nationwide promotion of sex education and condom use is viewed as essential for averting an epidemic (Zou, H. et al. 2012: 27).

The PRC government initially attracted trenchant criticism from scholars and international organizations for failing to respond to the policy imperatives of AIDS. A 2002 UN report, titled *HIV/AIDS: China's Titanic Peril*, claimed that the country was 'on the verge of a catastrophe that could result in unimaginable suffering, economic loss and social devastation' (UN Theme Group on HIV/AIDS in China 2002). Writing in the *New York Sociologist* in 2010, Zheng Tiantian claims that condom marketing is the acknowledged centrepiece of AIDS education and prevention in the western world, but 'this change has not yet occurred in China' because the Party-state defines 'condoms as a contraceptive tool that should be utilized only within the bounds of marriage rather than to prevent venereal diseases' (Zheng, T. 2010b: 51–2, 58). These negative assessments stem from the PRC government's reluctance to consider AIDS as a domestic and sex-related problem until the early 2000s.

However, the PRC government now acknowledges that the spread of HIV in China is driven by multiple domestic factors and actively promotes prevention work. Such work is directed at preventing individual 'risk-taking' behaviours, especially needle sharing among intravenous drug users, and engagement in unprotected heterosexual and homosexual intercourse (Detels et al. 2003: 803; Smith 2005: 67–8). This emphasis mirrors dominant paradigms in international social research with regard to the prevention of HIV and associated intervention programmes, which stress the identification of risk-taking behaviours and the subsequent provision of surveillance and education so that individuals can learn how to modify and self-regulate those behaviours (Altman 1999: 559; Smith 2005: 65–80).

Following the established parameters of international HIV prevention programmes, China's health authorities have become concerned about the potential spread of STIs-HIV from key populations at higher risk into the general population through the behaviours and practices of members of so-called bridge populations. Bridge populations include: intravenous drug users; former commercial blood donors; sex workers; long-distance drivers; people who engage in casual, pre-marital, extra-marital or non-monogamous sex; and men who have sex with men, that is, men who engage in sexual behaviours with other men, but who do not necessarily self-identify as 'gay' or 'bisexual'. These populations are categorized as key populations at higher risk and major routes of STIs-HIV transmission because of China's relatively low rate of condom use (Zou et al. 2012: 27).

Concerns about the spread of HIV from key populations at higher risk to the broader population have geographical dimensions in China. By 2011, there were six regions that accounted for over 75 per cent of the total number of HIV cases reported in the PRC (Ministry of Health of the PRC 2012: 21). In Henan Province, which has a high reported rate of infection because of previous commercial plasma collection practices, and in Guangdong, Guangxi, Sichuan, Xinjiang and Yunnan, where the incidence of needle sharing among intravenous drug users is high, new incidences of HIV infection are connected to heterosexual sexual transmission from persons living with HIV to their previously uninfected partners (Ministry of Health of the PRC 2012: 21–2). Although figures released by the PRC's Ministry of Health indicated a low HIV infection rate at the national level of 0.3 per cent among female sex workers in 2011, the prevalence rate is highest among those women who use drugs in the most affected provinces and autonomous regions (Ministry of Health of the PRC 2012:

37). Highlighting a different pattern, the rate of HIV infection among men who have sex with men in China is low by international standards but rising rapidly relative to other key populations at higher risk. Moreover, the reported incidence of new HIV infections among men who have sex with men is said to be high in major cities such as Beijing (Zhang, C. 2007: 5; see also Bates, Huang and Lu 2007: 21–4).

Concerns about the spread of HIV and STIs more generally have encouraged a focus on the perceived risk-taking behaviours of members of China's internal migrant population (Anderson et al. 2003: 177–85; Detels et al. 2003: 803–8; Smith 2005: 65–80; Zhao, R. et al. 2005: 848–52). The relationship between population mobility and the spread of STIs-HIV has been examined in many contexts around the globe (Herdt 1997; Hugo 2001; Mann and Tarantola 1996, Skeldon 2000; Wolffers and Fernandez 1995; Yang, Derlaga and Luo n.d.). Such research suggests that certain migrant populations are susceptible to risk-taking behaviours and represent one of the potentially most dangerous bridge populations in terms of the transmission of STIs-HIV from localized at-risk populations to the broader population (Smith 2005: 68–9). Given that China has experienced a population transfer of unprecedented proportions throughout the 1990s and into the new millennium, with an estimated 262 million people migrating mostly from rural to urban areas in search of work (Wang, Y. 2013), the broad parameters of such studies have been applied to an examination of the Chinese case.

Numerous English-language studies suggest that rural migrants labouring in China's cities are more likely to engage in high-risk activities and behaviours than permanent residents of both rural and urban areas (Anderson et al. 2003: 177–85; Detels et al. 2003: 803–8; Zhao, R. et al. 2005: 848–51). A standard claim is that rural migrants working in urban centres are predominantly young, poorly educated and sexually active men, who are not only socially isolated and far away from family constraints, but also have little knowledge of STIs-HIV, and virtually no access to preventative education or regular health care. Consequently, they are vulnerable to behaviours that place them at risk of acquiring an STI, such as needle sharing and engaging in unprotected sexual intercourse. Moreover, they are unlikely to abstain from further unprotected sexual contact or seek appropriate medical treatment if they acquire an STI ('China AIDS Survey' 2003; Yang, H. et al. 2005: 270–80). At the same time, the majority of China's estimated 3–10 million illegal sex sellers are said to be young, uneducated female migrants (Anderson et al. 2003: 177–8; 'China Aids Survey' 2003; Yang, H. et al. 2005: 270–80; Yu, Y. J. 2013: 350; see also chapter 5). Scholars therefore conclude that China's STIs and AIDS prevention strategies need to target (migrant) sex sellers and their clients, especially those who inject drugs (Chen, X. et al. 2005: 853; Zhou, J. 2006: 255; Zou, H. et al. 2012: 32).

International and domestic concerns over the *potential* risk posed to the national health by individual sexual behaviours have therefore encouraged the PRC government to establish standardized STI clinical services and develop a national surveillance system based on the informing logic of global HIV governance – the imperative to know those most at-risk, and thus the targeting of specific populations. Following the establishment of the Chinese National Centre for STD Control in 1986, the PRC's Ministry of Health launched a national STD surveillance system in 1987 (Chen, Z.-Q. et al. 2007). By 1994, forty-two sentinel sites were established in twenty-three provinces under guidance from the WHO with a focus on four populations designated as high-risk – patients of STI clinics, intravenous drug users, female sex workers and (male) long-distance truck drivers. By 2010, there were 1,888 sentinel sites across China's thirty-one provinces with a focus on eight key populations at higher risk – intravenous drug users, men who have sex with men, male clients of STI clinics, male drivers and conductors on long-distance coaches, male migrant workers, sex workers, pregnant women and young students (Ministry of Health of the PRC 2012: 67). Based on data collected from the national surveillance system, the PRC's Ministry of Health estimated that 780,000 people were living with HIV in China in 2011, including 150,000 people with AIDS. There were 48,000 reported cases of new infections and 28,000 AIDS-related deaths (Ministry of Health of the PRC 2012: 6).

The targeting of key populations at higher risk is providing much-needed public education on HIV and AIDS in China, while simultaneously pathologizing those groups of people who have been identified as 'most at-risk' and excluding others. Migrant workers, sex workers and men who have sex with men have become associated with disease, potentially exacerbating their already marginal position as people who are stereotyped as 'poor', 'lower-class', 'immoral' and/or 'unclean' citizens. Some studies suggest that middle-aged married men from the corporate and government sector are more likely to purchase commercial sexual services than migrant labourers (Pan Suiming et al. 2004; Uretsky 2008; Zheng, T. 2006). However, professional men have yet to be targeted by public education campaigns. The association of HIV by default with poverty, sex work and homosexuality may further encourage a distancing view of AIDS as a problem that affects other people rather than people like 'us' (Micollier 2012: 116).

CONTROLLING HIV AND AIDS

In keeping with the United Nations' vision of 'zero new HIV infections, zero discrimination and zero AIDS-related deaths', China's 2011–15 action plan for controlling, preventing and treating HIV/ AIDS aims to reduce the number of new HIV infections and control the number of people living with HIV in China at around 1.2 million people by 2015 (Guowuyuan bangongting 2012; Joint United Nations Programme on HIV/AIDS 2010). The action plan recommends implementing measures outlined in the 2010 Notice of the State

Council on Strengthening the Work of Preventing and Treating HIV/AIDS, which proposes curbing the spread of HIV in China by 2020 (Guowuyuan 2010). The Notice and action plan instruct government departments at all levels to: expand the coverage of surveillance and testing; improve accessibility to anti-retroviral treatments; improve the quality and scope of medical treatment; improve the management of blood; diversify sources of grant funding; and improve medical training and research capacity. They further instruct government departments at all levels to: increase public awareness of modes of HIV transmission; focus on key areas and key populations, such as intravenous drug users and men who have sex with men; expand the coverage of AIDS-related publicity and education; and introduce policies to guarantee the rights of people living with HIV, and their families, to freedom from discrimination (Guowuyuan 2010; Guowuyuan bangongting 2012).

Reversing the number of HIV infections and AIDS-related deaths requires universal access to testing and treatment, a costly and complicated strategy which has proved to be problematic in practice in China, as elsewhere. In 2005, the PRC adopted a system of standardized services at STI clinics, with funding from the World Bank's China Health Nine Project. Standardization is meant to facilitate more efficient monitoring and evaluation practices, such as case-reporting, clinical practice, laboratory diagnostics and health care, and the formation of routine work plans, training courses, and evaluation protocols within STI clinics (Xing ai zhongxin 2006). A real-name system of network reporting was also established to facilitate better record-keeping and better monitor the spread of STIs (Xing ai zhongxin 2006).

However, the standardization of clinical services has not necessarily resulted in more accurate information about STIs and AIDS trends across China's population. STI clinics are usually government-sponsored and staffed by qualified medical personnel who provide reliable services, whereas private/commercial clinics are renowned for using unqualified staff, that is, staff who do not possess a medical degree or diploma, and for providing unreliable and often fraudulent treatments (Detels et al. 2003: 803; Yu, Y. J. 2013: 359; Zhang, Mao and Xia 2004: 41). However, many people prefer the services of commercial clinics. This is because commercial clinics sometimes offer cheaper services than government-run hospitals (Yu, Y. J. 2013: 359). In addition, many people are wary of government-sponsored clinics, which are attached to the national sentinel system, because they believe that information about their activities may come to the attention of government authorities or work colleagues and family members (Detels et al. 2003: 803; Zhang, Mao and Xia 2004: 41). Hence, China's health authorities have begun to popularize sexual health awareness through public education campaigns that stress not only STIs-HIV prevention, but also the professional and strictly confidential nature of standardized STI clinical services.

In early 2003, the PRC government introduced a pilot programme called the China Comprehensive AIDS Response (China CARES); and, late that same year, it launched the 'Four Frees and One Care policy', making China one of the first countries in the world to have a free national AIDS treatment programme (Kaufman 2010: 78). The programme initially aimed to supply free domestically manufactured anti-retroviral AIDS medication to HIV patients in affected provinces characterized by severe poverty, a highly mobile population and a history of unsafe blood collection practices. Since then, the programme has been expanded to cover other regions and key populations at higher risk such as intravenous drug users and sex workers (Gu and Renwick 2008: 94). The 'four frees' are unified under the general policy of providing care and economic assistance to people living with HIV and involve: free voluntary counselling and testing; free anti-retroviral drugs to rural residents and poor urban residents living with HIV; free prevention of mother to child transmission; and free schooling for children orphaned as a result of AIDS (Kaufman 2010: 78).

However, the China CARES programme has not been implemented evenly and effectively. As Haiqing Yu (2012: 9) explains: 'in
some places there are multiple fees charged for HIV-related health
services; patients pay for tests and treatments of opportunistic infections such as tuberculosis and pneumonia; AIDS orphans do not
receive adequate care and schooling; and HIV patients have been
refused treatment'. These problems relate to the limited human
resources available to translate policy into action at the local level, and
to the ongoing influence of a history of social prejudice against people
living with HIV.

Most people learn about HIV and AIDS from the mass media and,
until the start of the 2000s, China's media typically presented AIDS
as an outsider's disease that affected foreigners and drug users, or
people whose actions made them somehow responsible for their fate
(Hood 2011, 2012: 127; Kaufman 2010: 73; Yu, H-Q. 2012: 17).
However, China's 2001–05 action plan for controlling, preventing and
treating HIV/AIDS stated that the broadcast media and central and
local newspapers should release news stories and PSAs about the work
of HIV and AIDS prevention at least once a week (Guowuyuan bangongting 2001: Item 3, Article 2). This led to a rapid increase in media
coverage of AIDS in China from 2002 onwards. In November 2000,
shortly before the release of that document, the *Southern Weekend*
newspaper ran a front-page exposé about the prevalence of AIDS in
rural communities in northern central China where poor farmers had
contracted HIV after selling blood for money. Local government inac-
tion on the issue had resulted not only in spouses and children being
infected, but also left orphaned children without support and welfare
services. The plight of these children challenged public perceptions of
AIDS as a 'foreigner's disease' that only affected 'deserving victims'
(Kaufman 2010: 73). This and the subsequent flood of stories about
the work of HIV prevention in China turned AIDS into an 'internal'
disease, albeit a 'distanced' internal disease that is presented as chiefly

affecting poor rural communities through blood contamination, ethnic minority communities through intravenous drug use, and internal migrants as consumers and providers of commercial sex (Hood 2012: 128; Yu, H-Q. 2012: 17–22).

More recently, China's media has begun to focus on the need to overcome the social stigma, and institutional and employment-related discrimination, experienced by people living with HIV. Government calls to implement anti-discriminatory measures, as stipulated in Article 3 of the PRC's 2006 Regulations on HIV/AIDS Prevention and Treatment (Guowuyuan bangongting 2006a), signify an acknowledgement that social and institutional discrimination against people living with HIV contribute to the continued spread of infection, by making people reluctant to access HIV testing, prevention and treatment services (Guowuyuan 2010; Guowuyuan bangongting 2012). Many people living with HIV in China have lost their employment or have been excluded from obtaining employment, and their children have been barred from attending schools or have experienced discrimination at school (Yu, H-Q. 2012: 21). A study conducted by the International Labour Office in China in 2011 found that 65 per cent of business owners felt that people living with HIV should not enjoy equal employment opportunities (Policy Research and Information Division of the National Center for AIDS/STD Control and Prevention, China CDC International Labour Office for China and Mongolia 2011: 6). As the UN estimates that many people living with HIV remain undiagnosed, health organizations view the reduction of social stigma and institutional discrimination against people living with HIV as a vital component of any strategy aiming to reverse the number of HIV infections and AIDS-related deaths (Settle 2003: 2; Ministry of Health of the PRC 2012: 12).

Anti-discriminatory messages about people living with HIV are now being promoted in China using celebrity-endorsed PSAs that gesture towards cultural and linguistic diversity. One series of posters and videos feature the famous basketball player Yao Ming with a group of HIV-positive fans. Coordinated by the UN and the PRC's Ministry of Health through public–private partnerships with China's commercial media and advertising sector, the posters present an image of Yao Ming with his arms around six young people. The text above the image states in Chinese: 'I have friends who are infected with the AIDS virus. So what? We are all in the fight against AIDS, let's eliminate discrimination together.' Another series shows Yao Ming with actor Pu Cunxin and children from AIDS-affected communities ('AIDS will not affect our friendship' 2007). The images are accompanied by slogans written in Chinese characters, or in Tibetan or Uyghur scripts, stating: 'We have the same feelings, the same dreams and the same life. HIV will not affect our friendship. We are friends' (see figure 6.2).

Recent policy changes suggest that anti-discriminatory measures are starting to be implemented in practice. In 2010, bans were lifted on the entry of people living with HIV into the PRC (Sun, X. et al. 2010: 4). In September 2013, government authorities in Guangdong Province overturned restrictions that prevented people diagnosed with STIs-HIV from working as teachers. Senior officials with the UN have praised these actions as a localized test-case of positive policy change that will gradually be adopted across the PRC ('China's Guangdong Province to lift HIV restrictions on teacher recruitment' 2013).

Although anti-discriminatory messages to date have focused on children from AIDS-affected communities, there is a growing recognition in China that social discrimination against homosexuals creates additional problems for the work of AIDS prevention. Rates of HIV infection among men who have sex with men in mainland China are low compared to other parts of the world; there were only fifty-seven cases reported in 2001 and around 14,100 in 2011 (Settle 2003: 98; Zhonghua renmin gongheguo weishengbu, lianheguo aizibing guihuashu, shijie weisheng zuzhi 2011: 5). However, the proportion of

一样的情感，一样的理想，一样的生活
艾滋病不会让我们的关系有任何不同

我们是朋友

来自富阳市艾滋病影响社区的儿童和蓝求明展览照片。若古真武项保护站在一起。欲取更多信息。请登录网站：http://uniteforchildren.youth.cn　http://www.chain.net.cn

Figure 6.2 People living with HIV are our friends
Source: Aaron Diamond AIDS Research Center, ChinaAidsInitiative.org.cn;
reproduced with permission

new cases arising from homosexual transmission increased from 0.2 per cent in 2001 to 2.5 per cent in 2006 and nearly 14 per cent in 2011, which represents a rapid increase when compared to other sectors of the population (Ministry of Health of the PRC 2012: 5; Settle 2003: 98). Studies suggest that men who have sex with men accounted for only 2 per cent of people presenting for voluntary HIV testing in 2008 (Xiong Ran et al. 2010). Moreover, some men who have sex with men, and may even self-identify as gay, marry women to meet parental and social expectations that they will marry and have a child (Tan 2013; Yu Yong 2006: 56; see also chapters 2 and 4). Reducing the social stigma and institutional discrimination experienced by men who have sex with men is therefore likely to be an important and complicated component of the PRC's evolving responses to AIDS.

POPULARIZING HIV AND AIDS EDUCATION

The popularization of public education about the utility of condoms in preventing the sexual transmission of HIV is now an integral component of government-supported efforts to stop the spread of AIDS in China. The PRC's action plan for controlling, preventing and treating HIV/AIDS for 2011 to 2015 stipulates that 90 per cent of key populations at higher risk, and 85 per cent of urban residents aged between fifteen and sixty, and 80 percent of rural residents of the same age group, should be educated about STIs and HIV by 2015. To realize this goal, the plan advocates sexual health education for secondary and tertiary students, and stipulates that condoms or condom-vending machines should be available in 95 per cent of hotels and other unspecified public areas by 2015 (Guowuyuan bangongting 2012). It also encourages the use of celebrities in 'easy-to-understand' PSAs about AIDS prevention.

The first celebrity-endorsed PSA series to promote safer sex and condom use was disseminated in 2008 in the run-up to the Beijing Olympic Games. Coordinated by the UN and the PRC's Ministry of Health through public–private partnerships with China's commercial media and advertising sector, the 'Life is too good' PSA series featured actors Jackie Chan and Pu Cunxin and soprano Peng Liyuan (wife of the PRC's President Xi Jinping). The PSAs provide a simple message about how to prevent the sexual transmission of HIV in the form of short video clips directed by Ruby Yang and Thomas Lennon – the director and producer respectively of an Oscar-winning documentary about AIDS orphans in China, called *The Blood of Yingzhou District* (Yang and Lennon 2006; http://www.bloodofyingzhou.com/). In one of these PSAs, Jackie Chan performs on a movie set to a script that states: 'I love making movies and I love life. An action movie needs danger but life needs protecting. Sexual transmission of AIDS is on the rise; condoms help reduce the risk. Life is too good, protect yourself' ('Life is too good' 2007).

Until the early 2000s, the public advertisement of condoms was restricted in the PRC, based on a 1989 regulation issued by the State Administration for Industry and Commerce, titled 'On Prohibiting the Advertising of Sex-Life Products' (Gongshang guangzi 1989). The 1989 regulation stated that it was permitted to produce products designed to cure sexual malfunction or aid sexual life, but such products should not be advertised because the advertising of vibrators and other sex products in unspecified regions of China had caused public offence (Gongshang guangzi 1989). Based on this regulation, the first public condom advertisement in reform-era China, which appeared on eighty Guangzhou buses on 7 November 1998, was removed thirty-three days later at the bequest of local government authorities. The advertisement, produced by a China division of the UK Jissbon Global Company, promised 'safe love without worry' (Zheng 2010b: 50). A cartoon condom made history in November 1999 by starring in the first condom PSA to air on state television. Produced by the PRC's Family Planning Commission for World AIDS Day, it featured a condom battling and chasing away HIV and other STIs, with a subtitle stating: 'Avoid unexpected pregnancy; condoms free you from worries' (Zheng 2010b: 50). The State Administration for Industry and Commerce stopped the PSA from being aired two days later because it violated the 1989 ban ('China bans condom advert' 1999). The 1989 regulation was rescinded in June 2002 after representatives from the Family Planning Commission petitioned the National People's Congress to overturn the regulation, arguing that bans on condom advertising prevented the circulation of public information about the functions of condoms, and prevented the market competition required to improve the cost and quality of condoms (Zheng 2010b: 65).

Bans on condom advertising were superseded by regulations that encouraged condom advertising for health-related purposes by the mid-2000s. In July 2004, the PRC's Ministry of Health and the Family Planning Commission issued guidelines titled 'On Promoting Condom Use for HIV Prevention' (Zhonghua renmin gongheguo guojia weisheng he jihua shengyu weiyuanhui 2004). The guidelines advocated the public promotion of condom use to prevent the spread of HIV through sexual transmission. In 2006, the State Council of the PRC issued the Regulations on HIV Prevention and Treatment (Guowuyuan bangongting 2006a). Article 28 of the 2006 Regulations states that all relevant government departments above the county level should promote the use of condoms with support from the broadcasting and print media, and they should also establish and improve the local supply of condoms. Article 29 stipulates that condoms should be made available in public places. Article 6 stipulates that the state should encourage and support the All-China Federation of Trade Unions, the Communist Youth League, the All-China Women's Federations, the Red Cross, and other organizations, to assist governments at all levels to carry out the work of AIDS prevention and control. It further stipulates that local residents' committees and villagers' committees should assist local governments and government departments to carry out and publicize the work of AIDS prevention. This explains the appearance of posters promoting condom use and safer homosexual sex on community noticeboards in urban residential areas, as noted in the introduction to this chapter.

Government-supported efforts to promote knowledge of HIV have helped to popularize a new Chinese-language term for condoms, *anquantao* or 'safety sheath'. Previously, the most common term was *biyuntao* or 'avoid pregnancy sheath', underscoring the association of condoms with the reproductive controls of the one-child-per-couple policy. The term 'safety sheath' emphasizes the use of condoms in relation to safer sex and disease prevention rather than solely in terms of preventing pregnancy. It also highlights a new understanding that monogamous marital sex is not the only legitimate form of sex, as illustrated by the recent provision of condom-vending machines on Chinese university campuses and in public entertainment venues (Yang, L. 2008). Figure 6.3 provides a graphic illustration of the increased frequency of the term *anquantao* in China's media from 2002 onwards, based on the number of hits for the keywords *biyuntao* and *anquantao* between 1999 and 2013 in the China National Knowledge Infrastructure database (CNKI), which contains full-text electronic articles from around 7,000 academic journals and more than 400 major Chinese newspapers.

Although public education about condoms and safer sex is a standard component of international AIDS prevention strategies, the

Figure 6.3 Publicizing condoms for safer sex and contraception: number of hits for 'Biyuntao' and 'Anquantao' in China National Knowledge Infrastructure (CNKI), 1999–2013

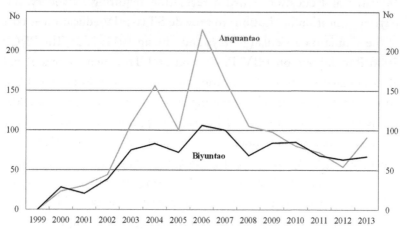

Source: Compiled with data from China National Knowledge Infrastructure (1999–), China core newspapers full-text database (cnki.net), Beijing: Tsinghua Tongfang Knowledge Network Technology Company Ltd

government-supported introduction of such strategies in the PRC initially encountered some resistance from 'concerned' parents and educators. This suggests that the PRC government is sometimes at the forefront of promoting positive social change rather than hindering it. For example, condom-vending machines placed near entertainment venues in Chongqing City in 2002 were vandalized by local residents reportedly because they feared that the public provision of condoms would encourage licentiousness and prostitution (Settle 2003: 118). Some universities in Guangdong Province refused to comply with requests from the Family Planning Commission to place condom-vending machines on campuses in 2004, arguing that it would encourage pre-marital sex ('Campus condoms vending machines stir debate again' 2004).

These concerns are embedded in HIV education materials designed for distribution in secondary and tertiary institutions. Following the introduction of China's 2001–05 action plan for controlling, preventing and treating HIV (Guowuyuan bangongting 2001), the PRC's Ministry of Education issued a regulation requiring secondary and tertiary education institutions to provide STIs-HIV education as part of the standard curricula (Jeffreys and Huang 2011: 163). The PRC's 2006 Regulations on HIV Prevention and Treatment reiterate that all secondary and tertiary education institutions should provide HIV education (Guowuyuan bangongting 2006a: Article 13). In May 2007, the Ministries of Health and Education approved a short brochure for dissemination in schools, colleges and universities, titled *Basic Knowledge of HIV Prevention for Youth*, replacing materials used since the early 2000s (Weishengbu bangongting, jiaoyubu bangongting 2007). The brochure provides basic information on what HIV is and how it is transmitted, and asserts that young people should care for and respect people affected by HIV (Weishengbu bangongting, jiaoyubu bangongting 2007: Items 1–4 and 9). It further stresses that HIV is not transmitted through general contact with others but rather through engaging in 'risky behaviours', which are identified as: pre-marital sex; serial pre-marital relationships; intravenous drug use; prostitution; and unsafe blood-collection practices (Weishengbu bangongting, jiaoyubu bangongting 2007: Item 5). However, the brochure only mentions condoms once and that is in the context of urging young people to be tested if they have engaged in unprotected sex or shared needles (Weishengbu bangongting, jiaoyubu bangongting 2007: Item 8).

Hence, while efforts to promote HIV-AIDS awareness among Chinese youth have increased dramatically, the promotion of sexual health awareness in schools and tertiary institutions tends to be conducted alongside moral education that stresses the importance of avoiding pre-marital sex as 'dangerous', rather than focusing on the efficacy of condom use and 'safe pleasure'. As in western societies, some of these programmes imply that engaging in pre-marital sex harms the individual and public health (Weishengbu bangongting, jiaoyubu bangongting 2007: Item 5). This approach follows from the American-style ABC strategy (Abstinence, Being Faithful and Condom Use) that informed and underpinned international AIDS campaigns in the early 1990s. Given survey-based claims in 2012 that over 70 per cent of Chinese youth have engaged in pre-marital sex (Wang, Q. 2012), this approach is clearly ineffective. An obvious qualification is that the survey in question does not specify the age range of the youth in question, which could be young adults anywhere between the ages of fifteen and twenty-eight according to Chinese definitions of 'youth' (Jeffreys 2012b: 39), and hence it may be referring predominantly to adults over twenty years of age.

In any case, recent developments suggest that information about HIV and condoms is increasingly being made available to people aged between fifteen and twenty-four years (Shan 2013a: 3). Celebrity-endorsed safer-sex PSAs offer informal educational tools that large sectors of the population can access through broadcast and social media (Hood 2010; 'Life is too good' 2007). Beijing is one of several Chinese cities that is now distributing free condoms for anyone aged between eighteen and sixty through user-friendly and more anonymous distribution channels, such as online ordering and automatic dispensers where personal ID cards can be swiped to access free boxes of condoms (Shan 2013a: 3). Shanghai family planning authorities have even designed a smartphone application that provides users with the addresses, telephone numbers and service hours of locations where free condoms are available ('Shanghai: City develops app for contraceptives' 2013). The government-funded provision of free condoms is designed to curb the rate of unwanted pregnancies and resulting abortions – China has an estimated 10 million abortions a year, half of which involve single women (Shan 2013a: 3; see also chapter 2). However, it also contributes to the normalization of pre-marital condom use and STIs-HIV prevention.

CONDOM PROMOTION AND COMMERCIAL SEX

Campaigns to promote condom use and prevent the spread of HIV and AIDS in the PRC now target sellers and buyers of sex, although the formation of a commercial sex industry is prohibited by Chinese law (see chapter 5). Based on the perceived success of Thailand's 100 Per Cent Condom Use Programme, the PRC's Ministry of Health, in conjunction with the WHO and the World Bank's China Health Nine Project, first implemented trial pilot programmes targeting female sex sellers in 1999 and 2000 (Disease Control Priorities Project 2006). Initially conducted on a pilot basis and without media publicity, such programmes have been promoted throughout China since the mid-2000s as part of a publicized national 100 Per Cent Condom Use Programme (Jeffreys and Su 2011: 326–7). These programmes aim to prevent the spread of STIs-HIV by encouraging a commitment from sex workers, and the owners, managers and employees of sex establishments, to 100 per cent condom use in all commercial sex encounters. They involve participatory workshops on the nature of STIs-HIV transmission and how to use condoms, and encourage the managers of public entertainment venues to provide visible supplies of condoms and put up 100 per cent condom use posters in their establishments (Jeffreys and Su 2011: 324).

As part of China's 100% CUP, state-affiliated municipal health authorities are running free STIs-HIV education classes for women who offer commercial sexual services in entertainment venues, providing them with free boxes of condoms and information about government-sponsored STI clinics and hotlines (Cai and Huang 2006; 'Condom promotion' 2007; 'Haerbin shi "xiaojie" peixunban' 2006; Qiu and Wang 2006). Health workers used a wide range of tactics to ensure attendance at such classes, primarily to limit the potential for low attendance flowing from the fact that the sex industry is banned in China and prostitution is stigmatized. These tactics included: seeking the active support of managers of entertainment venues; asking local police to halt anti-prostitution crackdowns temporarily and to refrain from arresting 'cooperative' managers, and attempting to gain the trust of sex workers by treating them with respect, taking them out for dinners and providing them with gifts (Cai and Huang 2006; 'Condom promotion' 2007; 'Haerbin shi "xiaojie" peixunban' 2006; Qiu and Wang 2006).

The PRC's Centre for Disease Control and Prevention, with the assistance of UNAIDS, has also published and disseminated a number of comic books that advise sex workers and their clients about the utility of condoms in preventing STIs-HIV (Zhongguo jibing yufang kongzhi zhongxin n.d.; Zhongguo xingbing aizibing fangzhi xiehui n.d.). These comic books, or low-literacy interventions, aim to minimize the effects of limited attendance at formal sexual health classes by encouraging those who engage in the prostitution transaction to share information about STIs and AIDS prevention among their peers. They not only stress the importance of safeguarding individual health by refusing to engage in unprotected sex, but also explain how STIs are transmitted, the long-term health implications of untreated STIs, how to use and dispose of condoms, and how to contact health authorities for further assistance.

For example, a booklet that promotes sexual health and STIs-HIV awareness for 'working girls' (*xiaojie*) begins by stating:

> Sisters, be careful! Pay attention to preventing HIV. Having multiple sexual partners is the most dangerous; protecting yourself is the most important. Always use a condom; it is very effective in preventing diseases. It also greatly reduces the risk of contracting STIs, HIV and Hepatitis B. (Zhongguo jibing yufang kongzhi zhongxin n.d.: 1)

The text uses catchphrases, often in the form of rhyming jingles, to aid memorization of the steps required to reduce the possibility of HIV infection. It reportedly was designed by speaking to sex workers who operate within commercial entertainment venues and incorporating the language that they use to negotiate the prostitution transaction, for example, referring to male consumers of commercial sexual services as *keren* (guests) who are after some 'fun' (*wan*) (Qiu and Wang 2006). The pictorial representations in the text also aim to match the sartorial and personal presentation style of the 'stereotypical prostitute' – young, pretty and wearing revealing clothes, short skirts, and lots of make-up and jewellery (Zhongguo jibing yufang kongzhi zhongxin n.d.: 1) (see figure 6.4).

Most importantly, the booklet has sections that tell 'working girls' how to encourage male buyers of sex to use condoms and how to say 'if it's not on, then it's not on'. Noting that many 'guests' will not want to use condoms, the text advises the prostitute-as-reader to say: 'Try

Figure 6.4 Preventing HIV: 'I have a method [a condom]'
Source: Photograph by Elaine Jeffreys, from Zhongguo jibing yufang kongzhi zhongxin [China Centre for Disease Control and Prevention] (n.d.), 'Yufang aizi: Wo you yi "tao"' [Preventing HIV: I have a 'method' [a condom], China Centre for Disease Control and Prevention and Qingdao-London Durex Company Ltd

it, it's really fun', and to be prepared to cajole or trick a reluctant 'client' into using them. These tricks include having different types of novelty condoms available for use and explaining that condoms not only help to prevent STIs-HIV, but can also prolong the 'fun' time expended before ejaculation. If these tactics fail, the prostitute-as-reader is encouraged to act like a spoilt or sulky child to induce compliance, or to state that they do not take the contraceptive pill and are worried about getting pregnant. If these appeals to masculinity and responsibility also fail, then the prostitute-as-reader is told to remember that their own health is of paramount importance and hence to say: 'no condom, no sex' (Zhongguo jibing yufang kongzhi zhongxin n.d.: 10–13). In short, the fundamental aim of the booklet is to empower female sex workers to protect their health and encourage peer-sharing of knowledge about the efficacy of condom use in preventing STIs-HIV.

While designed to empower sex workers, the implementation of the 100% CUP has also made female sex sellers responsible for the safer-sex practices of their clients. In China, as in many countries in the world, the 'invisibility' of male prostitute clients makes them a difficult target of government and other intervention strategies. Original plans to provide simultaneous trainings for sellers and buyers of sex in China's recreational venues were abandoned because of client mobility, and the refusal of targeted men to admit that they actually engaged in the prostitution transaction (Qiu and Wang 2006). Health workers subsequently focused their energies on women who provide commercial sex and the managers of the commercial venues in which they solicit their custom.

As a result, low-literacy interventions aimed at male buyers of sexual services are primarily targeted at (rural) migrant workers in the (urban) construction industry. Although there is little reliable data on the sexual consumption practices of male migrant workers, a government-sponsored project on HIV education for rural-to-urban migrant workers was launched in late 2005 (Guowuyuan fangzhi aizibing gongzuo weiyuanhui bangongshi 2005). The project stated that China had 120 million migrant workers from rural areas aged between fifteen and forty-nine years who may engage in unsafe sexual behaviours, or drug-related needle sharing, because of limited knowledge of HIV and sexual health issues. The project therefore aimed to popularize HIV education among male migrant workers in order to increase their capacity to protect their own sexual health, and to reduce the potential spread of STIs-HIV from this particular population to the general population.

A comic booklet for male buyers of commercial sex, who are characterized as rural-to-urban migrant construction workers, highlights the importance of avoiding unprotected sex in order to protect individual health, the health of one's spouse and children, and ultimately the health of China's future generations (Zhongguo xingbing aizibing fangzhi xiehui n.d.). The text opens with the somewhat improbable image of a group of people who are smiling and holding hands to signify their unity in the PRC's fight against the spread of STIs and HIV. As they say in unison: 'STIs and HIV can be prevented. Having respect for yourself and looking after yourself means protecting yourself.' This group is 'improbable' because it is comprised of five people who probably would not be smiling in the following circumstances: (1) the text's protagonist – the head of a (migrant worker) construction team; (2) a young man from the same village as the head of the construction team who has joined him to work in the city; (3) the wife of the protagonist, who lives in their native village; (4) a female sex seller from the rural hinterland who lives in the city where the protagonist is working, and from whom he has contracted an STI; and (5) a female doctor from a government-run STI clinic who treats and cures the protagonist, and tells him about the nature of HIV transmission and the potential threat that his engagement in unprotected sex poses to the health of his wife, his future children and that of the Chinese nation. The text concludes with an equally improbable image – the protagonist and his wife are smiling and standing with their arms round each other, saying: 'Learn how to protect yourself [be faithful or use a condom] and share what you know [about STIs-HIV and condom use] with others' (Zhongguo xingbing aizibing fangzhi xiehui n.d.).

However, commercial sex continues to be a focus of police-led crackdowns in China, which are now implemented in the name of disease prevention rather than solely addressing crime. Article 6 of the 2010 Notice of the State Council on Strengthening the Work of Preventing and Treating HIV/AIDS indicates that curbing the spread of HIV by 2020 requires the Chinese police to crack down on prostitution, debauchery and drug-related criminal activities (Guowuyuan 2010). The Notice urges local governments to crack down on these activities, arguing that such actions will significantly reduce the risk of the sexual transmission of HIV from members of key populations at higher risk to the general population. The PRC's 2011–15 action plan for controlling, preventing and treating HIV further states that combating the spread of HIV in China requires enhancing public education about sexual health, as well as continuing to implement police-led crackdowns on prostitution and drugs (Guowuyuan bangongting 2012). The combination of sexual health training and police-led crackdowns thus reinforces the social and legal marginality of people who sell sexual services in China, by suggesting that they are responsible for the spread of disease and crime.

The social and legal marginality of people who sell sexual services undermines the efficacy of China's 100% CUP in various ways. Some providers of local health services assign low priority to the work of HIV/ AIDS education among stigmatized groups such as sex workers, and hence the quality of interventions across the country is uneven (Jeffreys and Su 2011: 329). The high turnover and mobility of sex workers makes it difficult for health workers to monitor the outcomes of education on HIV prevention in recreational enterprises. Moreover, China has complicated rules regarding the registration of non-governmental organizations, which makes it especially difficult for such groups to liaise with people in the illegal sex industry, even when international funding is available. Police-led crackdowns against the sex industry exacerbate these problems by encouraging people who sell sexual services to move to evade apprehension, and may even reduce their capacity to insist on condom use. A sex worker who is experiencing lack of income because of police raids on recreational enterprises might find it difficult to turn away a new and non-compliant customer, or to reject a regular client who may insist on non-use of condoms as a perceived expression of trust and intimacy (Choi 2011: 112; Jeffreys and Su 2011: 329–30; Yu, Y. J. 2013: 358).

CONCLUSION

China's HIV governance strategy turns on the informing logic of international HIV prevention programmes – the imperative to know those most at-risk. International and domestic concerns about the potential threat of catastrophic disease have encouraged the PRC government to develop a national monitoring and surveillance system. The information derived from this system has resulted in the expansion of public education about both HIV and condom use, and the negative effects of AIDS-related social stigma and institutional discrimination, in order to curb growing rates of HIV infection from sexual transmission. At the same time, it has prompted a focus on (migrant) sellers and buyers of sex, which could function to further marginalize a population group that is already blamed for some of China's current social problems, for example, crime, on the grounds that their individual behaviours pose a threat to the collective health and wealth of the Chinese nation. As in other parts of the world, it appears that the success of these efforts is challenged by issues of shame, fear and secrecy, and the stigmatizing and often restrictive effects of identifying certain populations as being 'more at-risk' than others because of their sexual practices.

But the implementation of HIV education and condom promotion programmes in China also demonstrates that sexual health is now governed through market mechanisms and individual responsibilities rather than state-centred or bureaucratic controls. These programmes involve cooperation between the PRC government and the United

Nations and between diverse state and non-state actors, such as different government departments, CCP-affiliated mass organizations, business managers, condom manufacturers, advertising agencies and the media. They also involve the cultivation by individuals themselves of the capacity to regulate their own health and behaviours. Such cooperation challenges the widespread view that government in China refers to a monolithic Party-state that is somehow 'anti-sex'.

7   Sex Studies

This chapter fills a significant gap in the English-language scholarship on sex in China by examining the recent history and development of sex studies in the PRC. From the establishment of the PRC in October 1949 and up to the early 1980s, academic disciplines were subordinated to the organizing principles of Marxism-Leninism and the overarching goal of socialist development, which meant that sex studies were accorded a low priority. The early Chinese Communist Party was not exactly uninterested in sex-related matters. In the 1950s, the CCP banned prostitution, polygamy and arranged and mercenary marriages, with the aim of liberating Chinese women from age-old patterns of socio-sexual oppression (see chapters 2 and 5). It also provided married couples with sex-education pamphlets (Sigley 1998) and claimed to have eradicated sexually transmissible infections from mainland China by the early 1960s (see chapter 6). However, academic discussions of sex and sexuality were restricted throughout the Maoist period, and especially during the Cultural Revolution period, by the Party-state's overarching concern with revolutionary politics and control of channels of public information (Evans 1997: 11; Honig 2003: 143).

Sex became a new object of academic research in the PRC following the adoption of market-based economic reforms in December 1978. In the early 1950s, disciplines such as sociology were banned as 'anti-socialist', based on the assumption that since socialism had been realized in China there were no longer any socio-economic problems to study, especially from a non-Marxist perspective (Pei, Ho and

Ng 2007: 206). Deng Xiaoping (1904–97), the 'architect' of China's economic reforms, altered that situation in February 1980 when he called for academics to help fast-track the PRC's modernization by 'freeing the mind' from ideological fetters and 'seeking truth from fact' (*jiefangsixiang, shishiqiushi*) (Cai, Zhu and Deng 2011). This resulted in Fei Xiaotong (1910–2005), one of the PRC's most famous sociologists and anthropologists, being rehabilitated to direct the revival of sociology, both as a research discipline and as a subject taught at universities (Han Mingmo 1990: 55–66). Other scholars grasped the opportunity provided by the governmental call for intellectual innovation to open up new fields of academic inquiry such as sexology. Sexology refers to the multidisciplinary study of human sexual behaviour, but typically draws on concepts and terminology derived from medicine, biology, psychology, psychiatry and sociology. It attracted scholarly interest in the early reform period as a means to identify and address new medical conditions and social phenomena, such as rising rates of sexually transmissible infections and prostitution (see chapters 5 and 6).

While sex studies in reform-era China are predominantly medical in orientation and centred on identifying actual or perceived sex-related conditions and problems, a small but growing number of academics are working in the humanities tradition. Pei Yuxin, Petula Sik-ying Ho and Lun Man Ng's (2007) content analysis of sex-related academic articles obtained from four Chinese databases highlights some of the key trends in sex research after 1981. The authors searched the China Journals Net, the Renmin University of China Database, the China Doctoral Dissertations and Master's Theses Full-text Databases, and the China Proceedings of Conferences Database, for articles published between 1981 and 2004. Their findings reveal that most sex-related articles (more than 6,000) were published in the fields of medicine and hygiene, with the top five key words being AIDS, sexually transmitted diseases, sexual dysfunction, sexual precocity and sexual behaviour

(Pei, Ho and Ng 2007: 203). In comparison, around 1,600 articles were published in sociology and education, with the top five key words being sexual education, AIDS, sexual psychology, gender and sexual knowledge. Less than 800 articles were published in history and literature, with the top five key words being sexuality, sexual psychology, sexual culture, AIDS and sexual description. And around 500 articles were published in law and legal studies, with the top five key words being rape, AIDS, prostitution, sexual crime and sexual harassment.

Figure 7.1 provides a graphic illustration of the dominance of medicine compared to sociology, and of sociology compared to literature and law, in sex research in the PRC throughout the 1990s and early 2000s. Pei, Ho and Ng (2007: 203) conclude that reference to western 'science' helped to legitimize sex research in the early reform period.

Figure 7.1 The growth of Chinese sex studies

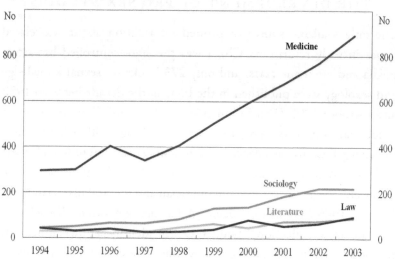

Source: Adapted by Elaine Jeffreys from figures provided by Y. Pei, P. Ho, and M. L. Ng (2007), 'Studies on women's sexuality in China since 1980: A critical review', *Journal of Sex Research* 44/2: 202–12

Some studies of sex as a historical and social phenomenon began to appear in the mid-1980s, and studies of sexual diversity and sexual rights emerged in the 2000s.

The chapter accordingly first provides an overview of the history of humanities and social science research on sex in reform-era China, with reference to some key authors and texts. It then looks at the blog of one of the PRC's most famous public intellectuals on sex-related matters – Li Yinhe, a female professor in sociology at the Chinese Academy of Social Sciences in Beijing and a renowned advocate of sexual rights. Finally, it discusses the new emphasis of sex studies in the PRC on indigenous or Chinese sexualities, with reference to conferences run by Pan Suiming, a male professor in sociology and Director of the Institute for Research on Sexuality and Gender at Renmin University in Beijing.

THE DEVELOPMENT OF PRC SEX STUDIES

The only available source of printed information about sex-related issues in early reform-era China was the state-controlled broadcast media and academic texts; and only 273 books on sexual knowledge and sexology were published in the PRC in the decade between 1982 and October 1992 (Pan Suiming et al. 2004: 40). Two of the most influential early texts were: urologist Wu Jieping's 1982 edited collection, *Xing Yixue* (*Sexual Medicine*), containing translations from Robert Kolodny, William Masters and Virginia Johnson's 1979 classic, the *Textbook of Sexual Medicine*; and physician and medical historian Ruan Fangfu's 1985 *Xing Zhishi Shouce* (*A Handbook of Sexual Knowledge*). Wu Jieping's collection about how to identify sexual functions, responses and problems reportedly was a best-seller on the black market, with non-medical professionals buying it along with another less 'salacious' text to hide the nature of their purchase (Yu Wei 2011). Ruan's work was listed under the classification of 'life, culture and education' as one of the Top 600 most influential books in the history of the PRC in 2009 ('Xin Zhongguo 60 nian' 2009). Other 'best-sellers' included: medical professor Hu Tingyi's 1980 *Xingzhishi Mantan* (*Informal Notes on Sexual Knowledge*), which was republished in 1985 and 1988, selling nearly 3 million copies in total (Zhong and Chen 2008); and the 1981 reprint of gynaecologist Wang Wenbin's 1955 text, *Xing de Zhishi* (*Sexual Knowledge*), which had sold over 9 million copies by 1986 (Wei Hong 1986). The popularity of these scientific texts suggests a strong demand for sex-related information.

Works in sociology and education began to appear in the late 1980s that included translations of canonical western texts and original research. In 1986, Pan Guangdan, a renowned sociologist and eugeni-cist, republished a 1944 translation with scholarly commentary of Henry Havelock Ellis's 1933 *Psychology of Sex*, titled *Xingxinlixue*. Between 1989 and 1990, Pan Suiming, professor in sociology at Renmin University, published translations of Alfred Kinsey's 1948 *Sexual Behavior in the Human Male* and 1953 *Sexual Behavior in the Human Female* (Kinsey, Pomeroy and Martin 1998a; Kinsey et al. 1998b; Pan Suiming trans. 1989, 1990). Two original texts were pub-lished in 1988 by two of the PRC's now most famous sociological sexologists: Liu Dalin's *Xing Shehuixue* (*The Sociology of Sex*); and Pan Suiming's history of western conceptions of sex, *Shenmi de Shenghuo – Xing de Shehui Shi* (*The Mysterious Flame – A History of Sex*). In 1989, Hong Jiahe, a professor in Chinese medicine, published *Xing de Jiaoyu* (*Sex Education*), the first reform-era text on sex education.

The newfound prominence of the 'science of sex' in 1980s China is demonstrated by the establishment of organizations promoting sexo-logical research. In 1986, Liu Dalin and Hong Jiahe set up the Shang-hai Sex Education Research Institute, which was followed by the founding by other scholars of the Society for Sexological Studies in Heilongjiang in 1987, and the Society for Sex Education Research in Shenzhen in 1988 ('Hong Jiahe' 2011; Kuan and Brosseau 1992: 14).

Liu Dalin and colleagues from the Shenzhen College of Education and the Hongkong University Medical School subsequently founded a short-lived academic journal called *Xingjiaoyu* (*Sex Education*) in 1988. The journal ceased publishing after three issues (Deng Mingyu 2008), presumably because of the repressive political climate in China immediately following the brutal crackdown on student protesters in Tiananmen Square in June 1989.

A national organization – the Chinese Sexology Association – was founded in May 1994 to promote 'China-focused' sex research and education (chsa.org.cn). The PRC's first large exhibition about sexual knowledge was also held in 1994 in Beijing, organized by the PRC's Ministry of Health, the National Population and Family Planning Commission of China, and the China Association for Science and Technology, among others, highlighting the newfound interest of China's governing authorities in sex-related issues. The widely publicized National Sexual Health and Sex Education Exhibition displayed more than 400 photographs, 100 posters and 30 videos for public viewing, and attracted an audience of 70,000 people – a much smaller audience than the organizers had anticipated (Li Daqing 1994). Liu Dalin established the PRC's first sex museum in Shanghai in 1999 (Yu Ying 2003).

Initially heralded as ground-breaking, many of these studies and activities have since been criticized for pathologizing 'sex' by promoting biomedical approaches and (moralistic) sex education (Huang et al. 2009; McMillan 2009). The expansion of knowledge about sex/uality in the medical arena was primarily concerned with identifying and curing sexual dysfunction. In turn, the expansion of sex education chiefly aimed to promote reproductive health and 'good marital sex', understood in terms of overcoming problems which were associated with stereotyped notions of men as dominant actors and women as passive and 'cold' (Pei, Ho and Ng 2007: 205). Such education also focused on promoting 'good' sexual conduct among China's youth, understood as discouraging pre-marital sex and encouraging self-restraint (Aresu 2009: 535–7).

However, alongside the development of 'sex science', Chinese anthropologists and historians began publishing texts on China's traditional sexual cultures and customs. These included ethnographic and folkloric studies of the sexual culture of ethnic minorities, such as the 'walking marriages' (*zouhun*) of the Mosuo (Naxi) peoples, who live near the border of Tibet in China's south-western provinces of Yunnan and Sichuan. Mosuo society operates according to a matrilineal system wherein 'husbands' and 'wives' do not live together as a couple or as the heads of a single household, and children are raised by the mother and her family. This system is referred to as a walking marriage because Mosuo women traditionally opened their doors to their lovers in the evening, and the men walked home to work in their mother's household in the morning in order to provide a livelihood for their mother, sisters and sisters' children (Yan and Song 1983; Zhan Chengxu et al. 1980; see also Zhou 2001).

Historians extended the study of China's ancient sexual culture during the 1990s with reference to manuscripts and artefacts retrieved from archaeological excavations. Li Ling (1993), a researcher at Peking University, traced the links between silk and bamboo manuscripts about sexual arts (re)discovered in 1972 at Mawangdui, an archaeological site containing the tombs of three people from the western Han Dynasty (206 BCE–9 CE), to what is now known as the Taoist 'Art of the Bedchamber'. This 'art' promotes specific forms of sexual activities, which often involve prolonged sexual stimulation without male ejaculation, to enhance vitality and longevity (Li Ling 1993). Shi Chengli (1999) published a text called *Dunhuang Xingwenhua* (*The Sexual Culture of Dunhuang*) based on an analysis of the 25,000 square metres of murals and 3,000 painted sculptures in the Mogao Caves near Dunhuang City in Gansu Province, which depict Buddhist-themed scenes from the fourth to the fourteenth century. These scenes include some semi-nudes (nudes are rare in traditional Chinese art), and Tantric figures in the ultimate state of enlightenment, symbolically represented by the state of sexual union.

Some academics also published general histories of sex in China, which, as in conventional western histories of sexuality, were presented as a history of escalating repression (see chapter 1). In *Zhongguo Gudai Xingwenhua* (*Sexual Culture in Ancient China*), Liu Dalin (1993) describes the history of sex in China in terms of relatively open attitudes towards sexuality from ancient times and up until the Tang Dynasty (618–907), followed by the imposition of an ideology of abstinence and sexual control based on neo-Confucian concepts of 'ritual' and 'propriety' (*li*) during the Song Dynasty (960–1279), and culminating in a culture of sexual repression during the Qing Dynasty (1636–1912). In 1995, Jiang Xiaoyuan, a professor of the history of science at Shanghai Jiaotong University, published a book called *Xingzhanglixia de Zhongguoren* (*Chinese People Living in a State of Sexual Tension*). Jiang (1995) similarly argued that an ancient culture of sexual openness was replaced by an increasingly repressive system of social and legal controls from the Song Dynasty onwards. He further concluded that such constraints conflicted with the cultural emphasis on reproduction to produce a male heir, which permitted men to have sex with multiple partners in the form of polygyny.

Such studies contributed to the opening of public debate on sexuality in reform-era China by suggesting that China's entry into the global economy had ended a prolonged period of sexual repression. Scholars claim that this period of sexual repression extended from the Song Dynasty up to the Qing Dynasty and, by implication, throughout the Mao era. The latter contention was not necessarily made explicit in Chinese-language publications in the 1990s because of the harsh political climate immediately after 1989. In fact, Ruan Fangfu published an English-language text in the USA in 1991 called *Sex in China: Studies in Sexology in Chinese Culture*. The book's preface claims that such a book would never be published in the PRC because it shows how the open sexual culture of ancient China was repressed by imperial and communist regimes, and exhorts the PRC government to adopt more modern and tolerant policies on sex-related issues (Ruan 1991: x).

The emerging field of Chinese Sex Studies was also boosted in the 1990s by media publicity surrounding large-scale sociological surveys of the sexual behaviours and attitudes of Chinese people (Pei, Ho and Ng 2007: 206). Between 1989 and 1990, Liu Dalin and a team of researchers from the Shanghai Centre for Sociology and Sexology, which was founded in 1988, conducted a pioneering national survey of 20,000 selected respondents from fifteen provinces about their sexual behaviours, relationships and norms, earning Liu the moniker of 'China's Alfred Kinsey' (Micollier 2005: 4). The interviewees included high-school students, college students, married people and convicted sex offenders. Questionnaires were distributed throughout rural and urban China through private businesses and government-affiliated organizations, with the aim of identifying issues new to the reform period. The survey findings were published in Liu Dalin et al. (1992) *Zhongguo Dangdai Xingwenhua: Zhongguo Liangwan Lie 'Xing Wenming' Diaocha Baogao* (*Contemporary Chinese Sexual Culture: Report on the Nationwide 'Sex Civilisation' Survey of 20,000 People*), and in English as Liu Dalin (1997), *Sexual Behaviour in Modern China*. It concluded that sex education should be a national priority, based on the ten major findings of the survey, which demonstrated increased rates of teenage romances, pre-marital sex, extra-marital affairs, sexual incompatibility between spouses, sexual crimes, commercial sex, STIs, HIV and reading pornography, and inadequate levels of public knowledge about sex.

In 1991, Pan Suiming and a team of researchers at Renmin University began a longitudinal study of the sex-related behaviours and attitudes of Beijing college students, which was replicated in 1995, and then extended to a national study in 1997, 2001 and 2006. The research examined student views and experiences of sex, love, autoeroticism, homosexuality, sexual harassment and sex education. The findings of the surveys were published in Pan Suiming and Zeng Jing (2000), *Zhongguo Dangdai Daxuesheng de Xingguannian yu Xingxingwei* (*The Sexual Attitudes and Behaviours of Contemporary Chinese College Students*); and Pan Suiming and Yang Rui (2004), *Xing'ai Shinian: Quanguo Daxuesheng Xingxingwei de Zhuizong Diaocha* (*Ten Years of Sex and Love: A Follow-up Investigation of Chinese College Students' Sexual Behaviours*). The major findings of the original survey were that a growing number of college students aged between eighteen and twenty-three years, and especially male students over twenty-one years of age, were engaging in pre-marital sexual relations, including serial pre-marital sexual relations. The follow-up surveys confirmed those findings but indicated that the incidence of pre-marital sex among college students remained at a relatively low rate: less than 37 per cent of male students and less than 27 per cent of female students in 2006 (Pan Suiming 2007b; see also chapter 3).

In the late 1990s, Xu Anqi, professor in sociology at the Shanghai Academy of Social Sciences, surveyed more than 3,200 couples about their mate selection preferences, expectations of marriage, the nature of their marital relationships and the role of sex within their marriages. The findings were published in Xu Anqi (1997), *Shiji Zhi Jiao Zhongguoren de Aiqing he Hunyin* (*Love and Marriage among Chinese at the Turn of the Century*); and Xu Anqi and Ye Wenzhen (1999), *Zhongguo Hunyin Zhiliang Yanjiu* (*Research on the Quality of Marriage in China*). The survey asked couples to assess their marriage based on indicators referring to their degree of emotional and sexual compatibility, and number of positive interactions regarding financial and recreational matters: 3 per cent of the survey respondents were categorized as enjoying a high-quality marriage; 75 per cent were categorized as having an average marriage, and 22 per cent were categorized as having a low-quality marriage. Despite concerns about the PRC's rising incidence of adultery and divorce, Xu concluded that the institution of marriage in China was stable, women have a more or less equal position to men, and mutual trust and harmony are essential components of a successful marriage ('Chengshi nüxing hunyin zhiliang ruhe' 2002).

Scholars have since conducted large-scale randomized surveys of the sexual behaviours and attitudes of Chinese adults. Between August 1999 and 2000, Pan Suiming, and a team of researchers from Renmin University and the University of Chicago, conducted the first randomized national survey of the sexual behaviours and mores of 5,000 people aged between twenty and sixty-four years of age (Pan et al. 2004: 22–3). The survey revealed that Chinese youth are entering puberty at an earlier age than previously, both single and married people reported a higher frequency of masturbation, and the average age of the first engagement in sexual intercourse had decreased to around twenty-two years of age (the legal age of marriage in China is twenty-two years of age for men and twenty years of age for women) (Pan et al. 2004: 405–6). In addition, a relatively high proportion of young urban men had viewed pornography and paid for commercial sexual services (Pan et al. 2004: 335–41).

Based on these observations, Pan Suiming and his co-authors concluded that a sexual revolution was taking place in China (Pan et al. 2004: 406). Another survey of more than 6,000 people aged between eighteen and sixty-one years of age was conducted in 2006 with funding from the Ford Foundation. That survey confirmed many of Pan et al.'s original findings and suggested that respondents had increased knowledge and experience of sexual techniques, positions and relationships (Pan Suiming 2007b). Media publicity about these surveys and the authors' conclusions has popularized the notion that the PRC is undergoing a belated sexual revolution ('Pan Suiming: Meiti' 2009).

Recent research on sexuality in China also includes a new focus on sexual diversity and sexual rights. Studies of female sexuality are no longer organized solely around issues of biological or sex-based differences and oppression (Evans 1997). They now include studies of how young Chinese women understand, experience and embody their sexuality as identity, for example, by 'being sexy' (Huang Yingying 2008; see also chapter 3). Although the academic study of homosexuality is primarily concerned with AIDS prevention (Zhang Beichuan 1994), novelists and film-makers are now documenting the life and cultural experiences of people who identify as lesbian, gay, bisexual, transgender and queer (Cui Zi'en 1998, 2000; see also chapter 4). Studies of commercial sex are no longer strictly about the history of prostitution and the PRC's prostitution controls (Public Security Bureau of Beijing 1998). Scholars are now using ethnographic interviews to highlight the diversity of sex sellers and consumers, and to advocate for public acceptance of sex work (Pan Suiming 1999, 2000; Pan and Huang 2005a, 2005b; Tong Ge 2007a, 2007b; see also chapter 5).

The growing focus on sexual diversity and rights is demonstrated in the work of Li Yinhe. China's changing sexual behaviours have made commentary from 'sex experts' a sought-after commodity by a new generation of journalists working in an increasingly commercialized and hence competitive media sector, and by an increasingly Internet-savvy population. Li Yinhe has become one of the PRC's most famous 'sexperts' not only because of her numerous sex-related publications, but also because of her willingness to talk to journalists and communicate her views in blogs.

ADVOCACY ON SEXUAL DIVERSITY AND RIGHTS

Li Yinhe is renowned in China for promoting the liberal view that sexual activities between consenting adults that are conducted in private, and entail no obvious harm to the individuals involved or to society in general, should be free from social condemnation and legal restraints (Li Yinhe (blog) 2006d). Li Yinhe is the first female sociologist to research and publish on sex-related issues in reform-era China. Her extensive and often ground-breaking publications include: a study of homosexuality with her now deceased husband, Wang Xiaobo (Li and Wang 1992); and sole-authored studies of homosexuality and sadomasochism, and of Chinese women's attitudes towards sexuality and love (Li Yinhe 2001, 1998a, 1998b, 1998c, 1996). She has also translated excerpts of works by western feminists, sexologists and queer theorists, as well as excerpts from Michel Foucault's famous histories of sexuality, thereby making such works accessible to broader audiences (Li Yinhe 2010, 2001; Li Yinhe (ed.) 2002a, 2002b, 1997; Foucault 1998, 1992, 1990).

Born in Beijing in 1952, Li Yinhe completed high school and went to Inner Mongolia in 1969, and subsequently to Shanxi Province as a 'sent-down youth'. In other words, she was one of the estimated 17 million urban youth with a secondary or higher education whose careers and lives were disrupted by being sent down to the countryside during the late Cultural Revolution period, theoretically to assist with rural construction and learn from the peasantry, while in practice easing the pressures of urban unrest and unemployment. Many such youth experienced hardship in the countryside and found it difficult to obtain permission to relocate to urban centres until after 1979.

In 1974, Li Yinhe started studying at the Department of History at Shanxi University, from which she graduated in 1977. After graduation she worked as an editor with a government newspaper, the *Guangming Ribao* (*Guangming Daily*), and then as a researcher with the PRC's State Council Research Office. In 1980, she married the now well-known author Wang Xiaobo. Li Yinhe went to the USA to undertake further study in 1982 and obtained a PhD in sociology from the University of Pittsburgh in 1988, which means that she was among the first group of students in reform-era China to study abroad. After returning to China, she worked as a post-doctoral fellow and instructor at Peking University. She is currently a professor, researcher and supervisor of doctoral students at the Institute of Sociology in the Chinese Academy of Social Sciences in Beijing – a prestigious government-affiliated think tank, where she started working in 1992 ('Li Yinhe' 2011).

Li Yinhe has been given numerous awards for bringing issues of sex and sexuality into the public arena. In 1999, Li Yinhe was listed by *Asiaweek* as a 'Nation Builder' – one of the fifty most influential people shaping the PRC in the new millennium, for being China's foremost expert on sexuality and trying to break the country's conservative, traditional attitudes on sex and sexuality (Gharemani and Stanmeyer 1999). In 2004, Li was ranked as one of 'China's 50 most influential public intellectuals' by the *Southern People Weekly* ('Li Yinhe' 2012). In 2006, she was described as a 'cutting-edge knowledge worker' by the *New Weekly Magazine*, for her use of empirical methods and tolerant standpoint on sex-related matters ('Xin Zhoukan' 2006). In 2008, she was ranked as a major contributor to 'China's 30 years of reform and opening up' by the China Economic System Reform Research Association ('Gaige kaifang 30 nian' 2008).

Li Yinhe is such a sought-after media spokesperson on sex-related matters that she claims to have started charging fees for interviews, in order to prevent journalists from wasting her time by failing to first research her opinions, which are publicly available via her publications and blog (Li Yinhe (blog) 2006a; Wang, Z. 2006). On 17 November 2005, she started a blog on Sina.com, one of China's most popular Internet portals. As of May 2014, her blog had more than 3,500 postings and had received over 75 million visitors ('Li Yinhe de boke' 2014).

Li Yinhe uses her blog as a public platform to advocate legal and social toleration of sexual practices that are viewed as unconventional in China (and elsewhere), a form of social activism that has earned her equal parts fame and notoriety. Her blog includes postings that encourage social acceptance of homosexuality, non-monogamous marital relations and sadomasochism. It also includes calls to decriminalize consensual adult activities that attract legal penalties in China, such as the organization of pornography, prostitution and orgies.

In blog postings, Li Yinhe advocates the legalization of same-sex marriage in the PRC on five grounds (Li Yinhe (blog) 2011a, 2011b, 2010g, 2007). First, it will promote social justice and citizen rights by helping to eliminate discrimination against China's estimated population of more than 40 million homosexuals. Second, it will reduce the spread of HIV and AIDS by promoting stable homosexual relationships and therefore safer sex. Third, it will revive China's proclaimed traditional culture of acceptance of (male) homosexuality, a culture that has been documented in Chinese literature from the Warring States period (475 BCE to 221 BCE) and throughout most of the imperial period (221 BCE–1911 CE). Fourth, it will enhance China's population control policies. Finally, it will build the PRC's international reputation as a progressive promoter rather than a backward violator of human rights by being the first superpower to follow the positive example of a small country such as Iceland (Li Yinhe (blog) 2011a, 2011b, 2010g, 2007).

Li Yinhe lobbied delegates at China's top political advisory body, the National Committee of the Chinese People's Political Consultative Conference, to submit proposals to legalize same-sex marriage in 2003, 2005, 2006, 2008 and 2012. All of these proposals failed to obtain sufficient support to be placed on an agenda for discussion. However, her opinions and actions in support of same-sex marriage have received widespread publicity, being praised for demonstrating China's modern progress and criticized for encouraging 'abnormal' behaviours (Li Yinhe (blog) 2007; 'Li Yinhe tongxing hunyin ti'an' 2011).

Li Yinhe has also used her blog to call for the decriminalization of group sex, pornography and prostitution. In April and May 2010, she defended online the activities of Ma Xiaohai, a fifty-plus-year-old computer science professor at Nanjing Technical University, who was arrested on charges of 'group licentiousness' (*juzhongyinluanzui*). Ma was tried for setting up an Internet chat room that initially was used by adults to discuss their marital problems, and eventually to organize eighteen group-sex parties between 2007 and 2009. Fourteen of these events took place in Ma's home, four in hotels and the rest in unspecified locations. On 20 May 2010, Ma Xiaohai was sentenced to three and a half years imprisonment for engaging in and organizing group licentiousness in accordance with Article 301 of the Criminal Law of the PRC (1997), under Crimes of Disrupting Public Order. Article 301 stipulates that: 'Whoever takes a lead in assembling a crowd to engage in promiscuous activities or repeatedly participates in such activities is to be sentenced to not more than five years of fixed-term imprisonment, criminal detention, or control'. It further suggests that a maximum sentence should be considered in cases involving minors.

Describing it as the 'last draconian law', Li Yinhe argued that Article 301 should be repealed for three reasons. First, the group-sex parties that Ma Xiaohai had organized and attended were private affairs, involving consenting adults not minors. Second, those activities had not harmed any of the single and married adults involved because they had engaged in such activities of their own free will. Finally, legal and social condemnation of adult group-sex parties reflects a 'mob-style' adherence to old-fashioned morality and demonstrates a disregard for the civil rights of individuals to choice and privacy. This upholding of a conventional moral code harms society by abrogating rights that should be protected rather than violated, and by encouraging the mob-style arbitrary rule of man that characterized the Cultural Revolution period rather than a modern and impartial rule of law (Li Yinhe (blog) 2010a, 2010d, 2010h). As with her support of same-sex marriage, Li Yinhe's defence of Ma Xiaohai attracted public support and criticism for promoting individual rights and undermining traditional family values ('Nanjing fujiaoshou' 2010).

Yet Li Yinhe is not an advocate of sexual libertarianism understood as the removal of all government controls over sex-related matters, as demonstrated by her views on pornography and prostitution. Li argues for the repeal of laws against the distribution and consumption of pornography in China on the grounds that adults should possess the civil right to consume pornographic materials in the privacy of the home. However, she supports government regulation of the content and dissemination of pornographic materials to protect children and youth from potential harm (Li Yinhe (blog) 2010b, 2010e, 2006b). Likewise, Li Yinhe advocates decriminalizing consensual adult prostitution to limit police corruption and give sex workers access to legal protections, but supports enhanced policing controls over forced prostitution and child prostitution to protect women and children (Li Yinhe (blog) 2006c, 2006d, 2010c, 2010f, 2011c; see also chapter 5).

While supporting the removal of legal controls over consensual adult prostitution, Li Yinhe adheres to the classic socialist feminist understanding that prostitution is an exploitative industry which has no place in a future society characterized by social and economic equality between women and men. For example, a leading member of the PRC's Ministry of Public Security proposed in 2010 that female sex sellers should henceforth be called 'women who have lost their footing in life' (shizunü), not women who sell sexual licentiousness (maiyin funü) as per legal documents. Contrary to critics who found this proposed shift in nomenclature insulting (see Jeffreys 2012b: 152), Li argues that it comprises an important step forward in legal terms because it implies that sex workers should be protected, rather than being viewed as law-breakers (Li Yinhe (blog) 2010c). She concludes that achieving the desired goal of reducing the incidence of prostitution in China will be achieved by encouraging social understanding of the reasons why women enter prostitution, providing sex workers with sexual health education, enforcing the mandatory use of condoms in all commercial sexual transactions with penalties for non-compliance, and providing sex workers with alternative skills training and welfare services so that they can return to a 'normal' professional and social life (Li Yinhe (blog) 2006c, 2006d, 2010c, 2010f, 2011c).

Indeed, as Li Yinhe explains on her blog, critics wrongly believe that she is advocating homosexuality, group sex, pornography, prostitution and extra-marital affairs, when she is simply arguing that the law should be used to protect impartial conceptions of individual rights, and not as a means to enforce arbitrary conceptions of social morality (Li Yinhe (blog) 2010a). Li believes that the private sexual activities of consenting adults should be free from legal constraints when they cause no harm to the individuals involved or to society in general, that is, in cases, unlike crimes of rape and sexual harassment, where there are 'no victims' involved. She also believes that responsible sexual ethics and practices, which she sometimes presents as abstaining from commercial and group sexual practices, should be fostered through education and awareness rather than legal punishment. Li Yinhe is therefore a proponent of liberal conceptions of sexual tolerance and rights; she is not a proponent of sexual libertarianism and sex radicalism.

RESEARCHING SEXUALITIES

Pan Suiming, another famous public intellectual, promotes arts and social sciences research on sex and sexualities in China in diverse ways. Born in Beijing in 1950, Pan worked on a state farm in Heilongjiang Province as a sent-down youth between 1968 and 1973. He then went to work in Inner Mongolia with the intention of preparing to undertake tertiary study. In 1985, he graduated with a master's degree in ancient and medieval world history from the Department of History at China's Northeast Normal University and started work as a lecturer in the History Department at Renmin University. As an early career academic, Pan Suiming was asked by the head of the history department to develop some new subjects in keeping with Deng Xiaoping's call for academics to 'free the mind'. This resulted in the creation and delivery of a subject called 'the developmental history of foreign sexual concepts' (*Waiguo xingguannian fazhanshi*), one of the first of its kind in reform-era China (Sigley and Jeffreys 1999: 51). In 1987, Pan joined the newly formed Department of Sociology at Renmin University, where he is now a professor and director of the Institute for Research on Sexuality and Gender.

Pan Suiming is an active researcher, media commentator and blogger. His extensive and often ground-breaking sole-authored and co-authored texts include: translations of Alfred Kinsey's work (Pan Suiming trans. 1989, 1990); histories of sex in China (Pan Suiming 1988, 1995); readers on sociological sexology (Pan Suiming 1998a, 1998b); ethnographic studies of sex work (Pan Suiming 1999, 2000; Pan and Huang 2005a, 2005b); and survey-based studies of sexual behaviours and mores (Pan Suiming 2006, 2007b; Pan and Zeng 2000, Pan et al. 2004, Pan and Yang 2004). Like Yinhe, Pan Suiming is frequently asked for his opinion on sex-related topics by journalists. He also started a blog on Sina.com on 23 July 2007 with the intention of making his opinions publicly available. As of May 2014, Pan Suiming's blog contained 360 postings and had received over 2.2 million visitors ('Pansuimingwww.sex-study.org' 2014).

Pan Suiming uses his blog as a public platform to advance public knowledge of sexual diversity and to promote China-focused sex studies. His blog includes postings on sex research, HIV and sex work. It also includes a smaller number of postings about homosexuality, hymen repair surgery, impotence, masturbation, pornography, sexual harassment and transsexuality.

Pan Suiming promotes humanities-style and China-focused sex studies in his role as Director of the Institute for Research on Sexuality and Gender. Founded in 1995, the Institute has hosted numerous domestic conferences and capacity-building workshops. In 2005, the Institute convened a conference on ten years of sexuality research in China (1996–2005), focusing on the emerging field's history and objectives. The Institute has also hosted four international conferences on sex-related issues in the PRC with funding from the Ford Foundation. In June 2007, the Institute convened the First International Symposium on 'Sex' Research in China (*Di yi jie Zhongguo 'xing' yanjiu guoji yantao hui*) ('2007.6.18–20 yu Beijing Renmin Daxue fabiao lunwen' 2007). The Institute convened a second symposium in 2009 titled 'Sex and Social Development' (*Xing yu shehui fazhan*); and it convened a third symposium in 2011 titled 'Sexual Rights and Diversity' (*Quanli yu duoyuan*). In 2013, the Institute convened a fourth symposium titled 'Toward Sexual Happiness' (*Zouxiang 'xingfu'*) ('Richeng biao' 2013).

The proceedings of the 2005 domestic conference were published as an edited collection by Pan Suiming (2005), titled *Zhongguo 'Xing' Yanjiu de Qidian yu Shiming (Discussion and Construction of the Concept 'Xing' [Sex]: The Elements and Mission of Sexuality Research in Contemporary China)*. The collection includes an introductory comment by Pan Suiming on the history and development of sex research in reform-era China, followed by chapters by Li Yinhe, Peng Xiaohui and Ruan Fangfu, on the problems associated with both the Chinese term *xing*, which translates as 'sex, gender and sexuality', and transporting western conceptions of a sexual revolution to China. It also includes chapters about cybersex, female sexuality, high-school students' sexuality, homosexuality, lesbianism, one-night stands and sex as a human right (Pan Suiming (ed.) 2005).

James Farrer (2007), an American sociologist and author of *Opening Up: Youth Sex Culture and Market Reform in Shanghai* (2002), notes that Li Yinhe concluded a keynote address at the 2005 conference by calling on China's sex researchers to be revolutionary. In Li's words:

> We have to pay attention to our own standpoint. Are we standing on the side of revolution or the side of counter-revolution? I am on the side of revolution, and I believe that everyone here in this room is also on the side of revolution. Our common purpose is through our

individual efforts to make the common people of China also choose the side of [*sexual*] revolution! (Li Yinhe, cited in Farrer 2007: 3; author emphasis added)

In short, Li Yinhe urged conference speakers and participants to promote social awareness and tolerance of different sexual behaviours and practices rather than promoting conventional and conservative views.

The lead author of this book attended both the first and second international symposiums on sex research in China in 2007 and 2009. At both symposiums, over fifty speakers representing universities, research centres and community organizations, based in Australia, Hong Kong, Japan, Taiwan, Thailand, the UK, the USA, and especially the PRC, presented papers on a broad range of historical and contemporary issues. However, the second conference was marked by an increased emphasis on themes relating to sexual diversity and sexualities, with several papers being presented by people who self-identified as gay, lesbian and queer. Also at the second symposium in 2009, a Chinese woman using the pseudonym 'Lanlan' represented herself as an autonomous scholar in a discussion about the negative impact of China's prostitution controls. Lanlan called for the repeal of police-led crackdowns against prostitution because they compound the vulnerability of female sex workers to crimes of robbery, rape and murder, as perceived 'social outcasts who get what they deserve'. Lanlan received a standing ovation when she concluded that she knew what she was talking about because she was a sex worker. This was perhaps the first time that a Chinese woman had talked in a formal public setting in the PRC as a self-identified sex worker, prostitution being an illicit and stigmatized activity (see chapter 5).

Speakers at the third symposium in 2011 presented papers about the sexual practices and associated rights of diverse people, including the disabled, elderly, lesbians, male homosexuals, rural-to-urban migrant workers, sadomasochists, sex workers, teenage girls, transsexuals and people living with HIV. Discussions focused on the heterogeneous rather than homogeneous nature of such populations. For example, the nature of homosexual identities and practices was debated in relation to men who have sex with men (men who are often married and have children) and men who self-identify as gay and queer, and the experiences of men from different generations in different cities and rural areas of China. Likewise, papers were presented on the lives and aspirations of both male and female sex workers, and consumers of sexual services. Speakers at the fourth symposium in 2013 focused on concepts of sexual pleasure using affirmative understandings of sexuality and rights-based approaches, and drawing on ethnographic and empirical research of sexualities and gender in China ('Richeng biao' 2013).

In short, a small but growing number of sex researchers in the PRC are exploring the specificities of Chinese sexualities. This point is underscored by the research activities of Huang Yingying, a former student of Pan Suiming and Deputy Director of the Institute for Research on Sexuality and Gender at Renmin University. Huang received a PhD from the Department of Sociology at Renmin University in 2005. She has published a monograph titled *Shenti, Xing, Xinggan: Zhongguo Chengshi Nianqing Nüxing de Richeng Shenghuo Yanjiu* (*Body, Sexuality and Sexiness: Research on Young, Urban Chinese Women's Daily Lives*) (Huang Yingying 2008). She has also published sole and co-authored ethnographic studies of sex workers, and presented arguments in favour of decriminalizing sex work in China's international media (Huang Yingying 2004; Huang and Liu 2010; Pan and Huang 2005a, 2005b). Apart from helping to coordinate the international symposiums mentioned above, Huang Yingying has organized numerous domestic workshops designed to develop skills and build capacity for sex researchers in China. For example, in 2007, she convened a workshop with Pan Suiming for over twenty university lecturers to develop multidisciplinary subjects with a focus on rights-based rather than biomedical sex education (Huang et al. 2009). In addition, she regularly travels overseas to present papers in English at sexualities conferences and to work as a visiting fellow on collaborative projects (e.g., Jeffreys and Huang 2011: 151–74; Huang, Y. 2010). Huang Yingying's research activities thus highlight the potentially altered and internationalized parameters of future research on sexualities in China.

CONCLUSION

Huang Yingying belongs to what some early career researchers of Chinese sexualities describe as the PRC's 'third generation' of sex researchers – the 'first generation' referring to famous scholars such as sociologist Liu Dalin and the second generation referring to famous sociologists such as Li Yinhe and Pan Suiming. Although the lines of demarcation in this particular typology are blurred, being based primarily on age, humanities-style research on sex in China is developing in new ways. The study of Chinese or indigenous sexualities is informed by a growing concern with sexual diversity and sexual rights, developing skills and capacity- building, and collaborating with scholars based at universities in China and overseas. It is also being pursued by scholars who are unlikely to become famous for speaking out about sex and sexual rights in public: such discussions now being a common, albeit unconventional, feature of life in China. However, given that academics in China are now expected to publish regularly in English-language journals, their work may eventually contribute to studies that disrupt the default tendency for western sex studies and western life-worlds to become the analytical yardstick for cross-cultural comparison.

8 | Concluding Comments

Sex and sexuality have become visible and publicly discussed components of everyday life in present-day China. The public visibility of sex, when compared to the perceived sexual austerity of the Maoist period (1949–76), has led numerous commentators to claim that China is undergoing a sexual revolution (Lynch 2003; Pan, S. 2009: 22; Zhang, E. 2011). This argument is popular because it appeals to common-sense understandings of how things were and are. It suggests that sex was repressed during the Mao era – the Communist Party-state confined sex to the institution of monogamous heterosexual marriage, and the political stress on revolution meant that 'to discuss any aspect of personal life, romantic relationships or sex was considered bourgeois and hence taboo' (Honig 2003: 143). In contrast, the 'natural' desires of the Chinese people have been liberated by the PRC's post-1978 opening up to international markets and western influences, as demonstrated by the growth of pre-marital sex, divorce, homosexuality, commercial sex, HIV and sex-related literature (Braverman 2002; Lynch 2003; Taylor 2012; Zhang, E. 2011).

Sex in China challenges the 'western-inspired sexual revolution narrative' by situating China's changing sexual culture in the socio-political history of the PRC. Chapter 2 examines the recent history behind the social expectation in China that everyone will marry and then have a child, a reality that is sometimes caricaturized as 'Chinese-style forced marriage' ('Zhongguoshi bihun' 2012). Marriage is virtually a universal experience for young adults in China. Data from the 2010 Population

Census of the PRC indicates that less than 2 per cent of men and women aged forty years and over have never married (Population Census Office under the State Council 2012b: 1862). The near universality of marriage, despite growing numbers of divorcees and people who self-identify as gay and lesbian, has led some scholars to suggest that marriage is a rigid, state-enforced means of effecting social control (Kam 2014). However, marriage and family structures in China, as elsewhere, are evolving and socially determined institutions, as illustrated by the history of the PRC's Marriage Law and the one-child-per-couple policy.

The newly victorious communist regime promulgated the PRC's first Marriage Law in 1950, banning polygamy and arranged and mercenary marriages, and instituting a new marriage and family system based on the free choice of (heterosexual) partners, monogamy and equality between the sexes (Zhonghua renmin gongheguo hunyin fa 1950). In doing so, the Party-state claimed to have revolutionized socio-sexual relationships by liberating women from China's age-old feudal-patriarchal marital and family system (Information Office of the State Council of the People's Republic of China 1994a, 1994b). This claim was supported by the large number of female-initiated divorces that took place in the 1950s (Johnson 1983). However, the PRC's adoption of a planned economy and associated restrictions on population mobility subsequently made it extremely difficult for Chinese citizens to exit a marriage from the 1960s until at least the 1990s (Woo 2009: 65–7). Divorce applications were restricted because married couples lived and worked in the same work unit. Potential divorcees could only access alternative accommodation by asking for permission from relevant workplace authorities; and resource-strapped workplaces concentrated on the mediation rather than dissolution of troubled marriages. Divorce applications were further restricted because people did not want their personal circumstances to become a matter of public discussion in the politicized socialist workplace. Divorce only became a practical option in contemporary China following the opening up of labour and housing markets in the 1980s and 1990s, and after revisions to the 2003 Marriage Registration Regulations removed the last vestiges of workplace authority over divorce proceedings (Hunyin dengji tiaoli 2003). The primacy of marriage in the PRC thus stems from a complex interweaving of factors that are not reducible to traditional Chinese culture or Party-state objectives.

The repressive hypothesis – the assumption that the relationship between 'sex' and 'government' is characterized strictly by repression – is also undermined by the example of the one-child-per-couple policy. Condemned by many commentators as the most extreme example of coercive government controls over the reproductive capacities and desires of individuals in the history of the world (Scharping 2003), the one-child-per-couple policy has severed the traditional link in China between sex and procreation and dramatically altered the lives of many Chinese women. Later and fewer pregnancies mean that Chinese women are living longer; they are also spending more time in full-time employment and other activities outside of the home (Riley 2004). Many women are therefore able to negotiate more equitable marital relationships than their mothers and grandmothers (Shea 2005). The widespread availability of contraceptives, and hence freedom from fear of pregnancy, has also expanded public discourses on marital sex for pleasure and eroded former restrictions on pre-marital sexuality (Pan, S. 2009: 29–30). The one-child-per-couple policy has thus played a significant role in promoting a new model of sex for pleasure in China, even as it has generated new problems such as skewed sex ratios – considerably more boys are born than girls ('New campaign targets gender ratio imbalance' 2011). It demonstrates that government policies do not operate strictly to repress 'sex'; they also create spaces for the emergence of new sexual subjects and subjectivities.

Choosing a marriage partner continues to be a family decision rather than a personal choice for many singles in urban China because parents and adult children are bound by considerations relating to financial security, housing and social welfare. Young professionals are often pressured by their parents to marry early and have a child while the retired parents are capable of providing childcare and allowing the couple to continue working. Senior cohabitation is reportedly increasing because adult children often discourage divorced or widowed parents from remarrying to avoid potential property disputes and additional responsibilities for aged care (Zhou, W. 2013: 5). While family pressures apparently push many homosexuals into actual or 'fake' heterosexual marriages (Kam 2013), marriage is not a sacrosanct institution in China. In 2013, civil affairs departments in Beijing and Shanghai reported a high number of uncontested divorces as couples with multiple properties divorced to avoid paying new taxes on the sale of second or investment properties (Feng Lanlin 2013; Xu, L. 2013: 3).

Chapter 3 questions the conflation of economic liberalization with youth-led sexual liberation by examining the sexualization of China's youth culture. According to a 2009 National Youth Reproductive Health Survey, the average age of first sexual intercourse in the PRC is just under twenty-three years (Guo et al. 2012). This suggests that most young adults view sex as largely occurring in the context of serious adult relationships, or as a precursor to marriage, and place a high value on virginity, fidelity and love. However, images of the young 'sexy' body now permeate China's urban spaces as young people explore and showcase their tastes and desires through the use of music and fashion, and in shopping malls, restaurants and nightclubs. Some Chinese youth are also using social media to talk about sexualities and sexual relations, including sex for leisure and without romantic attachment.

An examination of the performative sexualities of Chinese youth reveals that individual expressions of defiant sexuality question some conceptions about sex, but fail to significantly challenge gender roles, heteronormativity and the commercialization of human relationships.

Sexualities are performative in the sense that 'sex', 'gender' and 'sexual identity' can become markers of individuality and marketability, rather than being simply a biological trait. For example, female body-writers and sex bloggers such as Wei Hui (1999) and Mu Zimei (Goldkorn 2006) present Chinese women as sexy, sexually experimental and assertive, thereby countering traditional Chinese constructions of women as chaste and passive and Mao-era depictions of women as sexless labourers. Their presentations in novels, blogs and podcasts of young Chinese women as cosmopolitan individualists who love shopping, drinking and exploring their sexuality, have opened public debate on sexual morality, female sexuality and free speech (Farrer 2009: 102). However, they do not question the commercial re-feminization of women in reform-era China as sexualized objects of male desire (Zhong, X. 2006).

Likewise, pop star and actor Li Yuchun is adored by millions of fans for her performative persona as a *masculine* female artist. Li first rose to fame as the winner of a 2006 reality-television pop-music talent show called *Super Girl*. Part of Li's appeal lay in her cross-dressing and gender-blending persona which was perceived as 'rebellious' – she was tall, had short hair, wore baggy T-shirts and jeans, performed songs that were written for men, and called herself a tomboy (Yue and Yu 2008). Fans showed their admiration for Li's disruption of conventional sex roles by calling her 'Brother Chun'; they described her as 'handsome' rather than 'pretty' and generally imitated her fashion style. Some fans set up an online forum dedicated to the virtual romantic pairing of Li Yuchun and *Super Girl* contestants. Other fans responded by setting up a heterosexual romance postbar that paired Li Yuchun with men rather than women (Yang and Bao 2012). As fan responses to Li Yuchun suggest, the performative sexualities of Chinese youth sometimes stretch the conventional boundaries of male/female and masculine/feminine and encourage public expressions of homosociality. However, they typically fail to question the location of their 'rebellion' in the fashion and celebrity industries and stop short of accepting homosexuality.

Chapter 4 demonstrates that the politics of homosexuality in contemporary China is a product of the interplay between Chinese cultural traditions, the structural legacies of the Mao era and international influences. Historians have documented a history of government tolerance (or neglect) of homosexuality in imperial China (partly due to the absence of a monotheistic religion), which was replaced by more restrictive attitudes and legislation against homosexual rape after Manchu invaders established the Qing Dynasty (1644–1912) (Hinsch 1990: 143). Negative understandings of homosexuality became more prominent in China during the late nineteenth and early twentieth centuries along with the adoption of western science, and associated constructions of homosexuality as a form of sexual inversion or mental illness (Hinsch 1990: 168). After the PRC was founded in 1949, homosexuality became 'invisible' other than as a medical issue or perceived sign of degeneracy. That situation changed in the 1980s along with China's opening up to the global economy and the international 'discovery' of HIV.

Gay and lesbian lives are now a visible albeit peripheral focus of self-presentation and representation in China through online personal storytelling and independent film. The public presentation of homosexuality, whether that occurs in cinemas, through watching bootleg DVDs or in cyberspace, helps to foster alternative sexualities and lifestyles by revealing how same-sex attracted people express their sexual desires and manage social pressures to marry and reproduce (Berry and Pang 2010; Lim, S. H. 2006). However, it does not pose a direct challenge to heteronormative institutions and associated discrimination against homosexuals, being primarily directed at subcultural rather than general audiences to avoid censorship (Chase 2012).

New terms have entered the Chinese lexicon to identify same-sex attracted people, which highlight the heterogeneous and stratified nature of the PRC's homosexual community. The Mao-era term *tongxinglian* (same-sex love) is mostly used by older married men who have sex with men, and who look for sexual partners in venues such as public gardens, toilets and bathhouses (Bao 2012). The political appellation *tongzhi* (comrade), which was reappropriated by Hong Kong activists in the late 1980s as a Chinese and gender-neutral means to identify same-sex attracted people, is now used in mainland China to refer to homosexual people in general (Chou 2000, 2001). However, young same-sex attracted people who frequent upscale alternative venues often prefer to self-identify as 'gay' and some self-identified *tongzhi* maintain that rural-to-urban migrant men who provide male–male sexual services are not 'respectable', and hence are not *tongzhi* (Kong 2010a; Rofel 1999: 466, 2007: 105). Local terminology for same-sex attracted men is now also used in different parts of China, for example, 'rubber band' (*pijin*) in Shanghai and 'rabbit' (*tuzi*) in Beijing.

As with heterosexual youth, the capacity of young same-sex attracted people in China to openly express their sexuality is influenced by differences in family background, place of residence and employment. Some lesbians and gays can avoid or delay family and social pressures to marry by 'going out' (*chuzou*), literally moving away from their families or hometowns. Economic reform has created labour mobility, a private housing market and a service industry, enabling some people to live with their same-sex partners in major cities, to frequent gay venues and even to join advocacy groups for sexual rights. Gay men and women who have grown up in large cities can sometimes 'come out' because some parents of the one-child generation are willing to accept their only child's sexual and lifestyle choices. However, same-sex attracted people often practise a classical Chinese aesthetics of *hanxu* (implicitness, reticence or indirectness), or a 'don't ask, don't tell' approach, when dealing with their families and colleagues. The expression 'coming home' (*huijia*) refers in gay and lesbian circles to the act of going back to the family home with a same-sex partner but without declaring one's homosexuality, in order to obtain parental acquiescence for a same-sex relationship through non-confrontational means, such as eating and shopping together. Moreover, many Chinese homosexuals view entering a heterosexual marriage as 'the right thing to do' as evidenced by public concerns about women who are unwittingly married to male homosexuals, and by the alleged growth in pro-forma marriages between gays and lesbians who present themselves to family and work circles as heterosexual couples (Kam 2013: 99–103; Shan 2012). While complicated, the latter performance of heterosexual marriage arguably refers to 'an emerging queer private sphere that may offer alternative models and discourses to the heteronormative model of intimacy' (Kam 2010: 102).

Chapter 5 questions claims that prostitution in China is a taboo topic and unchanging object of punitive policing controls by examining the growth of the PRC's sex industry and public debate about its regulation. Commercial sex is a controversial subject in China, in part because the early Chinese Communist Party believed that prostitution had no place in a socialist country. In keeping with western Marxist discourses, the CCP viewed prostitution as a patriarchal-feudal-capitalist institution that oppressed women and therefore embarked on a series of campaigns to eradicate it (Jeffreys 2012b: 96–7). A PRC government white paper describes the abolition of prostitution in late 1950s China as effecting an 'earth-shaking historic change in the social status and condition of women' (Information Office of the State Council of the People's Republic of China 1994a). Although some historians question whether prostitution was truly abolished (Hershatter 1997: 332), the Mao-era system of centralized economic planning stopped a *visible*, organized prostitution industry from existing in the PRC until the mid-1980s by restricting the physical and moral spaces in which commercial sexual activities could occur.

A visible, albeit illegal, sex industry has developed in reform-era China along with labour mobility, growing income inequalities, changing sexual behaviours and a burgeoning hospitality and service industry. Disparate estimates suggest that between 2 and 20 million women aged mostly between seventeen and twenty-four years sell sexual services to men aged mostly between twenty-five and sixty years in venues across China ranging from upscale hotels to hair-washing salons, and for prices ranging from CNY 10 to more than CNY 1,000 (Liu, M. 2011: 109–20; Zheng 2010a: 35, 44; Jeffreys 2012a: 98). Originally restricted chiefly to adult heterosexual prostitution, the market for sexual services has expanded to include male–male prostitution, male–female prostitution, youth prostitution and child prostitution (Ding, Y. 2008: 95–6; Kong 2010a, 2010b; Jeffreys 2012b). While stereotyped as rural-to-urban migrant workers, people who provide and demand commercial sex come from diverse sectors of Chinese society as indicated by the multiple sites and prices for sexual services.

The growth of a sex industry in reform-era China, despite thirty-plus-years of police-led campaigns against it, has led academics, bloggers, journalists, police, sex workers, and even Party-state dignitaries, to advocate in favour of legalization or decriminalization. As they argue, adopting more tolerant approaches could limit policing abuses, promote tourism, raise tax revenue, prevent the spread of HIV, give sex workers legal protections and allow the police to concentrate on child and forced prostitution (Chang 2014; Huang and Liu 2010; Ji Ruijie 2009; Zhou Ruijin 2006).

The PRC government has not completely ignored criticisms of prostitution-related policing abuses and malfeasance. The 2005 Public Security Administrative Punishments Law, effective from 1 March 2006, addresses some of these criticisms by reducing the penalties for first-party involvement in consensual adult prostitution (Quanguo renda changwu weiyuanhui 2005). The Act recommends that first-time offenders should not be detained (Article 21). It stipulates a maximum of fifteen days' administrative detention in cases involving people with a prior record of multiple offences and five days in less serious cases (Articles 66–7), and gives suspected offenders the right of appeal (Article 102). It also limits the fines for those convicted of prostitution offences to a maximum of CNY 500 (USD 80), and to only CNY 200 (USD 32) in the case of on-the-spot fines, which must be issued with receipts (Articles 66–7; Article 100). These changes mean that people who are apprehended by the police on suspicion of first-party involvement in prostitution, but who have no prior record of being handled by the police, are unlikely to be penalized. Interviews with police officers also suggest that on-the-spot fines are now seldom meted because all fines and supporting documentation must be handed over to the state treasury, based on new administrative procedures designed to limit corruption (Liu, M. 2011: 180; see also Jeffreys 2012b: 95–110; Zhonghua renmin gongheguo gongan bu ling: di 88 hao 2006).

These changes are unlikely to halt public criticisms of China's prostitution controls for three reasons. First, the Criminal Law of the PRC (1997) continues to ban third-party profiteering from the organization of prostitution, with Article 358 stipulating sentences of between five and ten years' imprisonment for organizing or forcing other people into prostitution. Second, police-led campaigns against prostitution continue to attract negative media publicity because police officers often handle suspects inappropriately (Chang 2014; Jeffreys 2012b). This is despite repeated orders from the Ministry of Public Security that apprehended suspects must be treated in a lawful and respectful manner (Zhonghua renmin gongheguo gongan bu ling: di 88 hao 2006). Finally, government efforts to control the spread of HIV and AIDS have encouraged a new emphasis on sex work as a matter relating to public health rather than policing (Jeffreys 2012b).

Chapter 6 examines China's evolving responses to the governance of sexually transmissible infections to show that sexual health is now governed through market mechanisms and individual responsibilities rather than state-centred or bureaucratic controls. Sexual health is a recent object of government concern in the PRC. The PRC government made world history in 1964 when it announced to the World Health Organization that active venereal disease no longer existed in mainland China (Abrams 2001: 429–40; Chen, Z-Q. et al. 2007: 132–8). The Mao-era regime believed that syphilis and gonorrhoea were preventable social diseases caused by poverty, prostitution, ignorance and the subordinate status of women. It therefore initiated a series of campaigns to eradicate venereal disease, involving mass education, the virtual eradication of the prostitution industry and the large-scale provision of costly penicillin. Since the 1980s, the reported incident rate of STIs, including HIV, has risen dramatically in China. Figures published by the PRC's Ministry of Health in 2012 suggest that at least 780,000 people are living with HIV in China and nearly half of them were infected through sexual transmission (Ministry of Health of the PRC 2012: 5–6).

The PRC government attracted trenchant criticism from international organizations in the early 2000s for failing to respond to the policy imperatives of HIV. In fact, a 2002 United Nations' report, titled *HIV/AIDS: China's Titanic Peril*, claimed that the country was 'on the verge of a catastrophe that could result in unimaginable suffering, economic loss and social devastation' (UN Theme Group on HIV/AIDS in China 2002). This negative assessment stemmed from the PRC government's reluctance to consider HIV as a domestic problem until the early 2000s. In the 1980s, AIDS in China was portrayed in both policy and media frameworks as an outsider problem, stemming from foreigners (Hood 2011). The PRC government later recognized it as a problem for intravenous drug users in distant border regions, then as a problem stemming from commercial blood transfusions, and only after 2001 as a problem related to sex (Jeffreys and Huang 2011: 152–3).

The PRC's current action plan for controlling, preventing and treating HIV/AIDS is based on the United Nations' vision of 'zero new HIV infections, zero discrimination and zero AIDS-related deaths' (Guowuyuan bangongting 2012; Joint United Nations Programme on HIV/AIDS 2010). Instead of 'ignoring' AIDS, the PRC government is committed to reversing the number of HIV infections and AIDS-related deaths by providing universal access to education, testing and treatment. The PRC government has therefore adopted free care programmes and introduced policies to promote the acceptability of people living with HIV (Guowuyuan bangongting 2006a; Guowuyuan bangongting 2012; Kaufman 2010: 78). The PRC's Ministry of Health has also partnered with international organizations to introduce behaviour education programmes that promote safer sex and condom use for key populations identified as at higher risk, such as sex workers, men who have sex with men, college students and migrant workers (Jeffreys and Su 2011). Public–private partnerships have ensured that public-service advertisements promoting HIV awareness, condom use and anti-discriminatory messages, are an increasingly common feature of life in China ('AIDS will not affect our friendship' 2007; 'Life is too good' 2007).

As in other parts of the world, the success of China's AIDS prevention efforts is complicated by limited resources and issues of shame, fear and secrecy. People living with HIV in poor provinces cannot always access free health care as mandated by central government policies because local governments lack the capacity to provide such services, or are reluctant to relocate limited resources to help marginalized people (Yu 2012: 9). Many people are unwilling to present for testing at government-run clinics because of the social stigma attached to contracting an STI; sex workers and men who have sex with men are often afraid that their confidentiality will not be respected despite government assurances to the contrary (Fan, E. L. 2014; Yu, Y. J. 2013: 359; Zhang, Mao and Xia 2004: 41); and high-status people such as corporate elites and government officials are left out of HIV education programmes, which may encourage the view that AIDS is something that happens to 'other' people rather than people like 'us' (Micollier 2012: 116; Uretsky 2008). These problems highlight the importance of public debate on sex-related issues.

Chapter 7 surveys the history and development of sex studies in the PRC. Disciplines such as sociology were suppressed in universities and research institutes during the 1950s and 1960s as 'bourgeois science', based on the assumption that since socialism had been realized in China there were no longer any socio-economic problems to study, especially from a non-Marxist perspective (Pei, Ho and Ng 2007: 206). The study of sex was subsequently accorded a low priority, with available writings in the humanities tradition chiefly focusing on the CCP's liberation of women from traditional oppressive practices. As China's media was heavily controlled by the state until the 1990s, there was limited printed information available about sex-related issues during the Mao era.

Paramount leader Deng Xiaoping encouraged the revival of sociological, historical, anthropological and medical studies of sex in the early 1980s by calling on academics to assist China's modernization by 'opening the mind' (Cai, Zhu and Deng 2011). Sex studies in the reform period were legitimized initially with reference to 'western science' and focused on promoting reproductive health and 'good marital sex', identifying and curing sexual dysfunction, and providing morality-based sex education to discourage sex outside of marriage and halt the spread of STIs (Aresu 2009: 535–7; McMillan 2009; Pei, Ho and Ng 2007: 205). In the 1990s and 2000s, sociologists started conducting large-scale quantitative surveys to identify China's changing sexual behaviours and attitudes (Liu Dalin et al. 1992, Liu, D. 1997; Pan and Zeng 2000; Pan Suiming et al. 2004; Xu Anqi 1997; Xu and Ye 1999). Scholars also started publishing new histories and ethnographies of China's sexual culture and ethnic minority sexual cultures

(Jiang 1995; Liu Dalin 1993; Zhou 2001). More recently, there has been a shift to focusing on sexual rights, sex-related advocacy and indigenous sexualities.

The growing emphasis on sex-related advocacy and indigenous sexualities is demonstrated by the work of two of the PRC's most famous 'sexperts' – sociologists Li Yinhe and Pan Suiming. Both scholars are active researchers, media commentators and bloggers. Li Yinhe uses her blog, which has received over 75 million visitors, as a public platform to advocate legal and social toleration of sexual practices that are viewed as unconventional in China (and elsewhere), including homosexuality, same-sex marriage, group sex, commercial sex and sadomasochism ('Li Yinhe de boke' 2014). Pan Suiming's blog similarly contains postings that advocate legal and social acceptance of homosexuality, pornography, sex work and transsexuality ('Pansuimingwww.sex-study.org' 2014). As the Director of the Institute for Research on Sexuality and Gender at Renmin University, Pan Suiming also runs regular conferences and workshops to promote research on what it means as a Chinese woman or man who lives in mainland China to be sexy, homosexual, engage in one-night stands and so forth.

Hence, although humanities-style research on sex in China is influenced by the concerns and methodologies of western sex studies, some China-based researchers are exploring the specificities of gendered sexualities in the PRC with a view to developing indigenous or *Chinese* sex studies. These developments may contribute to a broader understanding of sexualities in China. They may also eventually contribute to studies that disrupt the default tendency for western sex studies and western life-worlds to become the analytical yardstick for cross-cultural comparison.

In summary, *Sex in China* demonstrates that the emergence of new kinds of sexual behaviours and the proliferation of sex-related discourses in reform-era China is bound-up with changing domestic policies and concerns, not just international influences. We should therefore question the 'western-led sexual revolution narrative', which has the added attraction in the case of China of presenting the speaker or writer as a fighter for democratic freedoms and civil liberties. Instead, we need to consider how diverse sexual subjectivities and communities are produced, supported and discouraged in different nation-states with varied governing strategies, economic formations, and consumer and media cultures, and in an increasingly globalized world.

Attention to the complexities surrounding the newfound prominence of 'sex' in China underscores the existence of tensions between how governmental authorities seek to shape the sexual conduct of Chinese citizens and the ways in which that conduct is enacted in practice. But it also demonstrates that the relationship between 'sex' and 'power' in the PRC is not always already conflictual: it is often a process of negotiation and contestation. Thus future research on sex in contemporary China should be directed towards tracking the interplay between the operations of the PRC government and the formation of new sexual subjectivities, and exploring the links between indigenous and international discourses on sex and sexualities, rather than focusing primarily on perceived sites of resistance to official discourses.

References

'2007.6.18–20 yu Beijing Renmin Daxue fabiao lunwen' [Papers at Renmin University, Beijing, 18–20 June 2007] (2007) *Chinavalue.net*, 4 June. At: <http://www.chinavalue.net>.

Abrams, H. K. (2001) 'The resurgence of sexually transmitted disease in China', *Journal of Public Health Policy* 22/4: 429–40.

'AIDS will not affect our friendship' (2007) United Nations Development Program: China, 18 April. At: <http://www.undp.org.cn>.

Altman, D. (1999) 'Globalization, political economy, and HIV/AIDS', *Theory and Society*, 28/4: 559–84.

An, B. (2010) 'Authorities to continue anti-vice campaign', *Global Times*, 13 December.

Anagnost, A. (2004) 'The corporeal politics of quality (suzhi)', *Public Culture* 16/2: 189–208.

Anagnost, A. (2006) 'Strange circulations: The blood economy in rural China', in E. Jeffreys and G. Sigley (eds), China and Governmentality, a special feature of *Economy and Society* 35/4: 509–29.

Anderson, A. F., Qingsi, Z., Hua, X. and Jianfeng, B. (2003) 'China's floating population and the potential for HIV transmission: A social-behavioural perspective', *AIDS Care* 15/2: 177–85.

Andrews, J. F. and Shen, K. (2002) 'The new Chinese woman and lifestyle magazines in the late 1990s', in P. Link, R. P. Madsen, and P. G. Pickowicz (eds), *Popular China: Unofficial Culture in a Globalizing Society*, Lanham and Oxford: Rowman and Littlefield, pp. 137–62.

Aresu, A. (2009) 'Sex education in modern and contemporary China: Interrupted debates across the last century', *International Journal of Educational Development* 29/5: 532–41.

Bakken, B. (2003) 'Norms, police and the problems of control', in T. Fisac and L. Fernandez-Stembridge (eds), *China Today: Economic Reforms, Social Cohesion and Collective Identities*, London; New York: RoutledgeCurzon, pp. 128–44.

Bao, H. (2011) 'People's Park: The politics of naming and the right to the city', in B. Scherer and M. Ball (eds), *Queering Paradigms II: Interrogating Agendas*, Bern: Peter Lang, pp. 115–32.

Bao, H. (2012) 'Querying/ queering cosmopolitanism: Queer spaces in Shanghai', *Culture Unbound: Journal of Current Cultural Research* 4: 97–120.

Bates, G., Huang Yanzhong and Lu Xiaoqing (2007) 'Demography of HIV/ AIDS in China: A report of the task force on HIV/AIDS Center for Strategic and International Studies', Washington DC: CSIS HIV/AIDS Task Force, July.

Beech, H. (2005) 'Sex and the single Chinese', *Time*, 5 December. At: <http://www.time.com/>.

Bergman, J. (2010) 'China's TV dating shows: For love or money?', *Time*, 30 June. At: <http://www.time.com/>.

Berry, C. (1996) 'Sexual disOrientations: Homosexual rights, East Asian films, and postmodern post-nationalism', in X. Tang and S. Snyder (eds), *Cultural Politics in East Asia*, Boulder, CO: Westview Press, pp. 157–83.

Berry, C. (2001) 'Asian values, family values: Film, video, and lesbian and gay identities', *Journal of Homosexuality* 40/3–4: 211–31.

Berry, C. and Pang, L. (2010) 'Remapping contemporary Chinese cinema studies', *The China Review* 10/2: 89–108.

Berry, C., Lü, X. and Rofel, L. (eds) (2010) *The New Chinese Documentary Film Movement: For the Public Record*, Hong Kong: Hong Kong University Press.

Biddulph, S. (2004) 'The production of legal norms: A case study of administrative detention in China', *UCLA Pacific Basin Law Journal* 20/2: 217–77.

Biddulph, S. (2007) *Legal Reform and Administrative Detention Powers in China*, Cambridge: Cambridge University Press.

Branigan, T. (2010) 'Chinese sex workers protest against crackdown', *Beijing guardian.co.uk*, 3 August. At: <http://www.guardian.co.uk>.

Braverman, A. (2002) 'Open-door sexuality', *University of Chicago Magazine* 95: 1.

Butler, J. (2009) 'Performativity, precarity and sexual politics', *AIBR* 4/3: 1–13.

Cai Liangzhi, Zhu Xianlin and Deng Wanqiong (2011) 'Deng Xiaoping "Jiefang sixiang, shishi qiushi" sixiang luxian de sixiang jiqi lilun shijian yiyi' [The theory and practical significance of Deng Xiaoping's concept of 'freeing the mind and seeking truth from facts'], *360.doc.com*, 11 June. At: <http://www.360doc.com>.

Cai Min and Huang Sui (2006) 'Guangzhou fang ai renyuan jiaban piaoke jiao maiyinnü yong anquantao' [AIDS prevention workers in Guangzhou City masquerade as prostitute clients to teach female sex sellers how to use condoms], *Xinxi Shibao*, 28 November.

'Campus condoms vending machines stir debate again' (2004) *People's Daily*, 16 March. At: <http://www.china.org.cn>.

Cao, Y., Zhang, Y., Chang, D., Yang, S. and Wang, G. (2011) 'Correlations between self-reported symptoms and psychosocial factors of perpetrators with domestic violence in China: A population-based sample', *Chinese Medical Journal* 124/4: 546–50.

Chan, K. (2008) 'Tactics of tears: Excess/erasure in the gay Chinese melodramas of *Fleeing by Night* and *Lan Yu*', *Camera Obscura* 23/2: 141–66.

Chang, B. (2014) 'Wuhan students demonstrate for dignified treatment of China's sex workers', *Beijing Cream*, 17 February. At: <http://beijingcream.com>.

Chao, S. Y. (2010) 'Coming out of *The Box*, marching as dykes', in C. Berry, X. Lü, and L. Rofel (eds), *The New Chinese Documentary Film Movement: For the Public Record*, Hong Kong: Hong Kong University Press, pp. 77–96.

Chapman, J., Cai, Y., Hillier, S. and Estcourt, C. (2009) 'Sex and sexuality in the Shenzhen tongzhi circle: HIV risk context and migrant men who have sex with men in China', *Culture, Health and Sexuality* 11/7: 689–702.

Chase, T. (2012) 'Problems of publicity: Online activism and discussion of same-sex sexuality in South Korea and China', *Asian Studies Review* 36/2: 151–70.

Chen Jieren (2003) 'Wuhan gaoxiao nüdaxuesheng maiyin xianxiang diaocha' [An investigation of sex selling by female university students in Wuhan], *Qingnian Cankao*, 21 May.

Chen Jiu (2006) 'Aizibingri de xingwenming sikao: Xiaojie wenti shi jiaoyu haishi chengjie' [Thinking about sexual civilization on World AIDS Day: Is the 'working girl' question an issue of education or punishment], *022.net.com*, 16 November. At: <http://www.022net.com>.

Chen, T. M. (2003) 'Female icons, feminist iconography? Socialist rhetoric and women's agency in 1950s China', *Gender and History* 15/2: 268–95.

Chen, W. (2013) 'More young adults living with parents', *China Daily*, 9 August, p. 10.

Chen, X., Yin, Y., Liang, G., Gong, X., Li, H., Poumerol, G., Nguyen, T., Shi, M. and Yu, Y. (2005) 'Sexually transmitted infections among female sex workers in Yunnan, China', *AIDS Patient Care and STDs* 19/12: 853–60.

Chen, Z.-Q., Zhang, G.-C., Gong, X.-D., Lin, C., Gao, X., Liang, G.-J., Yue, X.-L., Chen, X.-S. and Cohen, M. S. (2007) 'Syphilis in China: Results of a national surveillance program', *Lancet* 369: 132–8.

'Chengshi nüxing hunyin zhiliang ruhe' [The quality of marriage of urban Chinese women] (2002) *Chinatoday.com.cn*, March. At: <http://www.chinatoday.com>.

'China AIDS survey' (2003) *Casy.org*, Monterey, California. At: <http://www.casy.org>

'China bans condom advert' (1999) BBC News, 2 December. At: <http://news .bbc.co.uk>.

'China: Extensive use of torture – from police to tax collectors to birth control officials' (2001) Amnesty International, AI Index ASA 17/003/2001, News Service Nr. 10, 12 February. At: <http://www.amnesty.org>.

'China Internet Network Information Center (2010) '2009 survey report on Chinese youth online behaviors', April. At: <http://www.cnnic.com.cn>.

'China undergoing sexual revolution' (2003) People's Daily Online, 20 June. At: <http://english.peopledaily.com>.

'China's Guangdong Province to lift HIV restrictions on teacher recruitment' (2013) UNAIDS, 13 June. At: <http://www.unaids.org>.

'China's population, 1969–2009' (n.d.) Chinability. At: <http://www.chinability .com>.

Choi, K. H., Gibson, D. R. Han, L. and Guo, Y. (2004) 'High levels of unprotected sex with men and women among men who have sex with men: A potential bridge of HIV transmission in Beijing, China', AIDS Education and Prevention 16/1: 19–30.

Choi, S. Y. P (2011) 'State control, female prostitution and HIV prevention in China', The China Quarterly 205: 96–114.

Chou, W. S. (2000) Tongzhi: Politics of Same-Sex Eroticism in Chinese Societies, New York: Haworth Press.

Chou, W. S. (2001) 'Homosexuality and the cultural politics of tongzhi in Chinese societies', in G. Sullivan and P. A. Jackson (eds), Gay and Lesbian Asia: Culture, Identity, Community, New York: Harrington Park Press, pp. 27–46.

Chow, R. (1990) 'Listening otherwise, music miniaturized: A different type of question about revolution', Discourse 13/1: 129–48.

'Condom promotion at China's entertainment venues' (2007) Xinhua News Agency, 3 January.

Criminal Law of the People's Republic of China (1979) Adopted at the Second Session of the Fifth National People's Congress on 1 July 1979, promulgated by Order No. 5 of the Chairman of the Standing Committee of the National People's Congress on 6 July 1979, effective 1 January 1980. At: <http://www.novexcn.com>.

Criminal Law of the People's Republic of China (1997) Adopted by the Second Session of the Fifth National People's Congress on 1 July 1979; revised at the Fifth Session of the Eighth National People's Congress on 14 March 1997 and promulgated by Order No. 83 of the President of the People's Republic of China on 14 March 1997. At: <http://www.cecc.gov>.

Cristini, R. (2005) The Rise of Comrade Literature: Development and Significance of a New Chinese Genre, MA thesis, Leiden University. At: <http://leiden.dachs-archive.org>.

Croll, E. (1978) *Feminism and Socialism in China*, London: Routledge and Kegan Paul.

Cui, J., He, N., and Wu, W. (2013) 'Happily ever after until the divorce', *China Daily*, 16 September, pp. 1 and 5.

Cui, V. (2005) '"Money boys" become currency of pimps', *South China Morning Post*, 26 October, A6: 1.

Cui Zi'en (1998) *Meigui chuangta* [*Bed of Roses*], Guangzhou: Huacheng Chubanshe.

Cui Zi'en (2000) *Wo ai Shi Dabo* [*I love Shi Dabo*], Beijing: Huaxiao Chubanshe.

Cui, Z. (2002) 'Filtered voices: Representing gay people in today's China', trans. Chi Ta-wei, *IIAS Newsletter* 29: 13.

Cui, Z. (2010) 'The communist international of queer film', *positions: East Asia Cultures Critique* 18/2: 417–23.

Deng Mingyu (2008) 'Zhongguo dangdai xingxue fazhan gailun (3)' [Introduction to the development of contemporary Chinese sexology (3)], *Feminist.cn*, 7 March. At: <http://www.feminist.cn>.

Deng, S. (2013) 'China to merge health ministry, family planning commission', *Xinhuawang*, 10 March. At: <http://news.xinhuanet.com>.

Detels, R., Wu, Z., Rotherham, M. J., Li, L., Guan, J., Yin, Y., Liang, G., Lee, M., Hu, L. and the National Institute of Mental Health Collaborative HIV Prevention Trial Group (2003) 'Sexually transmitted disease prevalence and characteristics of market vendors in eastern China', *Sexually Transmitted Diseases*, November: 803–8.

Dikötter, F. (1995) *Sex, Culture and Modernity in China: Medical Science and the Construction of Sexualities in the Early Republican Period*, Honolulu: University of Hawaii Press.

Ding Li (2006) 'Maiyinpiaochang hefale ma?' [Is the selling and buying of sex now legal?], *Sichuan Xinwenwang*, 8 September. At: <http://comment.newssc.org>.

Ding, Y. (2008) 'Transitions and new possibilities of sex work: *Xiaojies'* perception of work and way of life in the Pearl River Delta', thesis submitted in partial fulfilment of the requirements for the Degree of Doctor of Philosophy at the University of Hong Kong.

Disease Control Priorities Project (2006) 'Thailand's 100 percent condom program'. At: <http://www.dcp2.org>.

Dong Xue (ed.) (2006) 'Fang ai xuanchuan jiaoyu yu guli maiyinpiaochang wushe' [Propaganda and education relating to the prevention of AIDS is not about encouraging the selling and buying of sex], *Nanfangwang*, 16 October. At: <http://www.southcn.com>.

Edwards, J. (2011) Sex in China: The Revolution, a dissertation submitted in partial fulfilment of the requirements of the degree of Bachelor of Arts (Asian Studies) with Honours, School of Social and Cultural Studies, University of Western Australia. At: <http://www.scribd.com>.

Edwards, P. (2013) 'China: First in cement', *Global Cement Magazine*, 23 July. At: <http://www.globalcement.com>.

Ellis, H. (1933) *Psychology of Sex*, London: William Heinemann.

Engebretsen, E. (2013) *Queer Women in Urban China: An Ethnography*, London; New York: Routledge.

Engels, F. ([1884] 1972) *The Origins of the Family, Private Property and the State*, New York: International Publishers.

Erwin, K. (2000) 'Heart-to-heart, phone-to-phone: Family values, sexuality, and the politics of Shanghai's advice hotlines', in D. Davis (ed.), *The Consumer Revolution in Urban China*, Berkeley: University of California Press, pp. 145–70.

Evans, H. (1997) *Women and Sexuality in China: Female Sexuality and Gender since 1949*, New York: Continuum.

Evans, H. (2008) 'Sexual bodies, sexualized identities, and the limit of gender', *China Information* 22/2: 361–86.

'Facts on American teens' sexual and reproductive health' (2013) *In Brief: Fact Sheet*, Guttmacher Institute, June. At: <http://www.guttmacher.org>.

Fan, C. (2008) 'Migration, hukou, and the city', in S. Yusuf and T. Saich (eds), *China Urbanizes: Consequences, Strategies, and Policies*, Washington, DC: World Bank Publications, pp. 65–89.

Fan, C. and Huang, Y. (1998) 'Waves of rural brides: Female marriage migration in China', *Annals of the Association of American Geographers* 88/2: 227–51.

Fan, E. L. (2014) 'HIV testing as prevention among MSM in China: The business of scaling-up', *Global Public Health: An International Journal for Research, Policy and Practice* 9/1–2: 85–97.

Fan, F. (2013) 'Spike in divorces linked to tax loophole', *China Daily*, 30 October, p. 3.

Fan, M. (2007) 'Oldest profession flourishes in China', *Washington Post*, 5 August.

Fan Xiaoling, Hu Fanzhu, Lin Jiejun and Ma Xiaoling (2004) 'Xiaojie chenghuyu de yuyong tezhong dili fenbu jiqi zouxiang' [The uses, features and geographic distribution of the appellation 'xiaojie' (Miss)], *Yuyan Wenzi Yingyong* 4: 41–7.

Fang Xiaoyi, Li Xiaoming, Yang Hongmei, Hong Yan, Zhao Ran, Dong Baiqing, Liu Wei, Zhou Yuejiao, Liang Shaoling, Stanton, B. and Beijing Normal University Institute of Developmental Psychology (2007) 'Profile of female sex workers in a Chinese county: Does it differ by where they came from and where they work?', World Health Population 9/1: 46–64.

Fang, X. (2012) Barefoot Doctors and Western Medicine in China, Rochester, NY: University of Rochester Press.

'Farenshenxing de Shanghai nüdaxuesheng maiyin an' [Thought provoking case of female university students selling sex in Shanghai] (2009) Dongfang Weishi [Dragon TV], 24 December. At: <http://news.xinhuanet.com>.

Farrer, J. (2002) Opening Up: Youth Sex Culture and Market Reform in Shanghai, Chicago: University of Chicago Press.

Farrer, J. (2007) 'China's women sex bloggers and dialogic sexual politics on the Chinese Internet', China Aktuell: Journal of Current Chinese Affairs 4: 1–36.

Farrer, J. (2008) 'A Chinese-led global sexual revolution', Contexts 7/3: 58–60.

Farrer, J. (2009 [2006]) 'Sexual citizenship and the politics of sexual storytelling among Chinese youth', in E. Jeffreys (ed.), Sex and Sexuality in China, Abingdon, Oxon: Routledge, pp. 102–23.

Feng Lanlin (2013) Shanghai minzhengju li pai gonggao: Luoshi you fengxian lihun xu jinshen' [Shanghai Civil Affairs Bureau announcement: The property market is risky, be careful when divorcing], Xinwen Wanbao, 21 March. At: <http://finance.sina.com.cn>.

Fong, V. L. (2004) Only Hope: Coming of Age Under China's One-Child Policy, Stanford CA: Stanford University Press.

Foucault, M. (1978) The History of Sexuality: An Introduction, trans. R. Hurley, Harmondsworth: Penguin Books.

Foucault, M. (1990 [1984]) The History of Sexuality Vol. 3: The Care of Self, London: Penguin.

Foucault, M. (1992 [1984]) The History of Sexuality Vol. 2: The Use of Pleasure, London: Penguin.

Foucault, M. (1998 [1976]) The History of Sexuality Vol. 1: The Will to Knowledge, London: Penguin.

Fowler, A. R, Gao, J. and Carlson, L. (2010) 'Public policy and the changing Chinese family in contemporary China: The past and present as prologue to the future', Journal of Macromarketing 30/4: 342–53.

French, H. W. (2006) 'Letter from China: The sex industry is everywhere but nowhere', International Herald Tribune, Asia-Pacific, 14 December.

Fu Jianfeng (2004) 'Fayuan panjue: Tongxingmaiyin zui chengli' [Court decision: The crime of same-sex prostitution exists], Nanfang Dushibao, 18 February.

'Gaige kaifang 30 nian jiechu renwu houxuan mingdan] [List of candidates for outstanding people in China's 30 years of economic reform and opening up] (2008) *Sports163.com*, 31 July. At: <http://sports.163.com>.

Geyer, R. (2002) 'In love and gay', in P. Link, R. P. Madsen and P. G. Pickowicz (eds), *Popular China: Unofficial Culture in a Globalizing Society*, Lanham, Maryland: Rowman and Littlefield, pp. 251–74.

Gharemani, Y. and Stanmeyer, A. (1999) 'Nation builders', *Asiaweek*. At: <http://edition.cnn.com>.

Giles, J. and Ren, M. (2007) 'Elderly parent health and the migration decisions of adult children: Evidence from rural China', *Demography* 44/2: 265–88.

Gittings, J. (2001) 'The AIDS scandal China could not hush up: Health officials' blood-for-cash scheme breeds HIV tragedy', *Guardian*, 11 June. At: <http://www.guardian.co.uk>.

Gold, T. (1993) 'Go with your feelings: Hong Kong and Taiwan popular culture in Greater China', *China Quarterly* 136: 907– 25.

Goldkorn, J. (2006) 'Muzi Mei sex blogger', *Danwei*, 27 April 27. At: <http://www.danwei.org>.

Gongshang guangzi (1989) Guojia gongshang xingzheng guanliju guanyu yanjin kan bo youguan xingshenghuo chanpin guanggao de guiding [Regulations of the State Administration for Industry and Commerce on prohibiting the advertising of sex-life products], Number 284, 13 October. At: <http://www.saic.gov.cn>.

Greenhalgh, S. (2003) 'Science, modernity, and the making of China's one-child policy', *Population and Development Review* 29/2: 163–96.

Greenhalgh, S. and E. A. Winckler (2005) *Governing China's Population: From Leninist to Neoliberal Biopolitics*, Stanford, CA: Stanford University Press.

Gu, J. and Renwick, N. (2008) 'China's fight against HIV/AIDS', *Journal of Contemporary China* 17/54: 85–106.

Guo, W., Wu, Z., Qiu, Y., Chen, G., and Zheng, X-Y. (2012) 'The timing of sexual debut among Chinese youth', *International Perspectives on Sexual and Reproductive Health*, 38, 4. At: <http://www.guttmacher.org>.

Guojia guangbo dianying dianshi zongju [State Administration of Radio, Film, and Television (SARFT)] (2007) 'Guangdian zongju guanyu tongyi Hunan Dianshitai juban 2007 nian "Kuaile Nansheng" huodong de pifu' [Reply from SARFT to Hunan Television Station on approving 2007 'Happy Boys'], 5 April. At: <http://www.sarft.gov.cn/>.

Guowuyuan [State Council] (2010) 'Guowuyuan guanyu jinyibu jiaqiang Aizibing fangzhi gongzuo de tongzhi guo fa (2010) 48 hao [2010 Notice of the State Council on Strengthening the Work of Preventing and Treating HIV/AIDS, No. 48], 1 March. At: <http://www.gov.cn/>.

Guowuyuan bangongting [Office of the State Council] (2001) Zhongguo ezhi yu fangzhi Aizibing xingdong jihua [China's action plan for controlling, preventing and treating HIV/AIDS (2001–2005)], 25 May. At: <http://www.gov.cn/>.

Guowuyuan bangongting [Office of the State Council] (2006a) Aizibing fangzhi tiaoli [Regulations on AIDS Prevention and Treatment]. At: <http://www.legaldaily.com.cn/>.

Guowuyuan bangongting [Office of the State Council] (2006b) Guowuyuan bangongting guanyu yinfa Zhongguo ezhi yu fangzhi aizibing xingdong jihua (2006–2010 nian) de tongzhi [Announcement from the State Council on China's 2006–10 Action Plan for Controlling, Preventing and Treating HIV/AIDS]. At: <http://www.gov.cn/>.

Guowuyuan bangongting [Office of the State Council] (2010) 'Guowuyuan changwu huiyi yanjiu bushu jinyibu jiaqiang aizibing fangzhi deng' [State Council Executive Committee on Research and Plans to Strengthen AIDS Prevention and Treatment], The Central Government of the People's Republic of China, 29 November. At: <http://www.gov.cn/>.

Guowuyuan bangongting [Office of the State Council] (2012) 'Guowuyuan ban-gongting guanyu yinfa Zhongguo ezhi yu fangzhi aizibing shi'erwu xingdong jihua de tongzhi guo ban fa (2012) 4 hao' [Office of the State Council Notice on the action plan for controlling, preventing and treating HIV/AIDS coter-minous with the twelfth national five year plan, document number 4, 2012], 13 January. At: <http://www.gov.cn/>.

Guowuyuan fangzhi aizibing gongzuo weiyuanhui bangongshi [State Council AIDS Working Committee Office] (2005) 'Guanyu lianhe shishi quanguo nongmingong yufang aizibing xuanchuan de tongzhi' [Announcement on HIV/AIDS education project among rural-to-urban migrant workers], China. com.cn. At: <http://www.china.com.cn/>.

'Haerbin shi "xiaojie" peixunban yinfa de zhenglun' [The 'working girl' training class in Haerbin City triggers debate] (2006) Haerbin Ribao, 15 October.

Han Mingmo (1990) 'Shehuixue de chongjian, ransuo he tupo' [Explorations and breakthroughs in the rebuilding of sociology], Zhongguo Shehuikexue 1: 55–66.

He, X. (2010) 'My unconventional marriage or ménage a trois in Beijing', in C. Yau (ed.), As Normal as Possible: Negotiating Sexuality and Gender in Mainland China and Hong Kong, Hong Kong: Hong Kong University Press, pp. 103–110.

Herdt, G. (ed.) (1997) Sexual Cultures and Migration in the Era of AIDS: Anthropological and Demographic Perspectives, New York: Oxford University Press.

Hershatter, G. (1996) 'Sexing modern China', in G. Hershatter, E. Honig and J. N. Lipman (eds) *Remapping China: Fissures in Historical Terrain*. Stanford, CA: Stanford University Press, pp. 42–93.

Hershatter, G. (1997) *Dangerous Pleasures: Prostitution and Modernity in Twentieth-Century Shanghai*, Berkeley, Los Angeles; London: University of California Press.

Hinsch, B. (1990) *Passions of the Cut Sleeve: The Male Homosexual Tradition in China*, Berkeley, Los Angeles; Oxford: University of California Press.

Ho, A. K. H. (2009) 'The lack of Chinese lesbians: Double crossing in *Blue Gate Crossing*', *Genders*, 49. At: <http://www.genders.org/>.

Ho, L. W. W. (2007) 'The gay space in Chinese cyberspace: Self-censorship, commercialisation and misrepresentation', *China Aktuell – Journal of Current Chinese Affairs* 36/4: 45–73.

Ho, L. W. W. (2008) 'Speaking of same-sex subjects in China', *Asian Studies Review* 32/4: 491–510.

Ho, L. W. W. (2010) *Gay and Lesbian Subculture in Urban China*, London; New York: Routledge.

'Homosexuality in China: Collateral damage, neither comrades nor spouses' (2010) *Economist*, 18 March. At: <http://www.economist.com/>.

Hong Jiahe (1989) *Xing de Jiaoyu* [Sex education], Shanghai: Shanghai Renmin Chubanshe.

'Hong Jiahe' (2011) *Hudong.com*. At: <http://www.hudong.com/>.

Honig, E. (2003) 'Socialist sex: The Cultural Revolution revisited', *Modern China* 29/2: 143–75.

Hood, J. (2010) 'Celebrity philanthropy: The cultivation of China's HIV/AIDS heroes', in L. E. Edwards and E. Jeffreys (eds), *Celebrity in China*, Hong Kong: Hong Kong University Press, pp. 85–102.

Hood, J. (2011) *HIV/AIDS, Health and the Media in China: Imagined Immunity Through Racialized Disease*, Abingdon, Oxon: Routledge.

Hood, J. (2012) 'HIV/AIDS and shifting urban China's sociomoral landscape: Engendering bio-activism and resistance through stories of suffering', *International Journal of Asia Pacific Studies* 8/1: 125–44.

Hooper, B. (1991) 'Chinese youth: The nineties generation', *Current History* 90: 264–49.

Hsu, J. H. (2012) 'Queering Chineseness: The queer sphere of feelings in *Farewell My Concubine* and *Green Snake*', *Asian Studies Review* 36: 1–17.

Hu Tingyi (1980) *Xingzhishi mantan* [*Informal Notes on Sexual Knowledge*], Nanchang: Jiangxi Keji Chubanshe.

Huang, P. (2005) 'Divorce law practices and the origins, myths, and realities of judicial "mediation" in China', *Modern China* 31/2: 151–203.

Huang Yingying (2004) 'A shi yu B shi falang xiaojie de zhuanye hua qingkuang yanjiu' [A study of the occupational practices of female sex workers based in hair salons in cities A and B], in Sun Liqing et al. (eds), *Beida Qinghua Renda san xiao lunwen ji 2002–2003* [*An Anthology of Masters Theses from Peking University, Tsinghua University and Renmin University 2002–2003*], Shandong: Shandong Renmin Chubanshe.

Huang Yingying (2008) *Shenti, xing, xinggan: Zhongguo chengshi nianqing nüxing de richeng shenghuo yanjiu* [*Body, Sexuality and Sexiness: Research on Young, Urban Chinese Women's Daily Lives*], Beijing: Shehuikexuewenxian Chubanshe.

Huang Youqin (2001) 'Gender, hukou, and the occupational attainment of female migrants in China' (1985–1990)', *Environment and Planning* 33: 257–79.

Huang, Y. (2010) 'Female sex workers in China: Their occupational concerns', in J. Jun and H. Worth (eds), *HIV in China: Understanding the Social Aspects of the Epidemic*, Sydney: University of New South Wales Press, pp. 43–66.

Huang, Y. and Liu, W. (2010) 'Debate: Prostitution', *China Daily*, 31 May.

Huang, Y., Pan, S., Peng, T., Gao, Y. (2009) 'Teaching sexualities at Chinese Universities: Context, experience, and challenges', *International Journal of Sexual Health* 21/4: 282–95.

Hudson, C. (2007) 'Big bad Chinese mama: Asian cyberfeminism and subversive textual strategies', *Genders* 46: 1–19.

Hugo, G. (2001) Population Mobility and HIV/AIDS in Indonesia, report prepared for the UNDP South East Asia HIV and Development Programme. At: <http://www.ilo.org/>.

Human Rights in China (1999) 'Not welcome at the party: Behind the "clean-up" of China's cities – a report on administrative detention under "custody and repatriation"', HRIC Arbitrary Detention Series, No. 2, September. At: <http://www.hrichina.org/>.

Hunyin dengji banfa [Marriage Registration Procedures] (1955) Ministry of Civil Affairs of the People's Republic of China, 1 June. At: <http://www.docin.com/>.

Hunyin dengji banfa (1980 nian) [Marriage Registration Procedures 1980] (1980) Ministry of Civil Affairs of the People's Republic of China, 11 November. At: <http://chengguan.mca.gov.cn/>.

Hunyin dengji banfa [Marriage Registration Procedures] (1986) Ministry of Civil Affairs of the People's Republic of China, 15 March. At: <http://www.people.com.cn/>.

Hunyin dengji guanli tiaoli [Marriage Registration Management Regulations] (1994) Ministry of Civil Affairs of the People's Republic of China, 1 February. At: <http://www.people.com.cn/>

Hunyin dengji tiaoli [Marriage registration regulations] (2003) State Council of the People's Republic of China, 1 October. At: <http://www.gov.cn/>.

Hyde, S. (2001) 'Sex tourism practices on the periphery: Eroticizing ethnicity and pathologizing sex on the Lancang', in N. Chen, C. D. Clark, S. Z. Gottschang, and L. Jeffery (eds), China Urban: Ethnographies and Contemporary Culture, Durham, NC: Duke University Press, pp. 143–62.

Hyde, S. T. (2007) Eating Spring Rice: The Cultural Politics of AIDS in Southwest China, Berkeley; Los Angeles; London: University of California Press.

Information Office of the State Council of the People's Republic of China (1994a) Chapter 1: Historic liberation of Chinese women, in The Situation of Chinese Women. At: <http://www.china.org.cn/>.

Information Office of the State Council of the People's Republic of China (1994b) 'Equal status in marriage and family life' White Paper on Women. At: <http://www.china.org.cn/>.

Institute of Sexuality and Gender (2007) 'Di yi jie Zhongguo 'xing' yanjiu guoji yantao hui' [First International Symposium on 'Sex' Research in China], Institute of Sexuality and Gender, Renmin University, 18–20 June. At: <http://www.sex-study.org/>.

Institute of Sexuality and Gender (2009) 'Xing yu shehui fazhan' [Sex and Social Development], Second International Symposium, Institute of Sexuality and Gender, Renmin University. At: <http://www.sex-study.org/>.

Institute of Sexuality and Gender (2011) 'Di san jie Zhongguo xing yanjiu guoji xueshu yantaohui richeng' [Schedule of the Third International Symposium on Sex Research in China], 'Quanli yu duoyuan' [Sexual Rights and Diversity] (Institute of Sexuality and Gender, Renmin University, 21–3 June. At: <http://www.sex-study.org/>.

Institute of Sexuality and Gender (2013) 'Zouxiang "xingfu"' [Toward Sexual Happiness], Fourth International Symposium, Institute of Sexuality and Gender, Renmin University. At: <http://www.sex-study.org/>.

Jeffreys, E. (2007) 'Querying queer theory: Debating male–male prostitution in the Chinese media', Critical Asian Studies 39/1: 151–75.

Jeffreys, E. (2008) 'Advanced producers or moral polluters? China's bureaucrat-entrepreneurs and sexual corruption', in D. S. G. Goodman (ed.), The New Rich in China, Future Rulers, Present Lives, Abingdon, Oxon; New York: Routledge, pp. 229–44.

Jeffreys, E. (2009 [2006]) 'Introduction: Talking sex and sexuality in China', in E. Jeffreys (ed.), Sex and Sexuality in China, Abingdon, Oxon: Routledge, pp. 1–20.

Jeffreys, E. (2012a [2004]) China, Sex and Prostitution, London; New York: RoutledgeCurzon.

Jeffreys, E. (2012b) *China's Prostitution Scandals: Policing, Media and Society*, Abingdon, Oxon: Routledge.

Jeffreys, E. and Huang, Y. (2011 [2009]) 'Governing sexual health in the People's Republic of China', in E. Jeffreys (ed.), *China's Governmentalities: Governing Change, Changing Government*, Abingdon, Oxon; New York: Routledge, pp. 151–73.

Jeffreys, E. and Sigley, G. (2011 [2009]) 'Governmentality, governance and China', in E. Jeffreys (ed.), *China's Governmentalities: Governing Change, Changing Government*, Abingdon, Oxon: Routledge, pp. 1–23.

Jeffreys, E. and Su, G. (2011) 'China's 100 Per Cent Condom Use Program: Customising the Thai experience', *Asian Studies Review* 35: 315–33.

Ji Ruijie (2009) 'Jinrong weijixia maiyin hefahua zheng dangshi' [The financial crisis: It's the optimum time to legalize prostitution], *Boke.com*, 12 January, reprinted in *Xiaojie*, No. 549, 24 February. At: <http://www.sexstudy.org/>.

Jiang Hongyan (2006) *Ershi shiji xifang wenxue piping lilun yu Zhongguo dangdai wenxue guankui* [Twentieth Century Western Literary Criticism Theory and Contemporary Chinese Literature Perspective], Chengdu: Sichuan Daxue Chubanshe.

Jiang, S. (2013) 'In China, activists fight for gay marriage', *CNN*, 30 June. At: <http://edition.cnn.com/>.

Jiang Xiaoyuan (1995) *Xingzhanglixia de Zhongguoren* [*Chinese People Living in a State of Sexual Tension*], Shanghai: Shanghai Renmin Chubanshe.

Jiangsu ji kong zhongxin xiang xiaojie xuanchuan fang ai bei zhi moren maiyin hefa' [Some people believe that Jiangsu police giving working girls education on how to prevent diseases is equivalent to saying the selling and buying of sex is lawful] (2006) *Nanjing Chenbao*, 18 October.

Jin Yan, Lei Jing and Wu Po (2002) 'Shaonü maiyin wenti diaocha: Shenti chengle shangpin jinxing maimai' [An investigation into female youth prostitution: Their bodies become the goods they sell] (2002) *Sanlian Shenghuo Zhoukan*, 9 January.

'Jiuyue wuri qi, Chongqing shi maiyinpiaochang hefale?' [From September 2006, is the selling and buying of sex legal in Chongqing City?' (2006) *Chongqing Chenbao*, 9 September.

Johnson, K. A. (1983) 'The 1950 Marriage Law: Popular resistance and organizational neglect', in K. A. Johnson, *Women, the Family and Peasant Revolution in China*, Chicago; London: University of Chicago Press, pp. 115–37.

Joint United Nations Programme on HIV/AIDS (UNAIDS) (2010) *Getting to Zero: 2011–2015 Strategy*. At: <http://www.unaids.org/>.

Kam, L. Y. L. (2010) 'Opening up marriage: Married lalas in Shanghai', in C. Yau (eds) *As Normal as Possible: Negotiating Sexuality and Gender in*

Mainland China and Hong Kong, Hong Kong: Hong Kong University Press, 87–102.

Kam, L. Y. L. (2013) *Shanghai Lalas: Female Tongzhi Communities and Politics in Urban China*, Hong Kong: Hong Kong University Press.

Kam, L. Y. L. (2014) 'The demand for a normal life: Marriage and its discontents in contemporary China', in M. McLelland and V. Mackie (eds) *Routledge Handbook of Sexuality Studies in East Asia*, Abingdon, Oxon: Routledge, pp. 77–86.

Kang, W. (2009) *Obsession: Male Same-Sex Relations in China, 1900–1950*, Hong Kong: Hong Kong University Press.

Kaufman, J. (2010) 'Turning points in China's AIDS response', *China: An International Journal* 8/1: 63–84.

Kinsey, A. C., Pomeroy, W. B. and Martin, C. E. (1998a [1948]) *Sexual Behavior in the Human Male*, Bloomington, IN: Indiana University Press.

Kinsey, A. C., Pomeroy, W. B., Martin, C. E., and Gebhard, P. H. (1998b [1953]) *Sexual Behavior in the Human Female*, Bloomington, IN: Indiana University Press.

Kipnis, A. (2006) 'Suzhi: A keyword approach', *China Quarterly* 186: 295–313.

Kolodny, R. C., Masters, W. H. and Johnson, V. E. (1979) *Textbook of Sexual Medicine*, University of Michigan, MI: Little Brown.

Kong, T. S. K. (2010a) *Chinese Homosexualities: Memba, Tongzhi and Golden Boy*, Abingdon, Oxon; New York: Routledge.

Kong, T. S. K. (2010b) 'Outcast bodies: Money, sex and desire of money boys in mainland China', in C. Yau (ed.) *As Normal as Possible: Negotiating Sexuality and Gender in Mainland China and Hong Kong*, Hong Kong: Hong Kong University Press, pp. 17–35.

Kuan, H. C. K. and Brosseau, M. (1992) *China Review 1992*, Hong Kong: The Chinese University Press.

Lagervist, J. (2006) *After the Internet, Before Democracy: Competing Norms in Chinese Media and Society*, Bern: Peter Lang.

Latham, K. (2007) *Pop Culture CHINA! Media, Arts, and Lifestyle*, Santa Barbara, CA: ABC CLIO.

Lau, S. (2010) 'Homosexuality in China', *US-China Today*, 10 March. At: <http://www.uschina.usc.edu/>.

Lavely, W. (1991) 'Marriage and mobility under rural collectivism', in R. S. Watson and P. B. Ebrey (eds), *Marriage and Inequality in Chinese Society*, Berkeley, CA: University of California Press, pp. 286–312.

Law of the People's Republic of China on the Protection of Minors (1991) Adopted at the Twenty-first Meeting of the Standing Committee of the Seventh National People's Congress on 4 September 1991, promulgated by

Order No. 50 of the President of the People's Republic of China on 4 September 1991, effective 1 January 1992. At: <http://www.unescap.org/>.

Law of the People's Republic of China on Protection of the Rights and Interests of the Elderly (1996) Adopted at the Twenty first Meeting of the Standing Committee of the Eighth National People's Congress on 29 August 1996, and promulgated by Order No. 73 of the President of the People's Republic of China on 29 August 1996. At: <http://www.china.org.cn/>.

Les Sky (2011) 'Xinghun, jiushi yi chang emeng' [Marriage is a nightmare], Douban.com, 20 September. At: <www.douban.com/>.

Leung, H. (2008) *Undercurrents: Queer Culture and Postcolonial Hong Kong*, Vancouver: University of British Columbia Press.

Leung, M. W. H. (2008) 'On sale in express package', in K. E. Kuah-Pearce (ed.), *Chinese Women and the Cyberspace*, ICAS publication series: Amsterdam University Press, pp. 223–48.

Li Daqing (1994) 'Xing jiaoyu tupo zuihou de jinqu' [Breaking through the final barrier to sex education], *Keji Ribao*, 20 November.

Li, F. (2006) 'AIDS lecture sparks prostitution row', *China Daily*, 17 October.

Li Ling (1993) *Zhongguo fang shu kao* [Textual Research on Chinese Divination Methods], Beijing: Zhongguo Renmin Chubanshe.

Li, L., Wu, Z., Rotheram-Borus, M. J., Guan, J., Yin, Y., Detels, R., Wu, S., Lee, S.-J., Cao, H., Lin, C., Rou, K., Liu, Z. and the NIMH Collaborative HIV/STD Prevention Trial Group (2009) 'Visiting entertainment venues and sexual health in China', *Archives of Sexual Behavior* 38/5: 814–20.

Li Yinhe (1996) *Zhongguo nüxingde xing yu ai* [Sexuality and Love of Chinese Women], Hong Kong: Oxford University Press.

Li Yinhe (ed.) (1997) *Funü: Zuimanchang de geming, dangdai xifang nüxingzhuyi lilun jingxuan* [Women, the Longest Revolution: Selected Contemporary Western Feminist Theories], Beijing: Sanlian Shudian Chubanshe.

Li Yinhe (1998a) *Nüelian yawenhua* [Subculture of Sadomasochism], Beijing: Zhongguo Jinri Chubanshe.

Li Yinhe (1998b) *Zhongguo nüxing de qinggan yu xing* [Sexuality and Love of Chinese Women], Beijing: Zhongguo Jinri Chubanshe.

Li Yinhe (1998c) *Tongxinglian yawenhua* [Subculture of Homosexuality], Beijing: Zhongguo Jinri Chubanshe.

Li Yinhe (2001) *Fuke yu xing* [Foucault and Sexuality], Shandong: Shandong Renmin Chubanshe.

Li Yinhe (ed.) (2002a) *Ku'er lilun: Xifang liushiniandai xing sichao* [Queer Theory: Western Theories on Sexuality in the 1990s], Beijing: Shishi Chubanshe.

Li Yinhe (ed.) (2002b) *Xifang xingxue mingzhu zhaiyao* [Western Sexology: Summaries of Famous Works], Jiangxi: Jiangxi Renmin Chubanshe.

Li Yinhe (blog) (2006a) 'Guanyu caifang shoufei' [On interview fees], *Sina.com*, 10 March. At: <http://blog.sina.com.cn/>.

Li Yinhe (blog) (2006b) 'Taiyuan yinhui wangzhan an zhiyi' [The challenges posed by the Taiyuan obscenity case], *Sina.com*, 23 March. At: <http://blog.sina.com.cn/>.

Li Yinhe (blog) (2006c) 'Wang liao maiyin wenti' [Web chat on the problem of prostitution], *Sina.com*, 4 December. At: <http://blog.sina.com.cn/>.

Li Yinhe (blog) (2006d) 'Xingquanli san yuanze' [Three principles of sexual rights], *Sina.com*, 16 August. At: <http://blog.sina.com.cn/>.

Li Yinhe (blog) (2007) 'Tongxing hunyin ti'an' [Same-sex marriage proposal], *Sina.com*, 26 January. At: <http://blog.sina.com.cn>.

Li Yinhe (2008) 'Di ershiqi jie: Zhongguo dangdai xingfalü pipan' [Section 27: Criticizing present-day China's sex laws], in Li Yinhe, *Xing, Aiqing ji Qita: Li Yinhe Zixuanji* [*Sex, Love and The Rest: Li Yinhe's Selected Works*], Inner Mongolia: Neimenggu Daxue Chubanshe. At: <http://book.qq.com/>.

Li Yinhe (2010) *Kuerlun* [*Queer Theory*], Beijing: Jishi Chubanshe.

Li Yinhe (blog) (2010a) 'Dui feichu juzhongyinluan fa ti'an de jidian jieshi' [Explaining my proposal to repeal the law against group licentiousness], *Sina.com*, 5 March. At: <http://blog.sina.com.cn/>.

Li Yinhe (blog) (2010b) 'Jianyi quxiao yinhuipinzui' [Proposal to abolish crimes relating to obscene merchandise], *Sina.com*, 19 March. At: <http://blog.sina.com.cn>.

Li Yinhe (blog) (2010c) 'Maiyinfunü gaicheng shizufunü shi zhongda jinbu [The renaming of 'women who sell sex' as 'women who have lost their footing' is a significant advancement], *Sina.com*, 17 December. At: <http://blog.sina.com.cn/>.

Li Yinhe (blog) (2010d) 'Quexiao juzhongyinluanzui hui baihuai shehui fengqi ma?' [Will rescinding the crime of group licentiousness harm society?], *Sina.com*, 7 April. At: <http://blog.sina.com.cn/>.

Li Yinhe (blog) (2010e) 'Shiqing zhengzai bian de yue lai yue huangdan' [Things are becoming more and more absurd], *Sina.com*, 24 March. At: <http://blog.sina.com.cn/>.

Li Yinhe (blog) (2010f) 'Zenyang jiejue maiyin wenti' [How to solve the problem of prostitution], *Sina.com*, 7 August. At: <http://blog.sina.com.cn/>.

Li Yinhe (blog) (2010g) 'Zhongguo zai tongxinglian wenti shang "qi da zao, gan wan ji"' [China got in early on homosexual issues, but has yet to deliver the goods], *Sina.com*, 1 July. At: <http://blog.sina.com.cn/>.

Li Yinhe (blog) (2010h) 'Zuihou de yanxingjunfa' [The last draconian law], *Sina.com*, 21 May. At: <http://blog.sina.com.cn/>.

Li Yinhe (2011) 'Lü Liping ni yinggai fansi' [Lü Liping, be reflective], Li Yinhe de geren kongjian [Li Yinhe's personal space], *Ifeng.com*, 6 July. At: <http://blog.ifeng.com/>.

Li Yinhe (blog) (2011a) 'Nan tongxinglian jiankang zhuangkuang ling ren youlu' [People are concerned about the health of male homosexuals], *Sina.com*, 9 July. At: <http://blog.sina.com.cn/>.

Li Yinhe (blog) (2011b) 'Pizhun tongxing hunyin jiang dada tisheng Zhongguo de guoji xingxiang' [Sanctioning same-sex marriage will greatly enhance China's international image], *Sina.com*, 26 February. At: <http://blog.sina.com.cn/>.

Li Yinhe (blog) (2011c) 'Yingdang zenyang kandai maiyin zhe jian shi' [How should we treat the matter of prostitution?], *Sina.com*, 16 February. At: <http://blog.sina.com.cn/>.

Li Yinhe and Wang Xiaobo (1992) *Tamen de shijie: Zhongguo nan tongxinglian qunluo toushi* [*Their World: An Examination of the Male Homosexual Community in China*], Taiyuan: Shanxi Renmin Chubanshe.

'Li Yinhe de boke' [Li Yinhe's blog] (2014) *Sina.com*. At: <http://blog.sina.com.cn/>.

'Li Yinhe tongxing hunyin ti'an' [Li Yinhe's same-sex marriage proposal] (2011) *Netease.com*, February. At: <http://blog.sina.com.cn>.

'Li Yinhe' (2011) *Baidu.com*. At: <http://baike.baidu.com/>.

'Li Yinhe' (2012) *Sina.com*. At: <http://vip.book.sina.com.cn/>.

Li Yunhong (2009) 'Chi Susheng: Tiyi zhendui "anchang" lifa' [Chi Susheng: Proposal to make 'prostitutes' legal], *Qzone.qq.com*. At: <http://user.qzone.qq.com/>.

Li, Y. (2009 [2006]) 'Regulating male same-sex relationships in the People's Republic of China', in E. Jeffreys (ed.), *Sex and Sexuality in China*, Abingdon, Oxon: Routledge, pp. 82–101.

Li Zidong (2011) 'Renkou yu jihua shengyu xuanchuan kouhao' [Population and family planning publicity slogans], National Population and Planning Commission of Yongcheng, 2 October. At: <http://www.ycsrkjsw.gov.cn/>.

'Life expectancy rises in China' (2012) Xinhua, 9 August. At: <http://news.xinhuanet.com/>.

'Life is too good' (2007) United Nations Development Program: China, 6 December. At: <http://www.undp.org.cn/>.

Lim, S. H. (2006) *Celluloid Comrades: Representations of Male Homosexuality in Contemporary Chinese Cinemas*, Honolulu: University of Hawai'i Press.

Lin, C., Li, L., Wu, Z., Guan, J., Xu, Y., Wu, D., Lieber, E., Rotheram-Borus, M. J. and the NIMH Collaborative HIV/STD Prevention Trial Group (2010) 'Entertainment venue visiting and commercial sex in China', *International Journal of Sexual Health* 22/1: 5–13.

Link, E. P. (2000) *The Uses of Literature: Life in the Socialist Chinese Literary System*, Princeton, NJ: Princeton University Press.

Liu Dalin (1988) *Xing shehuixue* [*The Sociology of Sex*], Jinan: Shandong Renmin Chubanshe.

Liu Dalin (1993) *Zhongguo gudai xingwenhua* [*Sexual Culture in Ancient China*], Yinchuan: Ningxia Renmin Chubanshe.

Liu, D. (1997) *Sexual Behaviour in Modern China*, London; New York: Continuum.

Liu Dalin, Ng, M. L., Zhou Liping and Haeberle, E. J. (1992) *Zhongguo dangdai xingwenhua: Zhongguo liangwanlie 'xingwenming' diaocha baogao* [*Contemporary Chinese Sexual Culture: Report of the 'Sex Civilisation' Survey on 20,000 People*], Shanghai, Sanlian Shudian.

Liu, F. (2011) *Urban Youth in China: Modernity, the Internet and the Self*, Abingdon, Oxon: Routledge.

Liu, L. and Liu, H. (2008) 'Boundary-crossing through cyberspace', in K. E. Kuah-Pearce (ed.), *Chinese Women and the Cyberspace*, ICAS publication series/Amsterdam University Press, pp. 249–70.

Liu, L. H. (1991) 'The female tradition in modern Chinese Literature: Negotiating feminisms across east/west boundaries', *Gender* 12: 22–44.

Liu, M. (2011) *Migration, Prostitution, and Human Trafficking: The Voice of Chinese Women*, New Brunswick; London: Transaction Publishers.

Liu, M. (2012) 'Speaking the unspeakable: An exploratory study of college women's sex communication in Shanghai, China', *Asian Journal of Communication* 22/2: 197–213.

Lu Xin (2007) 'Jiehun xiaofei diaocha wenjuan fabu: Jin 6 cheng xinren yusuan zai 2 wan yishang' [Marriage consumer survey released: Nearly 60 per cent of couples spend more than CNY 20,000], *Jing Yule Xinbao*, 5 March. At: <http://finance.sina.com.cn/>.

Lü, X. (2010) 'Rethinking China's new documentary movement: engagement with the social', in C. Berry, X. Lü and L. Rofel (eds), *The New Chinese Documentary Film Movement: For the Public Record*, Hong Kong: Hong Kong University Press, pp. 15–48.

Lu Yilong (2002) '1949 nian hou de Zhongguo huji zhidu: Jiegou yu bianqian' [The structure of and changes to China's household registration system after 1949], *Journal of Peking University* 39/2: 123–30.

'Lun maiyin buneng hefahua de zhenzheng yuanyin' [The real reason why prostitution cannot be legalized] (2004) *Taihaiwang*, 24 February. At: <http://bbs.taihainet.com/>.

Lynch, D. (2003) 'Move over Mao, today's Chinese revolution is sexual', *USA Today*, 15 September.

Ma Yiqun (2013) 'Shenme tuigao le hunyin chengben?' [What makes getting married so expensive?], *Xin Hangkong/New Air* (Air China inflight magazine) 8: 76–8.

McLaren, A. E. (2007) 'Online Intimacy in a Chinese setting', *Asian Studies Review* 31/4: 409–22.

McMillan, J. (2004) 'Doing it by the book: Natural tales of marriage and sex in contemporary Chinese marriage manuals', *Sex Education: Sexuality, Society and Learning* 4/3: 203–15.

McMillan, J. (2009 [2005]) *Sex, Science and Morality in China*, Abingdon, Oxon: Routledge.

Mann, J. M. and Tarantola, D. J. M. (1996) *AIDS in the World II*, New York: Oxford University Press.

Marriage Law of the People's Republic of China (1980) Adopted at the Third Session of the Fifth National People's Congress and promulgated by Order No. 9 of the Chairman of the Standing Committee of the National People's Congress on 10 September 1980, effective 1 January 1981. At: <http://www.unescap.org/>.

Mian, M. (2002) *Candy*, trans. A. Lingenfelter, New York: Little Brown.

Micollier, E. (2005) 'Aids in China: Discourses on sexuality and sexual practices', *Chinese Perspectives* 60: 2–14.

Micollier, E. (2012) 'Sexualised illness and gendered narratives: The problematic of social sciences and humanities in China's HIV and AIDS governance', *International Journal of Asia Pacific Studies* 8/1: 103–24.

Miège, P. (2009) '"In my opinion, most Tongzhi are dutiful sons!": Community, social norms, and construction of identity among young homosexuals in Hefei, Anhui Province', *China Perspectives* 1: 40–53.

Miller, T. (2006) 'Boys flocking to be "ducks" for China's bored housewives', *Observer*, 7 May 2006.

Milwertz, C. (2003) 'Activism against domestic violence in the People's Republic of China', *Violence Against Women* 9: 630–54.

Min, A. (2009 [1994]) *Red Azalea*, London: Bloomsbury Publishing.

Ministry of Health of the People's Republic of China (2012) '2012 China AIDS response progress report', 31 March. At: <http://www.unaids.org/>.

Moore, R. L. (2005) 'Generation *ku*: Individualism and China's millennial youth', *Ethnology* 44/4: 357–76.

Mu, G. (2013) 'Family policy deserves a rethink', *China Daily*, 15 August, p. 9.

Mu Haiyan and Xue Ming (2006) Haerbin jikong zhongxin gongkai peixun nüxing xinggongzuozhe yufang aizibing' [Harbin's CDC staff openly train female sex workers about HIV prevention], *Haerbin Ribao*, 15 October. At: <http://news.163.com/>.

'Nanjing fujiaoshou Ma Xiaohai zuzhi "huan youxi" shexian juzhongyinluanzui' [Associate Professor Ma Xiaohai's organization for 'swinger's parties' is suspected of engaging in the crime of 'group licentiousness'] (2010) *Szinfo.com*, 25 March. At: <http://jh.szinfo.com/>.

'New campaign targets gender ratio imbalance' (2011) *Global Times*, 17 August. At: <http://english.peopledaily.com>.

Noble, J. S. (2012) 'Youth culture in China: Idols, sex, and the Internet,' in T. B. Weston and L. M. Jensen (eds), *China in and Beyond the Headlines*, Lanham, MD: Rowman and Littlefield Publishers, pp. 50–68.

Oleson, A. (2011) 'China's abortion numbers grow,' *The Washington Times*, 13 January. At: <http://www.washingtontimes.com/>.

Palmer, J. (2013) 'The *balinghou*,' *Aeron Magazine*, 7 March. At: <http://www.aeonmagazine.com/>.

Pan Guangdan (1986) *Xingxinlixue* [*Psychology of Sex*], Beijing: Sanlian Shudian.

Pan Suiming (1988) *Shenmi de shenghuo – xing de shehui shi* [*The Mysterious Flame – A History of Sex*], Henan Renmin Chubanshe.

Pan Suiming (trans.) (1989) *Jinxi baogao – renlei nanxing xingxingwei* [*Kinsey Report: Sexual Behavior in the Human Male*], Beijing: Guangming Ribao Chubanshe.

Pan Suiming (trans.) (1990) *Nüxing xingxingwei – Jinxi baogao xupian* [*Kinsey Report: Sexual Behavior in the Human Female*], Beijing: Tuanjie Chubanshe.

Pan Suiming (1995) *Zhongguo xing xianzhuang – Pan Suiming xingxue zhuanti* [*Sex in China: Selected Topics by Pan Suiming*], Guangming Ribao Chubanshe.

Pan Suiming (1998a) *Xing, ni zhen dongle ma? 21 shiji xingxue duben* [*Sex, Do you Really Understand It? A Twenty-First Century Sexology Reader*], Zhongguo Jiancha Chubanshe.

Pan Suiming (1998b) *Zhongguo xingxue baikequanshu? Xingshehuixue juan* [*An Encyclopaedia of Chinese Sexology? Sexological Sociology Volume*], Zhongguo Dabaike Chubanshe.

Pan Suiming (1999) *Cunzai yu huangmiu – Zhongguo dixia xingchanye kaocha* [*Existence and Absurdity: A Study of China's Underground Sex Industry*], Guangzhou: Qunyan Chubanshe.

Pan Suiming (2000) *Shengcun yu tiyan, dui yige hongdengqu de zhuizong kaocha* [*Survival and Experience: Observational Study of a Red-light District in China*], Beijing: Zhongguo Shehuikexue Chubanshe.

Pan Suiming (ed.) (2005) *Zhongguo 'xing' yanjiu de qidian yu shiming* [*Discussion and Construction of the Concept 'Xing' [Sex]: The Elements and Mission of Sexuality Research in Contemporary China*], Gaoxiong: Wanyou Chubanshe.

Pan, S. (2002) 'Interview: Rough trade, rough justice', *China Development Brief*, 1 June. At: <http://www.chinadevelopmentbrief.com/>.

Pan Suiming (2006) *Zhongguo xinggeming zonglun* [*Discussing China's Sex Revolution*], Gaoxiong, Taiwan: Wanyou Chubanshe.

Pan Suiming (2007a) 'Jujue "xing" de zhengzhihua' [Stop politicizing 'sex'] (blog), *Sina.com*, 14 September. At: <http://www.blog.sina.com>.

Pan Suiming (2007b) Zhongguoren de xingxingwei yu xingguangxi: lishi fazhan 2000–2006 [Chinese people's sexual behaviours and sexual relations: Historical development 2000–2006], Ford Foundation, 11 May. At: <http://blog.sina.com>.

Pan Suiming (2008) 'Fansi "jinchang" zhengce' [Rethinking the policy of 'banning prostitution'] (blog), *Sina.com*, 13 September. At: <://www.blog.sina.com>.

Pan, S. (2009 [2006]) 'Transformations in the primary life cycle: The origins and nature of China's sexual revolution, in E. Jeffreys (ed.), *Sex and Sexuality in China*, Abingdon, Oxon: Routledge, pp. 21–42.

Pan Suiming and Huang Yingying (2005a) *Qingjing yu ganwu: Xinan Zhongguo sange hongdengqu* [*Situation and Inspiration: An Ethnographic Study of Three Red-Light Districts in Southwest China*], Gaoxiong, Taiwan: Wanyou Chubanshe.

Pan Suiming and Huang Yingying (2005b) *Chengxian yu biaoding: Zhongguo xiaojie shen yanjiu* [*Performance and Labelling: An In-Depth Study of China's 'Working Girls'*], Gaoxiong, Taiwan: Wanyou Chubanshe.

Pan Suiming and Yang Rui (2004) *Xing'ai Shinian: Quanguo Daxuesheng Xingxingwei de Zhuizong Diaocha* [*Ten Years of Sex and Love: A Follow-up Investigation of Chinese College Students' Sexual Behaviours*], Beijing: Shehuikexuewenxian Chubanshe.

Pan Suiming and Zeng Jing (2000) *Zhongguo dangdai daxuesheng de xing guannian yu xing xingwei* [*Sexual Concepts and Sexual Behaviors of College Students in Contemporary China*], Beijing: Shangwu Yin Shuguan.

Pan Suiming, Wang Aili, Parish, W. and Lauman, E. (2004) *Dangdai Zhongguoren de Xingxingwei yu Xingguanxi* [*Sexual Behaviour and Relation in Contemporary China*], Beijing: Shehuikexuewenxian Chubanshe.

Pan Suiming: Meiti zui guanxin shenme huati?' [Pan Suiming: What sex-related topics are the media most concerned about?] (2009) *Ifeng.com*, 4 September. At: <http://www.qisehuayuan.com/>.

'Pansuimingwww.sex-study.org' (2014) *Sina.com*. At: <http://blog.sina.com.cn/>.

Pei, Y. and Ho, S-Y. (2008) 'Sex and life politics formed through the Internet', in K. E. Kuah-Pearce (ed.), *Chinese Women and the Cyberspace*, ICAS publication series: Amsterdam University Press, pp. 203–22.

Pei, Y., Ho, P. and Ng, M. L. (2007) 'Studies on women's sexuality in China since 1980: A critical review', *Journal of Sex Research* 44/2: 202–12.

Policy Research and Information Division of the National Center for AIDS/ STD Control and Prevention, China CDC International Labour Office for China and Mongolia (2011) HIV and AIDS Related Employment Discrimination in China, International Labour Organization, 28 June. At: <http:// www.ilo.org/>.

Pomfret, J. (2003) 'A new gloss on freedom: Sexual revolution sweeps China's urban youth', *Washington Post*, 6 December. At: <http://www.highbeam.com/>.

Population Census Office under the State Council and the Department of Population and Employment Statistics, the National Bureau of Statistics (2012a) Zhongguo 2010 nian renkou pucha ziliao (shangce) [Tabulation on the 2010 Population Census of the People's Republic of China (Book I)], Beijing: China Statistics Press.

Population Census Office under the State Council and the Department of Population and Employment Statistics, the National Bureau of Statistics (2012b) Zhongguo 2010 nian renkou pucha ziliao (xiace) [Tabulation on the 2010 Population Census of the People's Republic of China (Book III)], Beijing: China Statistics Press.

'Prostitution thriving in Tibet as authorities look the other way' (2005) *AFP*, 1 September. At: <http://www.phayul.com/>.

Public Security Bureau of Beijing (1998) *Beijing fengbi jiyuan jishi* [*The True Story of the Closing of Beijing's Brothels*], Beijing: Zhongguo Heping Chubanshe.

Qiu Yulan and Wang Yequan (2006) 'Jiangsu jikong zhongxin jiaodao "xiaojie" youpian keren dai anquantao' [Jiangsu Centre for Disease Control and Prevention instructs 'working girls' on how to coax clients into using condoms], *Zhongguo Jiangsuwang*, 18 October. At: <http://www.news.qianlong.com/>.

Quanguo renda changweihui, xingfashi, fazhi gongzuo weiyuanhui [Criminal Law Office and the Legal Council of the Standing Committee of the National People's Congress] (1991) *Guanyu yanjin maiyinpiaochang de jueding he guanyu yancheng guaimai banjia funü, ertong de fanzui fenzi de jueding shiyi* [An explanation of the decision on strictly forbidding the selling and buying of sex and the decision on the severe punishment of criminals who abduct and traffic in or kidnap women and children], Beijing: Zhongguo Jiancha Chubanshe.

Quanguo renda changwu weiyuanhui [Standing Committee of the National People's Congress] (2005) Zhonghua renmin gongheguo zhian guanli chufa fa [Public Security Administrative Punishments Law of the People's Republic of China]. At: <http://news.xinhuanet.com/>.

Radio Free Asia (RFA) (2013) 'Zhongguo tongxinglian zhuangkuang diaocha – wo shi "la la"' [Survey of the situation of homosexuals in China – I am lesbian], 7 November. At: <http://www.rfa.org/>.

'Richeng biao: "Zouxiang xing fu" – di si jie Zhongguo xing yanjiu guoji yantao hui' [Schedule: 'Towards sexual pleasure', The Fourth International Symposium on Chinese Sexuality Studies] Institute of Sexuality and Gender (2013) Renmin University, Beijing, China, 24 June. At: <http://www.sex-study.org/>.

Riley, N. E. (2004) 'China's population: New trends and challenges', *Population Bulletin*, 59/2: 3–36. At: <http://www.prb.org/>.

Roberts, I. D. (2010) 'China's Internet celebrity: Furong Jiejie', in L. P. Edwards and E. Jeffreys (eds), *Celebrity in China*, Hong Kong: Hong Kong University Press, pp. 217–36.

Rofel, L. (1999) 'Qualities of desire: Imagining gay identities in China', *GLQ: A Journal of Lesbian and Gay Studies* 5/4: 451–74.

Rofel, L. (2007) *Desiring China: Experiments in Neoliberalism, Sexuality, and Public Culture*, Durham, NC: Duke University Press.

Rofel, L. (2010) 'The traffic in money boys', *positions: East Asia Cultures Critique* 18/2: 425–58.

Rojanapithayakorn, W. (2006) 'The 100% condom use programme in Asia'. *Reproductive Health Matters* 14/28: 41–52.

Rosenthal, E. (1999) 'Seriously, China learning sex is fun', *New York Times*, 11 April.

Rothman, A. and Wang, F. (2013) 'After the one-child policy', *CLSA Speaker Series: China Economics*, 13 May.

Ruan Fangfu (1985) *Xing zhishi shouce* [Handbook of Sexual Knowledge], Beijing: Kexuejishuwenxian Chubanshe.

Ruan, F. (1991) *Sex in China: Studies in Sexology in Chinese Culture*, New York: Plenum Press.

Ruan, F. F. and Bullough, V. L. (1992) 'Lesbianism in China', *Archives of Sexual Behaviors* 21/3: 217–26.

Sang, T. D. (2003) *The Emerging Lesbian: Female Same-Sex Desire in Modern China*, Chicago; London: University of Chicago Press.

Scharping, T. (2003) *Birth Control in China 1949–2000: Population Control and Demographic Development*, Abingdon, Oxon: Routledge.

Schein, L. (1997) 'Gender and internal orientalism in China', *Modern China* 23/1: 69–98.

Settle, E. (2003) *AIDS in China: An Annotated Chronology 1985–2003*, China AIDS Survey, 14 November, Monterey, California.

Shan, J. (2012) 'Millions of wives wed to gay men: Expert', *China Daily*, 3 February. At: <http://www.chinadaily.com.cn/>.

Shan, J. (2013a) 'Project focuses on unmarried youths, *China Daily*, 11 July, p. 3.

Shan, J. (2013b) 'Wait a minute baby', *China Daily*, 17 November, p. 1.

'Shanghai: City develops app for contraceptives' (2013) *China Daily*, 12 July, p. 2.

Shea, J. L. (2005) 'Sexual "liberation" and the older woman in contemporary mainland China', *Modern China* 31/1: 115–47.

'Shengnü' (2013) Baidu Baike. At: <http://baike.baidu.com/>.

Shi Chengli (1999) *Dunhuang xingwenhua* [*The Sexual Culture of Dunhuang*], Guangzhou: Guangzhou Chubanshe.

Shi, Y. (2013) 'Eager parents quick to learn marriage lines' and 'Matchmaking: Can't buy me love?', *China Daily*, 22 May, pp. 1 and 6.

Shutong de Gongzi (2011) 'Zhao BF nan, zhao xinghun nan shang nan – huashuo wo de 3 duan xinghun jingli' [It's hard to find a boyfriend, 'cooperative marriage' is really difficult, some words on my three experiences], *Tianya*, 19 January. At: <http://bbs.tianya.cn/>.

Sigley, G. (1998) 'Sex, state and the family: Guest editor's introduction', *Chinese Sociology and Anthropology* 31/1: 3–13.

Sigley, G. and Jeffreys, E. (1999) 'Interview: On "sex" and "sexuality in China: A conversation with Pan Suiming', *Bulletin of Concerned Asian Scholars* 31/1: 50–8.

Sima, Y. and Pugsley, P. C. (2010) 'The rise of a "me culture" in postsocialist China: Youth, individualism and identity creation in the blogosphere', *The International Communication Gazette* 72/3: 287–306.

Sinnot, M. (2010) 'Borders, diaspora, and regional connections: Trends in Asian "queer" studies', *The Journal of Asian Studies* 69/1: 17–31.

Skeldon, R. (2000) 'Population mobility and HIV vulnerability in South-East Asia: An assessment and analysis', a report prepared for the UNDP South East Asia HIV and Development Workshop, Chiang Rai, Thailand, November 1999. At: <http://www.hivdevelopment.org/>.

Sleeboom-Faulkner, M. E. (2011) 'Genetic testing, governance, and the family in the People's Republic of China', *Social Science and Medicine* 72/11: 1805–6.

Smith, C. J. (2005) 'Social geography of sexually transmitted diseases in China: Exploring the role of migration and urbanisation', *Asia Pacific Viewpoint* 46/1: 65–80.

Starr, J. B. (2001) *Understanding China: A Guide to China's Economy, History and Political Structure*, London: Profile Books.

Sun Hao (dir.) (2010) *Shengnü jiayou* [Come on Leftover Women!], Television series, 25 episodes (release date 3 April, broadcast on Hunan TV), China: Guangdong Huaxia Dianshi Chuanbo Youxian Gongsi.

Sun Jin, Deng Yinuo and Qin Li (2009) 'Zhongguo xinggongzuozhe quanyi zhuangkuang diaocha yu fenxi baogao – yi Zhongguo Wuhan jiangdi xinggongzuozhe wei kaocha zhongxin [A survey and analysis of the rights and interests of sex workers in China – a study of low-end sex workers in Wuhan], *Peking University Center for Legal Information*. At: <http://www.article chinalawinfo.com/>.

Sun Yi and Lu Yao (2012) 'Tianjin: Kong guizu guonian bu huijia, pa bei bihun deng cheng zhuyin' [Tianjin: Those who fear to go home for New Year family celebrations are afraid of being forced to marry] *Renminwang*, 20 January. At: <http://www.022net.com/>.

Sun, W. (2010) 'Sex, city, and the maid: Between socialist fantasies and neoliberal parables', *Journal of Current Chinese Affairs* 39/4: 53–69.

Sun, X., Lu, F., Wu, Z., Poundstone, K., Zeng, G., Xu, P., Zhang, D., Liu, K. and Liau, A. (2010) 'Evolution of information-driven HIV/AIDS policies in China', *International Journal of Epidemiology* 39: ii4–ii13.

Sun, Z., Farrer, J. and Choi, K. (2006) 'Sexual identity among men who have sex with men in Shanghai', *China Perspectives*, 64, March/April. At: <http://www.cefc.com>.

Tan, M. (2013) 'Co-operative gay marriage in China', *Dailylife*, 10 July. At: <http://www.dailylife.com>.

Tan, T. (2013) 'Lovebirds separate when the going gets rough', *China Daily*, 7 July, p. 3.

Tanner, M. S. (2005) 'Campaign-style policing in China and its critics', in B. Bakken (ed.), *Crime, Punishment, and Policing in China*, Lanham, MD: Rowman and Littlefield, pp. 171–88.

Taylor, A. (2012) 'China's sexual revolution has reached the point of no return', *Business Insider Australia*, 1 September. At: <http://www.businessinsider.com>.

'The second industrial revolution' (2004) *BBC News*, 11 May. At: <http://news.bbc.co.uk/>.

Tong Ge (2004) 'MSM renqun fangyu AIDS xiangwei ganyu fangfa yanjiu' [MSM (men who have sex with men) behavioural intervention and HIV/AIDS prevention and control study], Beijing Gender Health Education Institution: China-UK HIV/AIDS Prevention and Care Project.

Tong Ge (2007a) *Zhongguo nannan xingjiaoyi zhuangtai diaocha* [Report on Male Sex Workers in China], Beijing: Ji'ande Jiankang Zixun Zhongxin.

Tong Ge (2007b) *Zhongguoren de nannan xingxingwei: xing yu ziwo rentong zhuangtai diaocha* [Report on Men Who Have Sex With Men in China: Sexuality and Self-identity], Ji'ande Jiankang Zixun Zhongxin.

'Tuiguang anquantao fang aizibing yu daji maiyinpiaochang ying xiangfuxiangcheng' [The methods of popularizing the use of condoms to prevent HIV/AIDS and striking hard against prostitution are complementary] (2006) *Xinjing Bao*, 2 December.

UN Theme Group on HIV/AIDS in China (2002) HIV/AIDS China's Titanic Peril, June. At: <http://www.hivpolicy.org/>.

Uretsky, E. (2008) '"Mobile men with money": The socio-cultural and politico-economic context of high-risk behavior among wealthy businessmen and government officials in urban China', *Culture, Health, and Sexuality* 10/8: 801–14.

US Department of State (2009) '2009 Human Right Report: China'. At: <http://www.state.gov>.

Voci, P. (2010) 'Blowup Beijing: The city as a twilight zone', in C. Berry, X. Lü, and L. Rofel (eds), *The New Chinese Documentary Film Movement: For the Public Record*, Hong Kong: Hong Kong University Press, pp. 99–116.

Volp, S. (1994) 'The discourse on male marriage: Li Yu's "A Male Mencius's Mother"', *positions: East Asia Cultures Critique* 2/1: 113–32.

Wan, Y. (2001) 'Becoming a gay activist in contemporary China', in G. Sullivan and P. A. Jackson (eds), *Gay and Lesbian Asia: Culture, Identity, Community*, New York: Harrington Park Press, pp. 47–64.

Wang Anyi (1996) *Chang hen ge* [*The Song of Everlasting Sorrow*], Beijing: Zuojia Chubanshe.

Wang Dazhong (1995) 'Guanyu maiyinpiaochang renyuan de laojiao yu qiangzhi jizhong jiaoyu de wenti' [Some problems concerning the sending of prostitution offenders to education through labour and compelling them to undergo joint detention and education], *Fanzui yu Gaizao* 6: 57.

Wang, P. (2015) *Love and Marriage in Globalizing China*, Abingdon, Oxon: Routledge.

Wang, Q. (2004) 'The ruin is already a new outcome: An interview with Cui Zi'en', *positions: East Asia Cultures Critique* 12/1: 181–94.

Wang, Q. (2012) 'Premarital sex is common, survey finds', *China Daily*, 10 April. At: <http://english.peopledaily.com>.

Wang, Q. and Zhou, Q. (2010) 'China's divorce and remarriage rates: Trends and regional disparities', *Journal of Divorce and Remarriage* 51/4: 257–67.

Wang Wenbin (1981 [1955]) *Xing de zhishi* [*Sexual Knowledge*], Beijing: Renmin Weisheng Chubanshe.

Wang, Y. (2013) 'Chinese migrant workers exceed 260 mln by 2012, Xinhua, 27 May. At: <http://news.xinhuanet.com/>.

Wang, Z. (2006) 'Free speech? You have to pay', *China Daily*, 4 April. At: <http://www.chinadaily.com.cn/>.

Weber, I. (2002) '*Shanghai Baby*: Negotiating youth self-identity in urban China', *Social Identities: Journal for the Study of Race, Nation and Culture* 8/2: 347–68.

Wei Hong (1986) 'Zhanwang yijiubaliunian tushu shichang chuban yu faxing' [An overview of the 1986 book market: publishing and distribution], *Chuban Faxing Yanjiu* 1: 49–52. At: <http://www.cnki.com.cn/>.

Wei Hui (1999) *Shanghai baobei* [*Shanghai Baby*], Shenyang: Chunfeng Wenyi.

Weishengbu bangongting, jiaoyubu bangongting [Office of the Ministry of Health, Office of the Ministry of Education] (2007) 'Weishengbu bangongting, jiaoyubu bangongting guanyu yinfa "Qingshaonian yufang aizibing jiben zhishi" de tongzhi' [Notice of the Office of the Ministries of Health and Education, 'Basic Knowledge of HIV/AIDS Prevention for Youth'], 25 May. At: <http://www.moh.gov.cn/>.

Werff, T. (2008) 'The struggle of the tongzhi homosexuality in China and the position of Chinese "comrades"', in I. Dubel and A. Hielkema (eds), *Urgency Required: Gay and Lesbian Rights are Human Rights*. At: <http://www.hivos.net/>.

'What does the UN mean by "youth," and how does this definition differ from that given to children?' (n.d.) United Nations, Department of Economic and Social Affairs, Youth, Social Policy and Development Division. At: <http://undesadspd.org/>.

Whyte, M. K. and Parish, W. L. (1984) *Urban Life in Contemporary China*, Chicago: University of Chicago Press.

Wolffers, I. and Fernandez, I. (1995) 'Migration and AIDS', *Lancet* 346: 1303–4.

Wong, F. Y., Z. J. Huang, N. He, B. D. Smith, Y. Gin, C. Fu, and D. Young (2008) 'HIV Risks among gay- and non-gay-identified migrant boys in Shanghai, China', *AIDS Care* 20/2: 170–80.

Woo, M. Y. K. (2009 [2006]) 'Contesting citizenship: Marriage and divorce in the People's Republic of China', in E. Jeffreys (ed.), *Sex and Sexuality in China*, London: New York: RoutledgeCurzon, pp. 62–81.

Wu Jieping (1982) *Xingyixue* [*Sexual Medicine*], Beijing: Kexuejishuwenxian Chubanshe.

Wu, J. (2003) 'From "Long Yang" and "Dui Shi" to tongzhi: Homosexuality in China', *Journal of Gay & Lesbian Psychotherapy* 7/1–2: 117–43.

Wu Mindong (2006) '"Xiaojie xuexi ban": maiyin hefa' ['Working girl' training class: Is selling and buying sex lawful?], *Nanfang Luntan*, 18 October. At: <http://www.southcn.com/>.

Wu, W. and Wang, X. (2011) 'Lost in virtual carnival and masquerade: In-game marriage on the Chinese Internet', in D. K. Herold and P. Marolt (eds), *Online Society in China: Creating, Celebrating, and Instrumentalising the Online Carnival*, Abingdon, Oxon: Routledge, pp. 106–23.

Wyn, J. and White, R. (1997) *Rethinking Youth*, London: Sage.

Xi, J. (2006) 'Introduction to Chinese youth', in J. Xi, Y. Sun, and J. Jing (eds), *Chinese Youth in Transition*, Aldershot UK; Burlington USA: Ashgate, pp. 79–96.

Xiao, H. (2006) 'Narrating a happy China through a crying game: A case study of post-Mao reality shows', *China Media Research* 2/3: 59–67.

'Xin Zhoukan 2006 xinrui niandu zhidao fenzi: Li Yinhe' [Li Yinhe: The *New Weekly's* 2006 list of cutting-edge knowledge workers] (2006) *Xin Zhoukan*, 17 December. At: <http://ent.sina.com>.

Xin, R. (2003) *The Good Women of China: Hidden Voices*, Australia: Vintage, Random House Publishers.

Xing ai zhongxin [China Centre for Disease Control and Prevention (CDC)] (2006) '2005 nian quanguo aizibing shaodian jiance baogao' [2005 Report on national HIV sentinel surveillance, abstract]. At: <http://www.chinaids.org.cn/>.

Xinhua (2010) 'Cross-dressing "Happy Boy" stirs up debate on gender', *CRI English*, 31 May. At: <http://english.cri.cn/>.

'Xin Zhongguo 60 nian Zhongguo zuiju yingxiangli de 600 benshu mingdan jinri chulu!' [List of the 600 most influential books in the People's Republic of China is released today] (2009), China Publishing and Media Journal, 29 September. At: <http://www.cbbr.com.cn/>.

Xiong Ran, Wang Xiaodong, Yu Fei, Chen Yuan and Li Zhijun (2010) 'MSM aizibing ziyuan zixun jiance fuwu moshi tansuo' [Exploring the service model of HIV voluntary counseling and testing for men who have sex with men], *Zhongguo Gonggong Weisheng Guanli* 26: 251–3.

'Xishui piaosu younü an diaocha' [An investigation of the Xishui Case of buying sex from underage girls] (2009) *Nanfang Renwu Zhoukan*, 26 April. At: <http://news.163.com/>.

Xu Anqi (1997) *Shiji Zhi Jiao Zhongguoren de Aiqing he Hunyin* [Love and Marriage among Chinese at the Turn of the Century], Beijing: Zhongguo Shehuikexue Chubanshe.

Xu Anqi and Ye Wenzhen (1999) *Zhongguo hunyin zhiliang yanjiu* [Research on the Quality of Marriage in China], Beijing: Zhongguo Shehuikexue Chubanshe.

Xu, F. (2011 [2009]) 'Governing China's peasant migrants: Building xiaokang socialism and an harmonious society', in E. Jeffreys (ed.), *China's Governmentalities: Governing Change, Changing Government*, Abingdon, Oxon: Routledge, pp. 38–62.

Xu, J. (2013) 'Marriage attitudes slowly change', *China Daily*, 14 August, p. 4.

Xu, L. (2011) 'Poster boys of safe sex', *China Daily*, 19 December. At: <http://chinawatch.washingtonpost.com/>.

Xu, L. (2013) 'Matrimony and money', *China Daily*, Sunday Special, 7 July, p. 3.

Xu, X., Zhu, F-C., O'Campo, P., Koenig, M., Mock, V. and J. Campbell (2005) 'Prevalence of and risk factors for intimate partner violence in China', *American Journal of Public Health* 95/1: 79–85.

Yan Ruxian and Song Zhaoling (1983) *Yongning naxizu de muxizhi* [Matrilineal society in Yongning], Kunming: Yunnan Renmin Chubanshe.

Yan, Y. (2010) 'The Chinese path to individualization', *The British Journal of Sociology* 61/3: 489–512.

Yang Tao (2006) 'Yufang aizibing yu chachu maiyin' [Prevent HIV/AIDS and prosecuting prostitution], *Zhongguo Qingnianbao*, 17 October.

Yang, H., Li, X., Stanton, B., Liu Hongjie, Liu Hui, Wang, N., Fang Xiaoyi, Lin, D. and Chen, X. (2005) 'Heterosexual transmission of HIV in China: A systematic review of behavioural studies in the past two decades', *Sexually Transmitted Disease* 32/5: 270–80.

Yang, L. (2008) 'Shanghai campuses to get condom vending machines', *Shanghai Daily*, 18 August. At: <http://english.cri.cn/>.

Yang, L and Bao, H. (2012) 'Queerly intimate: Friends, fans and affective communication in a *Super Girl* fan fiction community', *Cultural Studies* 26/6: 842–71.

Yang, M. (1999) 'From gender erasure to gender difference: State feminism, consumer sexuality, and women's public sphere in China, in M. Yang (ed.), *Spaces of Their Own: Women's Public Sphere in Transnational China*, Minneapolis, MN: University of Minnesota Press, pp. 35–67.

Yang, R. (dir.) and Lennon, T. (prod.) (2006) The Blood of Yingzhou District, documentary film 40 minutes, Thomas Lennon Films.

Yang, X., Derlaga, V. J. and Luo Huasong (n.d.) 'Migration, behaviour change, and HIV/STD risks in China'. At: http://iussp2005.princeton.edu/>.

Ye Haiyan (2011) 'Zhongguo dalu xinggongzuozhe jigou Wuhan jietou changyi hefahua [Sex workers' organization from mainland China holds a protest on a street in Wuhan City to legalize sex work], *Liu Mangyan de Blog*. At: <http://blog.sina.com>.

'Yes, we do' (2013) *China Daily*, 14 August, p. 1.

Yu, H-Q, (2012) 'Governing and representing HIV/AIDS in China: A review and an introduction', *International Journal of Asia Pacific Studies* 8/1: 1–33.

Yu Wei (2011) 'Wu Jieping chuanqi rensheng: Xingyi Zhongnanhai wei Zhou zongli zhi bing' [The legendary life of Wu Jieping: the doctor who treated Premier Zhou Enlai at Zhongnanhai]. *Tianjin Ribao*, 4 March. At: <http://www.chinanews.com>.

Yu Ying (2003) 'Xingbowuguan guanzhang Liu Dalin' [An interview with the sex museum's director, Liu Dalin], *Nanfang Zhoumo*, 19 September. At: <http://www.china.com>.

Yu Yong (2006) 'Tongxinglian renqun de shengcun zhuangkuang yanjiu – yi Changsha nantongxinglian renqun weili' [A study on the living conditions of homosexuals – a case study of men who have sex with men in Changsha City], MA thesis, Central South University, Changsha, Hunan Province, People's Republic of China.

Yu, Y. J. (2013) 'Subjectivity, hygiene, and STI prevention: A normalization paradox in the cleanliness practices of female sex workers in post-socialist China', *Medical Anthropology Quarterly* 27/3: 348–67.

Yue, A. and Yu, H. (2008) 'China's Super Girl: Mobile youth cultures and new sexualities', in U. M. Rodrigues and B. Smail (eds), *Youth, Media and Culture in the Asia Pacific*, Newcastle, UK: Cambridge Scholarly Publishing, pp. 117–34.

Yue Xiaoli, Jiang Ning and Gong Xiangdong (2013) '2012 nian quanguo meidu yu linbing yiqing fenxi baogao' [2012 syphilis and gonorrhoea outbreak report], *Xingbing Qingkuang Jianbao* 1: 12–21.

Zeng Henglin (2007) '"2007 Kuaile Zhongguo Kuaile Nansheng" shengzhuang qihang' ['2007 Happy China Happy Boys' officially launched], *Hunan Ribao*, 23 March, p. B02.

Zhan Chengxu, Wang Chengquan, Li Jinchun and Liu Longchu (1980) *Yongning naxizu de a zhu hunyin he muxi jiating* [A Yongning Naxi 'A Zhu' Marriage and Matrilineal Family], Shanghai: Shanghai Renmin Chubanshe.

Zhang Beichuan (1994) *Tongxing ai* [Same-sex Love], Jinan: Shandong Kexue Jishui Chubanshe.

Zhang, B. and Kaufman, J. (2005) 'The rights of people with same sex sexual behaviour: Recent progress and continuing challenges in China', in G. Misra and R. Chandiramani (eds), *Sexuality, Gender and Rights: Exploring Theory and Practice in South and Southeast Asia*, New Delhi: Sage, pp. 113–30.

Zhang, C. (2007) 'Gay bars bring HIV awareness out of the closet', *China Daily*, 13 June, p. 5.

Zhang, E. (2011) 'China's sexual revolution', in A. Kleinman, Y. Yan, J. Jing, S. Lee, E. Zhang, T. Pan, F. Wu and J. Guo (eds), *Deep China: The Moral Life of the Person*, Berkeley, Los Angeles, and London: University of California Press, pp. 106–51.

Zhang, H. (2009 [2006]) 'Female sex sellers and public policy in the People's Republic of China', in E. Jeffreys (ed.), *Sex and Sexuality in the People's Republic of China*, Abingdon, Oxon; New York: Routledge, pp. 139–58.

Zhang Jing (2006) 'Zhongshandaxue jian tongxinliang shetuan zhi wei yanjiu, Li Yinhe biaoshi shiwang' [Sun Yat-sen University establishes association on homosexuality for research only, Li Yinhe expresses disappointment], *Renminwang,* 9 November. At: <http://society.people.com.>.

Zhang, K-L., Mao, S-J. and Xia, D-Y. (2004) 'Epidemiology of HIV and sexually transmitted infections in China', *Sexual Health* 16: 39–46.

Zhang, X. (2010) 'Chinese women putting off the family way', *China Today – Explaining China to the World,* 59, 12. At: <http://www.chinatoday.com.>.

Zhao, J. (2010) Imagining Queerness: Sexualities in Underground film in Contemporary P.R. China, MA thesis, Department of Communication, Georgia State University.

Zhao, R., Gao, H., Shi, X., Tucker, J. D., Yang, Z., Min, X., Qian, H., Duan, Q. and Wang, N. (2005) 'Sexually transmitted disease/HIV and heterosexual risk among miners in townships of Yunnan Province, China', *AIDS Patient Care and STDS* 19/ 12: 848–51.

Zheng, T. (2006) 'Cool masculinity: Male clients' sex consumption and business alliance in urban China's sex industry', *Journal of Contemporary China* 15/46: 161–82.

Zheng, T. (2009a) *Red Lights: The Lives of Sex Workers in Postsocialist China,* Minneapolis; London: University of Minnesota Press.

Zheng, T. (2009b) *Ethnographies of Prostitution in Contemporary China: Gender Relations, HIV/AIDS, and Nationalism,* New York: Palgrave Macmillan.

Zheng, T. (2010a) 'Complexity of female sex workers collective actions in post-socialist China', *Wagadu* 8: 34–70.

Zheng, T. (2010b) 'Vilifying and promoting condoms: Condom debate during the time of AIDS in China', *The New York Sociologist* 4: 50–74.

Zhong Gang and Chen Xuelian (2008) 'Huangse shouchaoben: 70 niandai xing qimeng' [Handwritten pornography: 70 years of sex instruction], *Nanfangwang,* 7 September. At: <http://news.ifeng.com/>.

Zhong, X. (2006) 'Who is a feminist? Understanding the ambivalence towards *Shanghai Baby,* 'body writing' and feminism in post-women's liberation China', *Gender & History* 18/3: 635–60.

'Zhonggong zhongyang wenjian zhong fa, 1970, 26 hao' [Chinese Communist Party Document No 26, 1970] (1970) Zhonggong zhongyang zhuanfa guojia ji wei jun daibiao guanyu jinyibu zuo hao zhishi qingnian xia xiang gongzuo de baogao [Report on work relating to sent-down intellectual youth, by Military Representatives of the National Planning Commission, and transmitted by the Central Committee of the Chinese Communist Party]. At: <http://blog.sohu.com/>.

Zhongguo jibing yufang kongzhi zhongxin [China Centre for Disease Control and Prevention] (n.d.) 'Yufang aizi: Wo you yi "tao"' [Preventing HIV/AIDS: I have a 'method' [a condom], China Centre for Disease Control and Prevention and Qingdao-London Durex Company Ltd.

Zhongguo xingbing aizibing fangzhi xiehui [Chinese Association of STD and AIDS Prevention] (n.d.) 'Huashuo "aizi"' [Talking about 'AIDS' with pictures], Beijing Xuanwu Qu, 27 Nanwei Road.

'Zhongguoshi bihun' [Chinese-style forced marriage] (2012) Baidu Baike. At: <http://baike.baidu.com/>.

Zhonghua renmin gongheguo gongan bu ling: Di 88 hao [Order No.88 of the Ministry of Public Security] (2006) 'Gongan jiguan banli xingzheng anjian chengxu guiding' [Regulations on the Procedures for Handling Administrative Cases by Public Security Organs], passed on 29 March 2006 and taking effect on 24 August 2006. At: <http://www.mps.gov>.

Zhonghua renmin gongheguo guojia weisheng he jihua shengyu weiyuanhui [Health and Family Planning Commission of the People's Republic of China (2004) Guanyu yufang aizibing tuiguang shiyong anquantao (biyuntao) de shishi yijian [Guidelines on Preventing AIDS and Promoting Condom Use]. At: <http://www.moh.gov>.

Zhonghua renmin gongheguo hunyin fa (2001 xuizheng) [Marriage law of the People's Republic China (2001 amendment)] (2001) Adopted at the Third Session of the Fifth National People's Congress on 10 September 1980, and amended in accordance with the 'Decision regarding the amendment (of the Marriage law of the People's Republic of China)' passed at the Twenty-First Session of the Standing Committee of the Ninth National People's Congress on 28 April 2001, Quanguo Renda Fagui Ku. At: <http://www.law-lib.com/>.

Zhonghua renmin gongheguo hunyin fa (xiuzheng) [Marriage law of the People's Republic of China (amendment)] (1980) Adopted at the Third Session of the Fifth National People's Congress and promulgated by Order No. 9 of the Chairman of the Standing Committee of the National People's Congress on 10 September 1980, effective 1 January 1981, Quanguo Renda Fagui Ku. At: <http://www.law-lib.com/>.

Zhonghua renmin gongheguo hunyin fa [Marriage law of the People's Republic of China] (1950) Promulgated on 13 April 1950 by the Central People's Government of the People's Republic of China, and enacted on 1 May 1950, Quanguo Renda Fagui Ku. At: <http://www.govyi.com/>.

Zhonghua renmin gongheguo minzhengbu [Ministry of Civil Affairs of the People's Republic of China] (2011) 'Lihun banli' [Divorce registration], Zhongguo Minzheng Tongji Nianjian, Beijing: Zhongguo Tongji Chubanshe, p. 106.

Zhonghua renmin gongheguo weishengbu, lianheguo aizibing guihuashu, shijie weisheng zuzhi [Ministry of Health of the People's Republic of China, UNAIDS and the World Health Organization] (2011) 'Weishengbu 2011 nian Zhongguo aizibing yiqing guji' [2011 estimates on the AIDS epidemic in China], November, Beijing. At: <http://www.moh.gov>.

'Zhongxuesheng maiyin "heiwang" yuanhe cunzai?' [What caused the high school prostitution group?] (2002) *Nanfang Zhoumo*, 10 January.

Zhou Huashan (2001) *Wufu wufu de guodu? [A Society without Fathers and Husbands?]*, Beijing: Guangming Ribao Chubanshe.

Zhou Jigang (2006) 'Dalu dixia xingchanye "hefahua" fengbo' [Debating the 'legalization' of China's underground sex industry], *Fenghuang Zhoukan* 9: 241.

Zhou Jinghao (2006) 'Chinese prostitution: Consequences and solutions in the post-Mao era', *China: An International Journal* 4/2: 238–62.

Zhou Ruijin (2006) '"Lianghui" daibiao bufang yiyi dixia "xingchanye"' [Delegates at the National People's Congress and the Chinese Political Consultative Conference should discuss [legalizing], the underground 'sex industry'], *People's Daily Online*, 19 January. At: <http://opinion.people.com>.

Zhou, R. (2013) 'Visit thy parents – it's the law', *China Daily*, 6 July, p. 11.

Zhou, W. (2013) 'Seniors share love without marriage', *China Daily*, 15 November, pp. 1 and 5.

Zhou, Y. (2014) 'Chinese queer images on screen: A case study of Cui Zi'en's films', *Asian Studies Review* 38/1: 124–40.

Zhu, Y., Keane, M. and Bai, R. (2008) 'Introduction', in Y. Zhu, M. Keane and R. Bai (eds), *TV Drama in China*, Hong Kong: Hong Kong University Press, pp. 1–18.

Zou, H., Xue, H., Wang, X. and Lu, D. (2012) 'Condom use in China: Prevalence, policies, issues and barriers', *Sexual Health* 9/1: 27–33.

Index